Making Up Our Mind

Making Up Our Mind

What School Choice Is Really About

SIGAL R. BEN-PORATH
AND MICHAEL C. JOHANEK

The University of Chicago Press
Chicago and London

The University of Chicago Press, Chicago 60637
The University of Chicago Press, Ltd., London
© 2019 by The University of Chicago
All rights reserved. No part of this book may be used or reproduced in any manner
whatsoever without written permission, except in the case of brief quotations in
critical articles and reviews. For more information, contact the University of Chicago
Press, 1427 E. 60th St., Chicago, IL 60637.
Published 2019
Printed in the United States of America

28 27 26 25 24 23 22 21 20 19   1 2 3 4 5

ISBN-13: 978-0-226-61946-0 (cloth)
ISBN-13: 978-0-226-61963-7 (paper)
ISBN-13: 978-0-226-61977-4 (e-book)
DOI: https://doi.org/10.7208/chicago/9780226619774.001.0001

Library of Congress Cataloging-in-Publication Data

Names: Ben-Porath, Sigal R., 1967– author. | Johanek, Michael C., author.
Title: Making up our mind : what school choice is really about / Sigal R. Ben-Porath
    and Michael C. Johanek.
Other titles: History and philosophy of education.
Description: Chicago : The University of Chicago Press, 2019. | Series: History and
    philosophy of education series | Includes bibliographical references and index.
Identifiers: LCCN 2018041631 | ISBN 9780226619460 (cloth : alk. paper) |
    ISBN 9780226619637 (pbk. : alk. paper) | ISBN 9780226619774 (e-book)
Subjects: LCSH: School choice—United States. | Education—Aims and objectives—
    United States. | Educational equalization—United States.
Classification: LCC LB1027.9 .B43 2019 | DDC 379.1/11—dc23
LC record available at https://lccn.loc.gov/2018041631

♾ This paper meets the requirements of ANSI/NISO Z39.48-1992
(Permanence of Paper).

Contents

Preface

Given the electrically charged topic of "school choice" in a politically polarized nation, we may be dancing around a "third rail." We invite your understanding of the particular nature of this book project on this contentious issue.

School choice, as with many other educational issues, is a topic which raises considerable passions as it touches on how we educate our children and what sort of society we wish to be; we would be surprised, even disappointed, if it were otherwise.

Through several decades of work, each of us has experienced myriad conversations around the many energized perspectives involved in "school choice"; not infrequently, a mix of views resides in the same person. Drawing composites from across half a century of experiences, we consider, for example:

- The deeply committed and anxious urban Mexican American mother pushing hard to find a more challenging and safer setting than her child's assigned elementary school. Extending the two-hour, multiple-bus-line commute to her hotel cleaning job, she found a smaller apartment for her family near the train station of a nearby suburban town, just within the school zoning boundary. She knew her third-grade daughter's primary school was considered the least desirable in town, and that it would be even more difficult to attend any activities now as a parent. For her son, the living room would now double as his bedroom. "But," she said, "I want my kids someday to be seen like those suburban ones, going to college and all, so they won't end up doing what I do." This limited form of residential choice is all that is available to her, and she wishes for better schooling options for her children.

- The African American single mother and services manager committed to working to improve her local public school. "My daughter will only be in third grade once," she underlined. She found what she saw as a better option: a seat at a recently opened charter. Yet she's angry at what she sees as the cultural cluelessness and disrespect of the young staff members in the charter to which her son transferred, none of whom live nearby. "If one more twentysomething suburban blonde tells me how to raise my kid, I may have to clock her," she said; she switched her son back to the neighborhood school the following year.

- A veteran African American public school administrator, now developing community-based charters in some of the most underserved communities in her city, is reenergized by her newfound flexibility to address student needs. Unleashed from stifling regulations, she weaves a powerful, cross-agency, community-revitalizing approach to nurturing the lives in her care. Yet she still feels a stranger in a foreign land when attending the suburban dinner parties that supplement her school's public funds.

- Or the white father in a semirural town whose solid but uninspiring local middle school reflects the starved resources of an aging community and flatlined local economy. He can't get decent guidance counseling or rich extracurriculars for his daughter, even with endless parent fundraising. Yet he reads of the six-figure salaries and endless revenue flowing to politically connected charter networks across his state; swollen neck veins tell the story of his anger at the opportunity robbed from his children by "private snouts in the public till."

- Or the working parents of four in a "universal choice" city, each of their children attending a different school in a different part of town—some district, some charter—each with its own schedule and transportation complications, its own culture, registration deadlines, parent contracts and requirements, open house nights, parent-teacher conferences. "We like most of the schools they got into," they note, "but a neighborhood school would have been nice. Having your siblings with you or coming up behind you, walking to school together, playing with kids in the neighborhood—that would have been nice." They would love to be more involved in their children's schools, but the various distances make it too hard.

Acknowledging the validity and mix of such deeply held emotions, beliefs, and perspectives, we seek in this volume to identify a useful common ground where the fellow citizens holding these different perspectives may meet. We hope to illuminate a bit, through the critical lenses of philosophy and history, some of the underlying tensions and trade-offs our society can discuss to work toward a richer mutual understanding. These tensions and trade-offs operate at both individual and collective levels, as present decisions and as products of past history, further complicating this task.

Even if this analysis does not resolve these differences, we hope it provides a place for an in-depth, multisided national discussion, setting a table at which we can sit together to make up our minds on the matter of school choice. Our children, our students, are hoping that we do.

If it were just introduced more thoroughly into our system, wouldn't "school choice" revitalize education and disrupt age-old bureaucracies with its innovative market forces? With proliferating charters and voucher schemes, would the United States then finally make a dramatic break with its past and expand parental choice? Or does the introduction of school choice usher in unprecedented attacks on our republic's traditions of schooling, sounding a novel and divisive challenge to the common good?

Wrong questions, wrong premises.

Market-driven school choices predate the republic. For centuries, parents have chosen to educate their young from an evolving mix of publicly supported, private, charitable, and entrepreneurial enterprises. Education in this country has arguably always been predominantly market-driven, especially by parental demand and by real estate interests. The question is then not *whether* to have school choice. The question is *how* we will regulate *who* has *which* choices in our mixed market for schooling—and what we want to accomplish as a nation with that mix of choices.

School choice as a term gives away the real debate. Describing the debate as for or against school choice masks the present realities of who already gets to choose, and among which options. *School choice* is a term for advocates of certain types of school reform today—principally concerning changes to governance and regulation, and primarily in the form of charters and vouchers. Who, especially in a culture of triumphant consumerism, really could oppose "choice," or more of it? But that's not the point. The proposed reforms are about very bounded choices available only to some people, within certain geographic borders, and with highly unequal resources. Consider that few if any choice advocates are lobbying for the rights of well-heeled suburbanites to have access even to high-performing urban schools.

Further, while this book focuses on the US, it is not even a particularly US question. The debate in the United States over the provision of compulsory schooling, including the relative roles of public and private sectors, relates to a parallel debate in many other countries. A growing push of private companies to provide low-cost private schooling in many of the world's developing countries like India, Pakistan, and Kenya focuses on the relative merits of public schools and of private entrepreneurs in education.[1] In countries where there is a considerable history of "market-based" approaches to schooling— for example, Chile—intensive arguments rage around proper public and private boundaries, public and private ends. The varied sides in Chile often focus on the equal access that public schools should provide to education, countered by claims of better quality and innovation (the result of a less bureaucratic structure) in privately managed schools for those who can afford them.

Thus, debates in other countries, as well as debates in the development community over how developing countries should reform their schools, mirror the central tenets of the debate on school choice in the United States. Public school supporters suggest that, while the public education sector is broken in many ways in the developing world, the best response is to help fix it, rather than bypass it by inviting the private sector to reorganize it according to its business models. The business community and its supporters counter that governments are unable or otherwise unlikely to effectively reform schools so that costs are reined in and outcomes improve significantly. Incentivizing the private sector by giving it an opportunity to benefit from providing education to the world's children can improve results while reducing the reach of sometimes-corrupt and often inefficient bureaucracies. One side argues for more independent voices in the schooling of youth; another fears the divisive potential of balkanized schooling. The two sides disagree about facts, especially regarding goals and how to measure them, as well as the values that the education system is expected to uphold and promote. Thus, some enthusiastic supporters of privatization define private school access as a human right, while some of their opponents view any private involvement in the education sector as undermining democracy. Some key values are shared across the divide— most important, the commitment to providing universal access to quality education—but disagreement remains on many aspects of education. As this discussion aims to clarify, the shared values may provide a middle ground on which a broadly acceptable policy could rest.

School Choice Today

Assessing how choice policies play out in the United States, then, requires an understanding of the current landscape of school choice. This book starts with that landscape, outlining the various ways parents exercise choice over schooling today. It then turns to some observations about this landscape, followed by the design trade-offs embedded in present policy, before diving into how the history and philosophy of school choice in the United States might shed some further light on the present.

Some quick data will frame the landscape. First, roughly nine in ten students attend public schools in the United States. Second, most parents of public school students—nearly 80%—consider the school their child attends as their "first choice" school; this percentage rises with parental education level, income and suburban location. In the United States, parents exercise school choice today essentially in seven ways, listed in order of their estimated prevalence:

1. Residential mobility: If you have the money and are not subject to housing discrimination, you can live in a neighborhood that feeds a desirable public school system. We know this drives housing decisions: the quality of schools influences 26% of all home purchases and 33% of suburban purchases, with higher rates for parents with children.[2] In 2007, the parents of 27% of public school students indicated that they chose their residence based on their choice of schools. If that percentage applied in 2014, then well more than thirteen million students attended schools as a result of residential choice—by far the most common way of exercising school choice.[3]

2. Open enrollment (inter- or intradistrict): Arguably the second most prevalent form of school choice—and pioneered by Minnesota before they started charters—open enrollment allows parents some power to decide which school or program within their public district their children will attend. Some districts also allow parents to send students outside their district, presumably if the district cannot meet specific needs. Most states (forty-six) now have some form of open enrollment. In addition, some larger school districts (like New York City and Philadelphia) offer "universal choice," usually to high school students, whereby each student applies to a list of preferred schools and is matched by the schools or the city according to grade, location, and other metrics; some districts also assign a neighborhood or "default" school to those who do not participate in the process or are not well matched. Stipulations regarding transportation, desegregation guidelines, or opt-out provisions vary considerably.

Twenty-two states have mandatory intradistrict open enrollment policies in place (seventeen voluntary), and twenty-five provide mandatory inter-district policies (twenty-eight voluntary).[4] In over 40% of school districts in the United States, parents may elect to send their children to schools in another district at no charge.[5] The 2002 federal legislation No Child Left Behind encouraged the transfer provisions of open enrollment poli-cies for those in low-performing schools.[6] However, no reliable national figures exist regarding the exact number of students leveraging this choice option.[7]

3. Private schools (including religious schools): The third most prevalent school choice option, and one of the most persistent, is private schooling. Generally tax-exempt and funded by tuition and donations, it serves a wide variety of populations and purposes. Private schools enrolled just over 9% of students when first recorded in 1889—a figure that peaked by 1960 at around 14%, has fluctuated within a fairly narrow band over the last four decades, and now stands just above 10%.[8]

4. Charter schools: Perhaps the most visible form of choice today, charters are funded by public monies, often in addition to funds raised from the philanthropic and business sectors. In this sense they are public schools; however, they receive a special charter from the state or other authorizing body that exempts them from various requirements, transparency, and rules by which traditional public schools must abide. These requirements can be related to admissions, operation, or curriculum. Significantly, char-ters are managed by their own governance structure and do not report to their public school district in the same way that other public schools do. In 2016, 5.7% of public school students attended more than 6,800 char-ter schools—a dramatic increase from a decade earlier.[9] Those charters were mostly serving urban areas (especially in poorer cities such as New Orleans; Detroit; and Flint, Michigan) where a significant portion of the children were part of the charter system.[10]

5. Magnet schools: From their origins in the late 1960s, magnets were "designed to attract students from diverse social, economic, ethnic, and racial backgrounds," though recently have been known more for a specialty theme, subject area, or instructional model.[11] Publicly funded and either open or selective, magnets allow applications from across a district and, in some instances, from across multiple districts. While more charter schools than magnets exist, magnets are on average much larger, and until the last few years, they enrolled more students at both the elementary and the secondary level, totaling 5.2% of K–12 enrollment nationally in more than 3,200 schools.[12]

6. Homeschooling: Homeschooling—parents choosing to educate their chil-dren at home—is legal today in most states (with some or no regulation

required) and has roughly doubled as a percentage of K–12 enrollment across the last decade or so. Nine in ten homeschooling parents cite concerns about the school environment as motivation, and about a third cite religious or moral reasons. In 2012, the last year for which federal data is available, 3.4% of American children were homeschooled, double the proportion of 1999.[13]

7. Vouchers, credits, and ESAs: School vouchers were inspired in recent history partly by Milton Friedman's writings from the 1950s, though Thomas Paine also had a similar idea, and Vermont and then Maine have provided vouchers since the late nineteenth century. While available only to a limited group of families, vouchers have gained some prominence in the United States in recent decades. Vouchers are generally public funds provided to families—either universally in a given location, or as a needs- or lottery-based opportunity—that can be used to pay tuition for their children's schooling in public or private schools. In some localities, private-voucher programs provide support for nonpublic schooling, or public schooling outside one's district. Some twenty-six voucher programs exist in fifteen states and the District of Columbia.[14]

In addition, a host of voucher-like schemes have arisen in which individuals or corporations get tax benefits for money they contribute to voucher-distributing funds. The advent of recent statewide tax credit scholarship programs in Indiana, Louisiana, and Nevada has raised the profile of this option, and eighteen states now provide tax credits for donations to nonprofit organizations through twenty-three programs that grant voucher-like scholarships for students to attend the school of their choice.[15] Similarly, five states, starting with Arizona in 2011, have provided individuals with access to government-authorized education savings accounts (ESAs) based on a set per capita state expenditure; parents can use those funds for a wide variety of educational purposes, not limited to tuition at a chosen school.[16] Finally, recent federal tax law changes allow, for the first time, use of pretax "529 accounts," established as state college savings accounts, for up to $10,000 in K–12 expenses, including private school tuition.[17] The impact of this change is, of course, unknown, though a 2018 analysis concluded that it will "primarily benefit affluent families, produce limited incentives for promoting private school choice, and come at a nontrivial cost to states."[18]

Summarized graphically, the mix of current school choice options then looks like this:

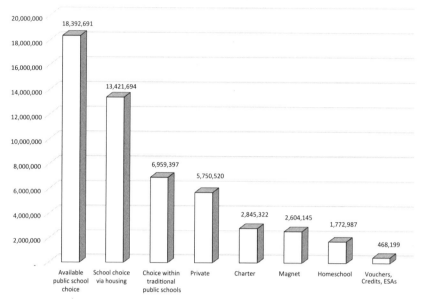

Estimated Enrollments for School Choice Options

FIGURE 1. School Choice Options: Enrollment Estimates.

Sources:

Available public school choice:

· The number is a product of total enrollment multiplied by the percent claiming public school choice.

· For total public school enrollment: US Department of Education, National Center for Education Statistics, "Table 216.20: Number and Enrollment of Public Elementary and Secondary Schools, by School Level, Type, and Charter and Magnet Status: Selected Years, 1990–91 through 2013–14," Digest of Education Statistics 2016, October 2016, https://nces.ed.gov/programs/digest/d16/tables/dt16_216.20.asp.

· For percentage claiming available public school choice: US Department of Education, National Center for Education Statistics. "Fast Facts: Public School Choice Programs," accessed July 27, 2018, https://nces.ed.gov/fastfacts/display.asp?id=6.

School choice via housing:

· The number is a product of total enrollment multiplied by the percent claiming their home selection was motivated by school quality.

· For total public school enrollment: US Department of Education, National Center for Education Statistics, "Table 216.20: Number and Enrollment of Public Elementary and Secondary Schools, by School Level, Type, and Charter and Magnet Status: Selected Years, 1990–91 through 2013–14," Digest of Education Statistics 2016, October 2016, https://nces.ed.gov/programs/digest/d16/tables/dt16_216.20.asp.

· For the percent of homeowners indicating they moved to the neighborhood for schools (27%): S. Grady and S. Bielick, Trends in the Use of School Choice: 1993 to 2007 (NCES 2010-004), National Center for Education Statistics, Institute of Education Sciences (Washington, DC: US Department of Education, 2010), table 7, 28, https://nces.ed.gov/pubs2010/2010004.pdf.

Choice within traditional public schools:

· The number is a product of total enrollment multiplied by the percent claiming they have choice within public schooling.

· For total public school enrollment: US Department of Education, National Center for Education Statistics, "Table 216.20: Number and Enrollment of Public Elementary and Secondary Schools, by School

FIGURE 1. (cont.)

Level, Type, and Charter and Magnet Status: Selected Years, 1990–91 through 2013–14," Digest of Education Statistics 2016, October 2016, https://nces.ed.gov/programs/digest/d16/tables/dt16_216.20.asp.

· For percentage claiming to be enrolled in a public school of their choice: US Department of Education, National Center for Education Statistics, "Fast Facts: Public School Choice Programs."

Private:

· US Department of Education, National Center for Education Statistics, "Table 205.20: Enrollment and Percentage Distribution of Students Enrolled in Private Elementary and Secondary Schools, by School Orientation and Grade Level: Selected Years, Fall 1995 through Fall 2013," Digest of Education Statistics 2016, May 2017, https://nces.ed.gov/programs/digest/d16/tables/dt16_205.20.asp.

Charter and magnet:

· US Department of Education, National Center for Education Statistics, "Table 216.20: Number and Enrollment of Public Elementary and Secondary Schools, by School Level, Type, and Charter and Magnet Status: Selected Years, 1990–91 through 2015–16," Digest of Education Statistics 2017, August 2017, https://nces.ed.gov/programs/digest/d17/tables/dt17_216.20.asp.

Homeschool:

· US Department of Education, National Center for Education Statistics, "Table 206.10: Number and Percentage of Homeschooled Students ages 5 through 17 with a Grade Equivalent of Kindergarten through 12th Grade, by Selected Child, Parent, and Household Characteristics: 2003, 2007, and 2012," Digest of Education Statistics 2015, November 2014, https://nces.ed.gov/programs/digest/d15/tables/dt15_206.10.asp. See also J. Redford, D. Battle, and S. Bielick, Homeschooling in the United States: 2012 (NCES 2016-096.REV), National Center for Education Statistics (Washington DC: US Department of Education, 2017), 5.

Vouchers and tax credits:

· The American Federation for Children website, accessed January 24, 2017, claimed "nearly 400,000" for 2015/16; that number is also used in congressional testimony in support of nominee Betsy DeVos, per C-Span, "Education Secretary Confirmation Hearing," January 17, 2007, video, 3:31:29, (testimony with the number at 12:26 and 33:11), and transcript, https://www.c-span.org/video/?421224-1/education-secretary-nominee-betsy-devos-testifies-confirmation-hearing.

· ESAs, vouchers and tax-credit scholarships sum to 468,199 at EdChoice, "Resource Hub: Fast Facts," accessed July 27, 2018, https://www.edchoice.org/resource-hub/fast-facts/#voucher-fast-facts.

Within those options most associated with "school choice," the recent trend lines are illustrated on the next page:

Given this landscape of choice, several notable patterns emerge. Amid all the options, nearly nine in ten school-age children in the United States still attend public school—a proportion that has been fairly consistent for decades. The percentage of K–12 students in private schools, after significant ups and downs, has settled roughly where it was when statistics first were collected in the nineteenth century.

Yet the debate on choice focuses heavily on what are in fact marginal options among current parental choices, charters and vouchers, which do not affect most families or districts. Nationally, 89% of districts report no charters within their borders, and an overwhelming majority of parents already claim

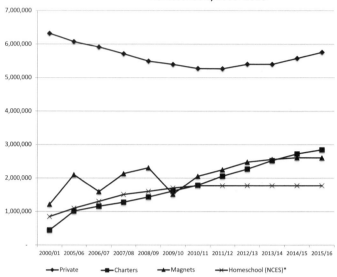

Enrollments for Private, Charter, and Magnet Schools and Homeschools, 2000–2016

Private — Charters — Magnets — Homeschool (NCES)*

FIGURE 2. Enrollments for Private, Charter, and Magnet Schools and Homeschools, 2000–2016.

Sources:

For private schooling: US Department of Education, National Center for Education Statistics, "Table 205.20: Enrollment and Percentage Distribution of Students Enrolled in Private Elementary and Secondary Schools, by School Orientation and Grade Level: Selected Years, Fall 1995 through Fall 2015," Digest of Education Statistics 2016, May 2017, https://nces.ed.gov/programs/digest/d16/tables/dt16_205.20.asp; supplemented by US Department of Education, National Center for Education Statistics, "Table 1: Actual and Projected Numbers for Enrollment in Grades PK–12, PK–8, and 9–12 in Elementary and Secondary Schools, by Control of School: Fall 1996 through Fall 2021," *Projections of Education Statistics to 2021*, January 2012, https://nces.ed.gov/programs/projections/projections2021/tables/table_01.asp.

For magnets and charters: US Department of Education, National Center for Education Statistics, "Table 216.20: Number and Enrollment of Public Elementary and Secondary Schools, by School Level, Type, and Charter and Magnet Status: Selected Years, 1990–91 through 2015–16," Digest of Education Statistics 2017, August 2017, https://nces.ed.gov/programs/digest/d17/tables/dt17_216.20.asp.

For homeschooling: US Department of Education, National Center for Education Statistics, "Table 206.10: Number and Percentage of Homeschooled Students Ages 5 through 17 with a Grade Equivalent of Kindergarten through 12th grade, by Selected Child, Parent, and Household Characteristics: 2003, 2007, and 2012," Digest of Education Statistics 2015, November 2014, https://nces.ed.gov/programs/digest/d15/tables/dt15_206.10.asp; see also J. Redford, D. Battle, and S. Bielick, *Homeschooling in the United States: 2012* (NCES 2016-096.REV), National Center for Education Statistics, Institute of Education Sciences, Washington, DC: US Department of Education, 2017) 5.

to be using their "first-choice" school.[19] Nearly 40% of parents indicate that school choice is available to them, and even 14% of traditional public school parents indicate they chose their school.[20] Even beyond residential selection, more than twice as many parents choose private schools and magnets, and have for decades, than attend all charters (see figure 1). For most of the last few decades, many more parents chose (and/or were chosen by) magnet schools as a way of exercising educational choice for their children than charters. Open enrollment policies may account for three times as many students as charters.[21]

Part of the present task, then, is to understand why, in light of this broader landscape, the dominant school choice policy discussion focuses on a narrow slice of those choice options, principally charters. Enrollment growth for charters since 2000 explains part of this; charter increases outpaced magnets considerably, increasing more than sixfold, though with slower growth since 2013. (Magnet enrollment increased, nonetheless, more than doubling during this time; see figure 2.) Private school enrollment, on the other hand, declined about 9%. Homeschooling has also scaled rapidly, roughly doubling in the last decade, but lacks the organized advocacy community of charters (less reliable enrollment data may be one result).[22] Thus, school choice trends in the last decade have favored charters and homeschooling, explaining, in part, their dominant role in current discussions, though still representing a minor part of how parents exercise school choice. Vouchers have faced ongoing legal and political challenges related to persistent concerns regarding public/private boundaries, though they may be set to expand.

Indeed, charters and vouchers disproportionately serve minority families in poor and highly segregated cities—urban contexts reflecting the failed desegregation and funding equity efforts over several decades. According to what has become known as "Nixon's compromise" regarding local control versus desegregation, that administration "compromised" by agreeing to spare the suburbs from further desegregation while saving the cities from their decline; sadly, the second half never quite happened in many cities. Historically, charters have often exacerbated segregation by race and income, and therefore tend to concentrate wealth and opportunities in some schools while leaving others—especially those which serve poor and minority students— lagging in funds and opportunities.

Across the school choice landscape, choice options often serve distinct audiences and geographies. In New York State, for example, 80% of all charter schools are in New York City; 93% are in just four districts, among the poorest in the state and the nation.[23] Charter school populations tend to include more African American, Hispanic, single-parent, and low-income heads than the general public school population. Over the last decade, a growing share of charter schools have become 50% or greater African American or Hispanic, relative to noncharters.[24] Homeschooling households, in contrast, tend to be more rural and more white, with higher incomes and more likely to have two parents than the overall school population.[25] The distinct communities served by different school choice options reflect the interplay of several decades of suburbanization, desegregation struggles, school financing reform, deunion-ization, consumerism, and the coproduction of public services by private and public entities.

Not Your Parents' Schooling

Part of our challenge in understanding this complex landscape arises from the fact that we often view schools to be unchanging, stagnant institutions in a world of constant change and innovation. Technology revolutions and dynamic markets, according to this perception, are contrasted with staid teachers standing in front of kids in classrooms. Indeed, the pedagogical challenges of the classroom seem in many ways a perpetual daily tussle between what adults want for children and what children want for themselves.

However, a great deal has changed regarding US schooling over the last two hundred or so years; by understanding those multiple shifts, we can decipher the constant versus distinctive elements of our current debate. As historian Carl Kaestle observes, history helps us resist the easy, but often wrong, quick analogies, and can help us raise more interesting questions about the present.[26] Despite the attention given to the recent growth of charters, for example, chartered schools operated in our colonial era, alongside for-profit venture schools and a vast array of other institutional forms of schooling. Debates over the appropriate role of different institutional forms of schooling have raged in other eras, particularly in the nineteenth century. Even more fundamental, perhaps, is the fact that the prevalence of schools themselves among educating agencies has radically changed; arguably, it may be time to radically change their relative role again. Consider, for example, student makeup: as recently as 1870, with nearly a third of the population of school age, only two-thirds of those children attended school, and for an average of 132 days per year, with wide deviations from that average; today, with the present school-age population a much smaller proportion of our population (18%), 92% of them attend school for an average of 179 days per year—nearly a third longer. We now view daily attendance as the norm, and right up until those students can vote. As we hear a lot today about "college readiness," only since World War II has a majority even graduated from high school. Our present "schooled society," "sending ever-greater proportions of successive cohorts of children and youth to attend ever-longer and more sophisticated levels of formal schooling[,] is an astonishingly different approach to formal education from that of past societies," including our own.[27] In this purported era of "choice," student options in schooling have expanded dramatically, especially when considering the curricular and nonschool options available. Yet in other respects, students have less choice about it; a longer period of their life has been bounded by compulsory schooling and, increasingly, by required courses and tests.[28]

How we have organized and governed schools in the United States has changed considerably as well: there were 117,108 school districts in the United States in 1940, serving roughly twenty-four million students; most elementary schools still employed a single teacher.[29] In 2010, there were barely 12% that number of districts serving over twice as many students, and only .3% in one-teacher elementary schools.[30] Even how we understand the notion of choice itself—including the boundaries of our public and private realms—seems to have shifted considerably; the terms themselves have histories, and we must allow other eras to inform us in that way as well.[31]

What does seem familiar, though, and a constant in several eras, is the way our present controversy around school choice overlaps with a period of accelerating social, economic, and technological change, reflecting a deep thread within US history. Educational foment arises as adults attempt to address an uncertain environment and an unpredictable future for their offspring. Debates around the choices parents should have regarding the education of their children, or of others' children, inevitably reflect the anxieties over the future direction of the community or society, and of youth in particular. Even institutions that remain intact through a crisis may begin to serve quite different purposes, as the framing of choices shifts as well. In our design of school choice, in any era, fundamental trade-offs apply.

Design Trade-Offs

Given the current landscape sketched above, how should we think about school choice, especially in light of the recent growth of options like charters and vouchers? We need to start by thinking about what goals are promoted or hindered by the introduction and expansion of specific school choice programs, and how small design details carry large implications.

Those goals and details get complicated quickly by the fact that education is a unique kind of good—private, public, *and* "positional." It is both a private good, conferring benefits on the individuals who pursue it, and a public good, helping maintain a productive, well-organized, and democratic society.[32] Additionally, education is a positional good, creating ordered benefits to those who get more or better education and placing them ahead of those who got less or worse kinds of education.[33] In other words, your education is worth more simply by virtue of me having less education; in a way, you benefit by my weaker education. Your education would be worth less if I attain more education than you. If we're both interviewing for the same job, for example, all other things being equal, whoever has more years of schooling, more degrees, or fancier diplomas is more likely to get the position.

If education were an entirely private good, however, it would make sense for families to purchase it on the free market, the same way we purchase food, shelter, tickets to arts and cultural events, and other material things. Of course, the state would in such a case regulate some basic aspects of it, the same way that the state works to ensure food or building safety, and the same way that it can subsidize some basic provisions in these areas. But parents would be allowed to decide what kind of education they would like their children to have, what content the schooling should have, and at what cost, in the same way that they make decisions about which groceries to buy and how to cook them. The view of education as a private good—one that is beneficial especially to the individual who has it—is close to the vision John Stuart Mill had for education when he suggested that "if the government would make up its mind to require for every child a good education, it might save itself the trouble of providing one. It might leave to parents to obtain the education where and how they pleased, and content itself with helping to pay the school fees of the poorer classes of children."[34] While Mill focused his advocacy on the passage and enforcement of compulsory attendance laws (or the requirement of universal education)—an aim that has since been largely fulfilled in much of the Western world—his vision was one of private choice. It was based on the view that since education is primarily a private good, full school choice is the only reasonable policy approach to organizing it.

On the other hand, if education is seen primarily as a public good, then it makes more sense for the state not only to regulate it but also to provide it, as a way to ensure the full benefit to society as a whole. Society needs adults with certain types of knowledge who can then participate effectively in the economy. The nation needs citizens with certain types of attitudes to be part of the system of governance; society may even decide that it requires certain types of sentiments from its members (for example, love of country), and it can breed those sentiments through the curriculum. If that were the case, parents would have a hard time raising a serious argument for school choice.

However, given that education is a mixed public/private good, with important benefits to both individuals and society, there is a strong argument to be made for a mixed approach—one that would share the responsibility for the education of the young between their parents and the state. Moreover, since education is positional, the benefits of their education depend on how much and what kind of education others around them obtain. The personal and the social benefits of education depend on everyone's access, and the outcomes of education policy and personal decisions about schooling affect everyone in society. As a public/private/positional good, personal and public decisions intertwine deeply.

All this makes the specific design of educational choices and opportunities especially important, because it will impact the outcomes to each person as well as to society as a whole. For instance, if choice happens only within racially separate attendance zones ("catchment areas"), then choice cannot impact diversity or integration. If religious schools are included within the palette of choices, public funds will support religious schooling and parents will have a different set of choices in front of them than they did before. If we want school choice to advance more equitable schools but we wall off resource-rich suburbs from fiscally challenged cities, then our public policy continues to position higher-income families more favorably. If we further open up geographic boundaries of school choice but provide disparate access to transportation, then we bound the choices of time- and resource-strapped parents, positioning some families ahead of others regarding access. If we fully open up boundaries and school options but make application systems and school information more accessible to some households over others, then we diminish the odds that equality will truly advance.

Our design choices create concrete options that will be available to specific people, and these are crucial to the goals that the choice of schooling will promote. Some localities have made innovative design choices that promote key democratic values within their boundaries. Cambridge, Massachusetts, has refined since the 1980s a "controlled-choice" system, seeking to bound parental school choices with community values, such as integration. No zoned elementary schools exist. Parents can choose, but admission depends in part on whether the resulting mix reflects the wider community. New Orleans tapped the thinking of two Nobel Prize–winning economists to design a centralized admissions system that appears to be diminishing the degree to which better-connected and better-informed parents can game the system. The city's more careful approach to closing and turning around low-performing schools, so as to assure more quality options—for example, assuring students transfer to higher-performing schools, minimizing the disruption students experience—accounted for an estimated 25–40% of the positive impact of school reform efforts there since hurricane Katrina.[35] Even within the broader inequitable frame of residency-driven choice, design decisions matter.

Unfortunately, nuance and careful design considerations don't usually characterize the public debate on school choice, which is usually split between those who prioritize the free market as the most effective mechanism to disseminate education, and those who see public schools as an irreplaceable democratic structure. Free market advocates suggest that democratic values are expressed by allowing individual parents to enact their preferences for their children by selecting the schools they would attend. This view of democratic values, though, is limited by its neglect of democratic accountability—the ability of a community to control and demand a response from the institutions that serve it. It also fails to commit to core democratic values such as nondiscrimination in that it allows school choice policies to resegregate schools by race (a result Friedman anticipated when he first wrote about choice). Public schools are far from ideal in terms of segregation versus integration, but most remain better in this regard than charters.

On the other hand, those who advocate for the primacy of parental authority avert their eyes from the fact that parents often shield their children from knowledge and values that are necessary for the functioning of a democratic society. Preferring scripture alone over any exposure to scientific knowledge (including, as in Indiana, public funding for schools which teach that humans and dinosaurs roamed the earth together[36]) represents a failure of democratic politics, and undermines the future ability of children to engage in public debate or even to participate as equals in the job market. This does not mean that public school advocates reject the role of parents in educating their children; nor do they reject the value of varied religious perspectives. Rather—as has always been the case in US history—they call for the institutions that represent the values and principles of democratic governance to provide families with appropriate choices, and to continue regulating the quality of schools and of the curriculum. It means that exposing children to content beyond that which their parents espouse is still seen as a necessity for the continued progress of this pluralistic society. Moreover, as public schools are accountable to the communities they serve (and not just the parents) whereas charter and private (voucher-funded) schools are not, the opportunity to sustain a democratic community is significantly depressed by the introduction of these choice mechanisms. In this way, parents who are offered a choice of privately managed schooling can take it only if they also choose to limit their—and their neighbors'—right to hold their schools publicly accountable.

Some suggest that choice is the only way to achieve equality. If some can choose a desirable but expensive school by moving to its pricey attendance zone, those who cannot afford it must have choice too. This argument fails to recognize that more-affluent parents are better able to game the system and gain access to more desirable schools, and that choice in fact provides them with more opportunities to do so. From the mounds of research that already exists on school choice programs, it is clear that even if the act of choice becomes equally available to all, quality schools themselves are not equally available. Rather, schools become more segregated and less equally funded; additionally, the outcomes in terms of course and activity availability, achievement on standardized tests, graduation rates, and college attendance and completion all become less equal. School choice strategies would need to deliberately design counterforces to these evident tendencies—uniform curricular access, sufficient transportation incentives, cross-district transfer rights, and so on—to address these positional effects.

In sum, the design of school choice surfaces unavoidable trade-offs for policy and practice. How we design choice will reveal, in any era, how we have made up our minds regarding these fundamental tensions. How we design school choice policy will provide our answers to the following core questions:

1. Whose education is it? In what ways should parents, students, and/or the state decide? How should decisions be made about how and where to educate children?
2. How much innovation do we want, and how much accountability? By what measures? How will we hold compulsory schooling accountable for both our public as well as private educational goals?
3. What role do we seek for our schools in building a more inclusive, equitable and integrated plural society? How will our design of school choice advance or retard our collective progress?

School choice policy essentially designs the school market, with substantial implications akin to other regulatory challenges. For example, with greater choice amid a proliferation of charters and of vouchers, some nonpublic schools will not succeed—for lack of students, financial malfeasance, or other causes. When that failure occurs, local public schools must pick up the enrollment. There is no FDIC equivalent for failed schools; individual schools are not protected by a broader regulatory structure as a bank. In this way, school regulation carries a great collective risk, reminiscent of where financial markets were before 2008. Thus, whereas deregulated school choice may affect some families negatively, it has been a boon for various businesses and investors. In 2017, for example, ed tech firms alone raised nearly $3.5 billion in investments; venture capital investments grew tenfold in the last decade.[37] Choice gains get privatized, but losses are inherited by the public system. Further, as charter school management companies grow in size, will they then become "too big to fail," as districts hesitate in closing large poorly performing charters and overburdening already strained public systems?[38]

Most current school choice programs are bound to increase inequality, limit democratic accountability, and reduce students' exposure to shared values; this will be the effect unless such programs are deliberately designed to counter these market tendencies. Design details matter greatly if we want market means to yield more equitable collective outcomes—something markets do not "naturally" do. Communities, local governments, and states would do best to think about these consequences before implementing existing forms of choice that might push districts and states well beyond where most educators, families, and other taxpayers would like to go.

What Follows

The issues informing the school choice debate are central to the democratic debate: who has the authority to make decisions on children's education, and what norms and values should inform these decisions.[39] Who gets to choose a school for one's child, and at what stage in schooling do they get to do that? Since early in the history of the republic, states have enacted compulsory attendance laws, thus restricting parents' and children's choices about whether and when to attend school. What is the relationship between the aims that society attaches to schooling and the opportunity families have to select the institution where their children would be educated? And most significant for our project: how can the history of school choice help us think through our current policies and practices?

These questions are at the heart of this book, and have been the focus of policy and public debates for a long time. It aims to offer a balanced account of the history and philosophy of school choice in the United States—one that looks beyond the ideological divide between those (usually on the right, as well as both left and right libertarians) who seek to avoid government intervention and allow parents to choose any educational context for their children, and those (usually on the progressive left) who wish to support public education as a way to nurture a democratic public sphere, promote integration, or advance other public aims. We suggest that there are valid personal and public considerations on both sides, which partly explain the unusual coalitions sometimes forged in public struggles around this topic. Given the variety of ways in which parents choose schooling, we make the case for a "structured landscape" of choice in schooling, one that protects the interests of children first, and that supports a vibrant public sphere. Throughout this book we intend to put aside preconceived perspectives, taking careful stock of the policies and practices as well as values and commitments that have made the American school choice landscape what it is today. Pushing past the polarizations, we suggest a productive path forward.

What can several centuries of US history tell us about school choice today? We cannot presume to copy and paste lessons from the past, but we can see the present in fresh ways. Instead of a broad sweep, the historical section that follows explores three different eras, so as to highlight some trade-offs and tensions that persist. For example, we first look at the colonial and early republic periods. Why such a long leap back? The period illustrates that parents and communities have chosen a variety of ways to educate their children since our national beginnings, often in a mix of home, church, workshop, or school environments. Those schools might be free, tuition-driven or some combination thereof. This mix is not new; indeed, establishing and requiring schooling outside the home became an early collective "school choice" worth revisiting, as is the way in which that choice shapes our system still. Next, we shift to the period in which common schools—the roots of our present public school systems, had finally triumphed as an institutional form over a variety of competing institutions. But as publicly funded, publicly operated schools expanded, and a nation sought to unify via them, a large minority of families chose otherwise. Catholics essentially established a parallel, private mass schooling system, offering a choice that significant percentages of residents in some cities took up. Cities and towns were forced to somehow manage both public and private institutions as compulsory attendance expanded. Here was an early experience of regulating diverse providers, balancing wider parental choice with public accountability and quality. There is a lot that we can learn today from how this dual system of mass schooling emerged, including its early precedents in cross-sector regulations and accommodations. Finally, we turn to our more recent past, from the 1950s forward. How might the last sixty years help explain today's profile of school choices sketched above? What emerged in the dramatic decades following the horrific conflagration of World War II, as the United States grew dramatically, shifted demographically, and tested its democratic vision? In what ways has school choice today been shaped by trends in housing, desegregation, counterculture visions, institutional experimentation, and ideological shifts?

Following this historical analysis, the philosophical chapter looks at the justifications for school choice and discusses them in light of the empirical evidence within the framing ideals of democratic equality. While the historical section lends broader context, the philosophical section delves more deeply into the arguments themselves. In what ways does school choice promote or hinder democratic equality, which serves as the basic premise of the effort to provide access to quality education for all? The chapter explores in some detail the three core questions noted above: Whose education is it? Should the system remain stable, or keep innovating? And what are the social goals of schools?

We conclude the book by discussing the collective and individual aims of education, and how policy, by affecting the configuration of school choice, in turn affects these aims. In essence, we contend that education must be recognized as both a private and a public good, and as such the role of choice in its distribution cannot be summarized as a yes/no answer to the question, Should parents have choice in their children's schooling?

The aspects we consider along the way are related to the kinds of benefits schools can confer and the access to those benefits, as well as to the role of the state in providing education and regulating its provision. School choice today is often framed in terms of its role as an economic transaction—parents pay taxes, and they therefore deserve to choose the product they use; children will take part in the workforce, and therefore need to be prepared for its demands. While these are all recognized here, this book aims to broaden the lens used to look at school choice to include other public dimensions of education. We consider in this context preparation for civic participation, the boundaries and value of community membership and racial equity and access. This expanded framework for thinking about the history and philosophy of school choice provides a fuller and clearer view than the common ideologically driven debate permits. It clarifies why there is an important role for the parents in deciding about their children's schooling, while not shying away from discussing the limitations that parents have in serving their children's or society's best interests. The combined public and private roles of education necessitate state regulation of schooling, including the design of choice sets and processes, and demand attention to the growing role of private operators in this realm as well as to the effects that specific types of choice have on equal access to quality education.

School choice in the United States has long been a contentious issue, reflecting the internal struggles built into a federal system with authority over education distributed across parents, communities, states, and federal agencies, all aiming to serve the best interests of children as interpreted through personal, religious, community-based, and national lenses. Through considering the historical evolution of school choice and the enduring values that inform the debate, we hope to provide a framework that accounts for these different perspectives and provides a way forward. Our goal is to focus on a nuanced understanding of the role of choice in education policy making in the United States, and the principles that should inform school choice policy in order to do it right. We see the current phase of school choice history as both a continuation of historical trends—in the effort to balance government regulation with parental authority, which has endured over the life of the republic—and a breaking from it, characterized by the centrality of international financial and business considerations that go beyond the ongoing public/personal tension. The main normative tension we see in the current historical moment of school choice, as differentiated from earlier ones we surveyed, is that private business and philanthropic entities play a growing role not only in providing options to parents (which often happened historically in less cohesive ways), but also in shaping public policy and designing the choice landscape available in different ways to different communities.

The design of choice policy will define significant aspects of the future of the republic. How we shape those choices will shape the minds and profile of our citizenry, of our children and our neighbors. We make our society through such choices, and we must make up our minds about which shared vision we seek to construct.

School choice predates this republic; we turn now to that history.

Historical Reflections on School Choice

But do you really want a skeptical, slow complexifier at the table when you're trying to sort through important policy dilemmas? Well, yes, you do.
—CARL F. KAESTLE, "Clio at the Table"

Arguments around school choice date back at least several centuries, and often with odd bedfellows sharing positions, as is the case today. Just in terms of voucher plans, for example, an ideological range of thinkers urged support in the eighteenth century. Thomas Paine, in *The Rights of Man* (1791), advocated a plan to provide the poor ten shillings a year for six years of schooling, which included "half a crown a year for paper and spelling books." In a rhetorical flurry on behalf of more schooling in the new democratic republic, he argued that "it is monarchical and aristocratical government only that requires ignorance for its support." Paine also noted the varied interests to be advanced, on both the supply and the demand side: "To [the children] it is education, to those who educate them it is a livelihood," noting that "there are often distressed clergymen's widows to whom such an income would be acceptable." Though not fond of what John Adams called Paine's "yellow fever" of egalitarian "democratical" philosophy, Adam Smith also supported a "wide dispersal of educational expenditure and decision making," emphasizing it as an efficient way of letting the market's creative energy stimulate stuffy pedagogues. John Stuart Mill advocated a voucher program, but emphasized it as a means of guarding personal liberty: "A general State education is a mere contrivance for molding people to be exactly like one another. . . . [It] should only exist, if it exist at all, as one among many competing experiments."[1] He almost sounds like an early advocate for portfolio approaches to public school management.[2]

Yet the history solely of the arguments and theories about school choice will likely yield limited insights, for reasons a colleague of John Dewey noted early last century. In an attempt to understand the "controlling ideas in American education," George Counts decided to avoid the "natural temptation to write the educational theory of a people . . . in terms of the names and the thoughts of its great educational theorists."[3] Certainly, claimed Counts, their ideas seldom shaped actual practices, as "again and again the evolution of American educational institutions has proceeded with but little regard for the pronouncements of leading educators."[4] Instead, we should "endeavor to abstract from the actual practice of education the principles to which it gives expression"—in this case, regarding school choice.[5] For it is "through its concrete program of education a nation must give conscious or unconscious answer to every important question of theory"; indeed, "these practical responses of society . . . constitute the living theory of education of a country, the theory which has been made flesh and endowed with the breath of life."[6] Years later, historian and school reform leader Ted Sizer urged attention to actual practices over time; we should look at "what the people do for their young citizens. There are lessons in chalkdust."[7]

Following Counts's direction and Sizer's urging, this chapter examines a few of the choices made by parents over time in the United States, so as to unearth what underlies Counts's "practical responses of society," particularly looking at three historical "moments." Each section, each "moment," foregrounds an aspect of our history worth recalling in the current school choice debate. The first section reminds us of both the fundamental choice of schooling relative to other means of education, as well as the wide mix of "providers" evident since our early colonial days. It highlights the question, To whom does education belong? The next section shines light on parents who chose to opt out of the public system, forming a private mass schooling system to compete with the public. What affected this, and how did both public and private systems develop within, and benefit from, an emerging shared regulatory environment? That section also highlights the struggles over innovative approaches to schooling and to the design of choice sets for parents, and illustrates the tensions between innovation and accountability and the ways in which regulation aims to permit both. Regulation of schools, as in numerous other sectors, became the means for balancing private and public interests across public and private providers. A final section reminds us that our extended history of alternative school choice struggles—intensified by schooling's growing impact on economic and social aspirations—has long reflected the impact of other social policies. How we sort and select our neighbors, for example, has long affected how we balance public purposes and private choices in schooling, usually reflecting adult political choices. This section illustrates the centrality of questions about shared or collective aims of education in the making of policies about schooling.

Moving chronologically across the republic's history, the first section discusses colonial/early republic origins, first of schooling as a more deliberate choice among educating agencies, and then of the great variety in the school-ing market through the early national period, prior to the common schools. From the nation's birth, its educational pluralism reflected a decentralized political system, shifting roles among educating institutions, and a diverse range of providers and purposes for an uprooted people. A second section examines the coexistence of parochial and public schools as a single market, post–common school triumph, roughly 1870 to 1930, in selected northern cities where Catholic schools enrolled significant percentages of students. The period illuminates schooling trade-offs between assimilation and pluralism, the appropriate integration of private values and common schooling, the role of often invisible local adjustments, community leaders, and school boards, and the enabling role of cross-sector regulations in facilitating choices. A final section examines the drivers of the school choice landscape from World War II to recent years. Amid the intertwining influences of desegregation struggles, residential shifts, alternative school models, and growing conser-vatism, the nation shifted its educational pluralism to a bounded system of differentiated choices.

Our collective question is not whether to have choices for parents—we do, and always have—but how we will regulate who has which choices in this always-mixed market for schooling. To start, we turn back to eastern North American shores nearly four centuries ago; what choices did parents face then about the education of their children, and what echoes do we hear today?

Original Choices

Forasmuch as the good education of children is of singular behoof and benefit to any Common-wealth; and wheras many parents & masters are too indulgent and negligent of their duty in that kinde . . .

MASSACHUSETTS BAY SCHOOL LAW, 1642

Debates around the choices that parents should have regarding the education of their children, or of others' children, inevitably reflect the anxieties over the future direction of a community or society, and of its youth in particular. Even institutions that remain intact through a crisis may begin to serve quite different purposes, as their position in the ecology of educational agencies may shift. What does this mean?

One of the most striking examples arose in the early colonial period, in the fundamental crisis adults faced in transferring their European lives into, for them, a strange, new and often inhospitable wilderness setting. Historian Bernard Bailyn described what he saw as perhaps the "most important . . . transformation" ever to affect US education, a set of primordial choices that set fundamental patterns in place which still shape US schooling. To understand the educational choices he uncovered, including who had what authority over schooling, requires "a broader definition of education," beyond "formal pedagogy" to "the entire process by which a culture transmits itself across the generations . . . [as] when one sees education in its elaborate, intricate involvements with the rest of society."[8]

In post-Reformation England—especially among the middling classes, whose offspring would emigrate to the North American colonies from England and northern and western Europe—printing and literacy had spread considerably. Indeed, one sixteenth-century writer, Thomas Nashe, even complained that "every gross-brained idiot is suffered to come into print."[9] (And this was more than four hundred years before blogs were invented!) Children were raised in an instinctive, intuitive tradition of child-rearing closely tied to community and religious life. So then imagine that you, as an English colonist, survive the stench, disease, and weather perils of the boat ride over, settle into this strange new territory (strange and new to you, at least), and begin to implant your familiar institutions, habits, norms, and community life. You try to recreate the world you knew, in some way. For many, this meant patriarchal kinship communities, with youth taught to read and write, socialized to adulthood, and even taught their trade by family and friends, aided by the explicit moral instruction of the local church and, likely, a short spell of instruction in something we would recognize today as a brief, ungraded primary school.

But the colonists were not in anything like the world they were in before, though they struggled to recreate it. In many respects, it seems they were remarkably successful. Yet such a dramatically different environment did challenge some central tenets of how children were educated in the European countries they had left behind, leaving, says Bailyn, some permanent marks on US education. What was for centuries past an integrated ecology of extended family, community and church, with borders blurred, introducing youth unconsciously into a future of known roles largely defined by the past—all this crumbled given the pressures in a new land. Between the early days of European settlement and the end of the colonial period, the educational system was "dislodged from its ancient position in the social order."[10] An unforgiving environment wreaked havoc on family discipline, often advantaging youthful energy, as abundant land offered an easy escape for white males.[11]

Without the support of other established institutions as they had in England—local churches, universities, and so on—especially in the towns and urban areas, the colonial family seems to have taken on added importance as an educator. Many were alarmed at what they saw as a moral crisis among the young, were worried about their ability to raise their children in the faith of generations, and, for all their patriarchal trappings, turned increasingly to women to play a role in educating and catechizing the children in this new world.

The forbidding new surroundings challenged parental authority, where youth might adapt more easily than adults; bouts of starvation and disease could shatter traditional family discipline, even beliefs in Divine Providence; available land could loosen the bonds of familial allegiance; the demands of adapting to a harsh new physical environment might distract families from religion and home education. The fate of the culture, of civilization breaking down before it was passed down, was seen as hanging in the balance. Elders and clergy condemned the disorder, the moral breakdown of familial hier- archies, and even "the great neglect of many parents and masters in train- ing up their children in learning and labor."[12] The choices seemed dire. If the family broke down, then, per Ulysses in Shakespeare's famous speech, "the rude son should strike the [sic] father dead," and

> What plagues and what portents, what mutiny,
> What raging of the sea, shaking of earth,
> Commotion in the winds, frights changes horrors,
> Divert and crack, rend and deracinate
> The unity and married calm of states
> Quite from their fixure.[13]

To face this moral threat, colonists increasingly turned to schools to com- plement an already increased burden that families felt in educating youth, especially for proper moral upbringing—an echo we still hear so often today. Parents might not be trusted to carry out their duty, and the challenges grew.[14] Massachusetts's "Old Deluder Satan Act" of 1647, following on the heels of its 1642 mandate, required towns of fifty or more households to appoint a teacher for the children, to be "paid either by the parents or masters of such children, or by the inhabitants in general."[15] At one hundred households, Massachusetts towns were required to set up grammar schools in order to prepare students for university. Lack of compliance brought possible fines, though compliance proved very incomplete.[16] Clear student outcomes were sought; all students should be "able to answer unto the questions that shall be propounded to them out of such catechism by their parents or masters or any of the Select men when they shall call them to a tryall of what they have learned of this kinde."[17] An early restraint on parental choice, then, appeared in the form of the first school laws, as well as in early publicly set educational standards for youth.[18] The jolt of a new context surfaced a core question: Who can be entrusted with the decisions of how to educate the children?

But the new environment also challenged the natural order of educating youth to the world of work. You might learn your trade at home, or often, with a friend or relative, as an apprentice in their shop. The master tradesman, consequently, would also assist in your moral upbringing, with his own rules and guidelines, serving *in loco parentis* for the apprentice away from home. This was, in Bailyn's words, part of an "extensive network of mutual obligations."[19] Yet, as the colonies grew, labor grew more scarce, youth were more in demand, and the legal servitude that the master could insist on diminished. Apprentices now had a few more options; they could leave and find another placement if life was too strict or the promised benefits not realized. For example, at age 17, a disgruntled Benjamin Franklin, who was to become the greatest printer of colonial America, threw down his apron, bolted from his apprenticeship to his overbearing brother James in Boston, and headed down to Philadelphia to seek his fortune.[20] More broadly, shops urgently needed apprentices as much if not more than young laborers needed apprenticeships. In turn, apprentices sought greater options by furthering their own learning in evening schools or clubs, as in Franklin's famous Junto—a "club of mutual improvement" and North America's first subscription library—and many others.[21] Cut off from an inevitable place in the social order, many coalesced in various self-improvement efforts, what Bailyn saw as "the beginnings of a permanent motion within American society by which the continuity between generations was to be repeatedly broken."[22] In the northern colonies especially, young Americans and their families responded to shifting conditions, shaping their own educational paths, with new institutions arising and old ones evolving to support new paths and patterns. The increased demand outpaced the traditionally private means of financing schools, marking them early on as an institution subject to the designs of their funders as much as their pedagogues. Lacking sufficient state moneys or independent benefactors in this hardscrabble world, schooling depended on those who would pay, on "repeated acts of donation," creating a deep tradition of local dependency, reinvention, and a lack of self-direction.

The English colonies also had a greater religious, cultural, and ethnic heterogeneity than northern and western Europe. Religiously and culturally diverse groups of colonists jostled for their place in the colonies and early republic, including among them a motley variety of infidels, "Papists," defiant sectarians, varied nationalities, royalists, and revolutionaries, as well as various "backsliders into savagery."[23] Native tribes represented ethnicities, world views, and ways of life quite alien to colonists.

As committed denominational Christians, many colonists felt compelled to proselytize to, as well as to educate, their native brethren and other wayward souls. Perhaps the most aggressive and systematic early use of formal education during the colonial period had been for missionary work with the native tribes. While we may view such efforts as tragic, farcical, or horrific—especially when conjoined to the spread of European diseases across the continent— there is no doubt of the resulting transformation of education into a more explicit tool of indoctrination, persuasion, and transmission of culture.

In the eighteenth century, sectarian enthusiasts noted a useful precedent for the competitive denominational landscape in the colonies, where persuasion had to triumph over compulsion, even in territories with established churches. The use of schooling to nurture, protect, and extend a group's place in society became another legacy in the transformation of education by the end of the colonial era. In addition to schooling as a choice in the individual's increasingly uncertain life trajectory, the expanding of school options also became a tool for advancing the collective purposes of religious, ethnic, racial, vocational, and women's groups—affirming identity, subverting exclusions, extending moral agendas. The availability of land, along with increased demand for labor over time, gave restless youth and noncompliers an outlet from moral submission. Traditional approaches to moral and cultural enforcement became much less reliable in keeping youth in the fold, placing a premium on persuasion and education. Religious and other groups saw in schooling, and in other educational efforts, the essential tools to defend and advance their interests.[24] Education was now "an instrument of deliberate group action," preserving or advancing group identities, norms, and values.[25]

By the War for Independence, then, an education revolution had taken place; what had been an assumed, tradition-guided process, followed unconsciously across generations, became a matter of deliberate choice. Amid the "jarring multiplicity, the raw economy, and the barren environment of America," a "process whose origins lay in the half-instinctive workings of a homogeneous, integrated society was transformed. No longer instinctive, no longer safe and reliable, the transfer of culture, the whole enterprise of education, had become controversial, conscious, constructed: a matter of decision, will, and effort."[26]

Schooling the young, in other words, became an intentional decision in a manner in which it had not been—for parents, for religious groups, for communities, for students themselves. Deeply implicated in the cultural identity of the soon-emerging republic, education "tended to isolate the individual, to propel him away from the simple acceptance of a predetermined social role, and to nourish his distrust of authority."[27] Sought as a bulwark against change, schooling often became its accelerator. For the new nation, the form in which education would occur had become a matter of choice, both individual and collective, and a facilitator of a constant—and contested—social and cultural reconstruction. The question of who should have what choices, and how it related to that larger societal reconstruction, would shape discussions up to the present.

An Educational Ecology Emerges

> In the home or local system of schools, the aim is really private education, and for ends more or less personal, though it be obtained at the public expense. In the academical or collegiate system of schools, the aim is a true public education, though it may be obtained by means legally private; that is, such as furnished by individuals or corporations.
> —CHARLES HAMMOND, principal, Monson Academy, 1868

If we accept Bailyn's thesis of an early radical transformation in US education, how then did early Americans develop their choices, once education was "controversial, conscious, constructed"?

By the late colonial era, schooling was "plentiful," if "unorganized . . . haphazard and temporary; people in all ranks of society gained their education in a patchwork, rather than a pattern, of teachers and experiences."[28] Driven largely by popular demand, literacy—basic reading and writing—became nearly universal in New England by the end of the eighteenth century.[29] A wide variety of educational institutions emerged during the seventeenth, eighteenth, and early nineteenth centuries to support both basic and advanced learning.

Throughout this early time period, most families lived in sparsely populated rural areas, supported by local district schools, which were often located on land useful for little else.[30] In the early nineteenth century, over 90% of the population lived in towns under 2,500; the population also skewed much younger than it is today, and with considerably larger families.[31] With considerable variation across colonies (and later, states), most free youth, from roughly ages 5 to 14, would attend some form of schooling seasonally, alternating with family obligations on the farm. Transient teachers—often untrained and scarcely older than their elder charges—held forth several months a year in unpainted clapboard or log buildings, cramming in the most students during winter days, when farming duties waned. The youthful and itinerant pedagogues would usually work another job to make ends meet, and rotated their lodging among the community's families; they rarely stayed at any one school for long. Many communities preferred men during the winter months, when rowdy older boys could be an issue, employing female teachers during other times of the year, especially for younger children. Localities funded the schools through a combination of parental contributions (in-kind included, such as fuel, room, and board), tuition, proceeds from public land sales, and local taxes (often after state permission was granted). Most funding came from private sources prior to the Civil War, with contests of control embedded. The authority of parents ran high—they could decide or influence whom to hire as the teacher; monitor the teacher's habits, including his or her social life; select the texts and curriculum; and determine when the school would be open or closed. These early schools sufficed to provide basic levels of literacy and numeracy, at low cost and under tight local control.[32]

Across their careers, students might attend a mix of schools, for varying spells of time (if they attended formalized schooling at all; some apparently learned basic numeracy and literacy informally, from family, work, and church). Depending on one's locality, a *church* school, sponsored by a religious denomination, might provide basic education, with particular attention to the children of local parishioners, and often for a fee. Some missionary societies provided free schooling to indigent children and, in some areas, to African American children through charity or Sunday schools. In many northern and southern towns, local communities—with varying support from state, local, and private funds—established *town* schools to provide basic numeracy and literacy preparation, overseen by local officials.

Implanting a familiar pattern from England, initial schooling in the colonies often included time in a petty or dame school, on and off for perhaps two to three years, at times in the home of the teacher. Using paddle-shaped wooden hornbooks, students would learn the alphabet and basic words through simple prayers and catechetical lessons, work on basic writing and reading, and learn a bit of basic arithmetic, perhaps some singing, music, and manners. The next level of formal schooling, the grammar school, aimed to instill a basic knowledge of Latin, with some Greek and Hebrew likely, toward university preparation, and might last roughly seven years; few completed these studies. Towns often preferred the teacher who could switch across levels and content, a bit of Latin here, reading and writing there; the shortage and instability of enrollment made a blurred, petty/grammar model more sustainable.[33]

Even given the variety of ways in which basic schooling was carried out locally in the early republic, the next level of schooling—"higher learning," in the broad, flexible space across what we understand now as elementary school through college—provided an even richer field of educational choice. Parental options varied widely as education markets developed, especially in the eighteenth and early nineteenth centuries. A closer look at these options, and their mutual evolutions prior to the Civil War, illuminates some enduring trade-offs and tensions relevant to current questions of school choice, markets, and funding.[34]

What were the basic options for schooling beyond grammar school? In addition to options that might be available through local colleges or tutors, a family might send their child to a *venture* school—an entrepreneurial operation, usually small, and entirely dependent on tuition; the school often offered only one or two subjects, such as dancing, surveying, or needlework, based on student interest. Venture schools would arise, then shift subject or disappear. There appears to have been "something of a flowering of venture schools" in the second half of the eighteenth century, responding to desire for schooling in areas of commercial demand —writing, basic math, keeping books, surveying, navigation, and so on—as the new republic's economy grew.[35] In some cities, they competed successfully against existing grammar schools. In Boston, for example, venture writing schools' enrollment exploded from 1727 to 1767, growing 241%; grammar school enrollment dropped 16% in the same period.[36]

Finally, once their child mastered basic literacy, the parents might also select an academy—a broad range of incorporated educational entities, often characterized by a self-perpetuating board and funded by tuition and other funding, including in-kind support. Many academies held a state "charter," "basically a government-endorsed statement permitting institutions to hold property and to direct their own affairs."[37] Many were founded by colleges, towns, counties, societies, and religious groups.[38] Many served students between the ages of 8 and 18, though some would limit enrollment to those over 12; others would admit whoever could pay tuition.[39] Given the local nature of so many of these early educational institutions, we still have much to learn about the academies, though a considerable literature has arisen in more recent years.[40]

The academies became the "dominant institution of higher schooling from the late eighteenth to the late nineteenth century," before schools and school systems began to structure themselves more like they do today.[41] Even before the United States formed as an independent nation, *academies* formed in various parts of the colonies, as well as in the French and Spanish territories— largely by religious groups and congregations initially, but eventually also by local communities, societies, counties, and individuals. The first recorded academy in what is now the United States dates back to the 1727 founding of the Ursuline Convent School in French New Orleans, and in the English colonies, back to Philadelphia's Franklin's academy in 1753.[42] The academies flourished particularly between the Revolutionary and Civil Wars. As the young republic grew rapidly—the US population tripling between 1790 and

1830 — and as a "market revolution" transformed daily life, academies flowered across prosperous hub towns that connected the rising web of early turnpikes, state roads, and canals.[43] While the new state governments proved unwilling or unable to provide significant tax support, they often would incorporate the growing numbers of proposed academies; aided by local boosters, states thus could expand schooling with little cost to the state treasury. By 1786, Yale College president Ezra Stiles noted the "Spirit of Academy making"; and by the mid-1800s, more than six thousand academies operated across the nation.[44] In other words, more chartered schools existed in 1850, when the United States had roughly 7% of its current population, than existed in 2010.[45] As historian J. M. Opal notes, the academy "emerged as the primary educational innovation of the new republic, a conspicuous departure from the common [town] school."[46]

Academies, while located most frequently in small towns, were a "fundamentally rural institution," often attracting students from considerable distances; perhaps as many as 65%–85% of students would come from outside the town.[47] For this reason, most of these schools generally included boarding options. Students, broadly drawn from the rural middle classes, probably came on average from better-heeled families; tuition, board, and travel would add up, even if students attended sporadically. Families often had some property of their own, used for household production purposes, and the mix of students appears to have included a considerable range of wealth. While "solidly middle class," "most academies drew a fair share of hardscrabble youth from farming and artisanal families," and "represented a range of levels of property ownership."[48] In this way, they could be understood as "rather cosmopolitan."[49] Overall attendance rates appear to have rivaled or exceeded rates in more urban settings at the time.[50]

Indeed, "most academies would accept all students who could pay the fees, a rudimentary grasp of reading being the only academic entrance requirement."[51] Academy students sought to advance both personal and professional ends, and academy curricula varied considerably. Competing with the practical focus of many venture schools as well as the Latin-heavy grammar schools, academies represented a synthesis of those curricula, and often blended a variety of curricula, including by different tracks within the school. Academies also appeared responsive to market demands. The Philadelphia School of Design for Women, for example, even developed a sliding-scale tuition schedule based on student aims and wealth. The highest tuition came from those studying "fine arts" simply "for accomplishment"; the next level for those studying "commercial design," intending a professional career, or "normal art," for future teachers; and the lowest was reserved for those intending to work, yet without the means for even modest tuition.[52] In other schools, low-cost approaches such as the Lancasterian system—where a single teacher monitored advanced students who taught younger ones in a prescribed, structured format—might serve those paying modest tuition, while more traditional instruction applied to those at higher rates.[53] Beyond curricular innovations, academies also advanced other new approaches for their occasional, middling class clientele. They kept strict attendance rules and charged tuition for the full term to discourage daily turnover (town schools might lose students day to day, based on home farming needs). They grouped students more by ability level, and some provided curricular guides that would allow students to progress when not attending in person—perhaps assisted by a local tutor, if the family had the means. Finally, unlike the town schools and like the venture schools, they excluded those who could not pay, building an "engineered public of comparable others."[54] As an institutional form evolving over time, and with variation across distinct regions and family economies, the academy reflected the myriad purposes and contexts of schooling in a rapidly developing country.

In some ways, academies represent a peculiarly American educational institution. Historian Ted Sizer argued that "few social institutions in American history better exemplify the grand optimism of the people of this republic."[55] Institutions adapting to competing venture schools and town grammar schools, with a curricular variety to meet a range of clients pursuing an equally mixed set of purposes—from aspiring teachers to future surveyors—academies reflected well the hustling new nation as it scrambled to build itself.[56] Embedded across this range of rural-serving, town-located institutions were trade-offs and tensions that would mark US education to the present. Academies brought together families from across many towns and districts, and thus "promoted the expansion of middle-class culture and education."[57] Rev. Charles Hammond of Monson Academy in Massachusetts argued that academies, in gathering students from across communities, also served the republic by extending social bonds across classes and communities, countering the perspective-limiting "power of home associations."[58]

Yet that cosmopolitan mix included largely those who could foot the bill and spare children's labor—in sum, academy curricula reflected a pragmatic people hustling to develop a new nation. However, the academies retained grammar school elements for personal refinement. In this way, they contributed to what De Tocqueville found paradoxical:

> I do not believe there is a country in the world where, in proportion to the population, there are so few uninstructed and at the same time so few learned individuals.[59]

As Sizer argued, "The academy fit the American ideal: it provided a smatter-ing of both useful studies and traditional book learning, a veneer of educa-tion."[60] With this curricular mix, academies appeared further to promote a new American ethic of "emulation," encouraging children to seek distinction among their peers and in the increasingly evident expanded public.[61] Youth might aspire to emerging mercantile careers while also seeking the means for self-definition as familiar identities slid away, along with familiar ties, in a more mobile, unsettled world.

Beyond curriculum, academies also reflected tensions regarding what served private and public purposes in the new republic, what balanced col-lective ends in a tax-wary nation suspicious of governmental authority. Acad-emies argued that they more nimbly served the demand for schooling, and in more innovative ways, than did public institutions.[62] At the dedication of a new hall at Williston Seminary in Massachusetts in 1845, an invited speaker noted that

> we do not . . . see here the fruit of governmental patronage. Had its founders waited for this, I fear that the materials which now constitute these noble edi-fices, would have still remained unwrought in the mountains.[63]

An agile, messy nation needed flexible solutions to education, competing for student interest and resources. Yet many academies grew out of dissatisfac-tion with highly entrepreneurial venture schools. Indeed, some grew directly out of those schools. Venture schools could be too unstable, frustrating parents and community; their increasing segmentation raised questions of the com-monweal served in this new republic. Towns saw the benefit of academies for other reasons: reinforcing their standing as economic and cultural entrepôts, advancing local booster agendas. Thus, academies could meet demand as venture schools might, but also, with funding beyond tuition, create a more stable market for schooling and the communities they served. The volatility of the market for parental and student choices would be moderated by the academy's nonmarket sources of support.

As the nineteenth century progressed, with rising challenges of urbaniza-tion, immigration, regional tensions, and class divisions, configurations of schooling that moderated market and denominational impulses gained fol-lowers. While the story of the common schools has become familiar—with a triumphant Horace Mann on horseback in Massachusetts—the transition reflected competing and persistent concerns worth recalling. For example, as Mann served in the Massachusetts Senate, Bronson Alcott opened the short-lived, conversation-based Temple School (where he greeted each young charge on day one by asking what he or she was there to do) in sharp rebuke to the wide popularity of the rote Lancasterian monitorial system in the 1830s that had scaled rapidly across resource-strapped communities.[64] The notion of "public" and "private" was also shifting. While the early national period countenanced privately run academies, along with other private institutions, as "public" in their social functions—and, indeed, worthy of public funding—by the Civil War, "public" increasingly meant publicly supported *and* controlled, freely accessible on equal terms, and subject to state supervision. To consider these terms otherwise, warned Mann, was to abandon education "to the hazards of private enterprise, or to parental will, ability, or caprice."[65] By the end of the century, and unevenly across regions, one public system slowly emerged. Intended to be aligned with the needs of a rapidly developing, industrializing, and diversifying state, all other school providers were portrayed and eventually perceived as suspiciously private institutions amid pressing public concerns.[66]

By the onset of the Civil War, then, and particularly in the leading cities, a much more hierarchical, sequential, ordered, and publicly provided system of schooling had begun to settle into place. Pay schools—at one time the de facto common schools—became increasingly elite. As the still-young, expanding republic of new immigrants struggled with unity, common schools bridged prior denominational divisions. The "common school movement" of the antebellum period also sought to bridge the widening gulf between the broad middling classes attending pay schools and those attending free charity schools. As the nation hurled toward its most bloody chaos, reformers sought order in the provision of schooling. By 1860, many students who might have attended less pricey pay schools now attended free public common schools; much more tuition-free schooling had become available during the previous three decades.[67]

The messy mix of autonomous pay schools contributed critical pieces to the more centralized, standardized, and professionalized system of public-provided schooling that emerged in its place. Historian David Tyack called the emerging urban school structure the "one best system": a unified administrative control meant to bring the new scientific educational expertise to bear on what was once the realm of local stakeholders.[68] Despite this trend, some local academies survive to this day as elite independent schools, such as Andover Academy, and public schools inherited various practices from them.[69] Overall, though, pay schools disappeared as common schooling expanded and as decision-making shifted away from localities, sponsors, and parents to local elected officials and superintendents. Equity arguably increased, as did conformity to emerging professional norms. Yet voices of dissent from the one best system remained, in rural districts protective of local control, and in the growing Catholic school system, to which we now turn.[70]

Between Rome and Albany: The Catholic Challenge to Common Schools

During the mid-nineteenth century, dramatic shifts took place in the United States, with the quadrupling of city populations, the arrival of large new immigrant groups, the dramatic expansion of territory, an explosion in transportation, changes in social norms, a rise in regional tensions, increased class segregation, and so on. The sheer scale of the changes seemed to warrant institutional-size solutions, from incarceration to charity to schooling. To many, leaving individuals to act independently within this larger scale seemed a recipe for chaos. The "free publicly supported common schools" became one response, a "moral crusade" for reformers, one that would

> unite Christian morality with democratic patriotism; . . . stamp out the evils of ignorance, crime, vice, and aristocratic privilege; and finally, . . . not only assimilate the immigrants but also transform them into virtuous, productive American citizens.[71]

As reformers advanced their efforts, they left compulsory schooling laws in their wake, with most states enacting a wide variety of laws, often several per state. Obligatory schooling, claimed the courts, simply extended the state's "legitimate police power regulation on behalf of the public interest."[72] Enforcement, however, lagged far behind; parental choice still held sway locally, with little will or machinery to insist otherwise; overall schooling rates stayed flat in the latter half of the nineteenth century.[73] As the US commissioner of education lamented in 1889, "All experience goes to show that the complaints of voters or taxpayers have never yet set in motion the machinery for enforcing a compulsory law."[74]

By the early twentieth century, however, the juggernaut of school expansion accelerated, as did the pace of an urbanizing industrializing nation. On average, one new high school opened every day in the United States between 1890 and 1920; enrollments rose 812%. In addition, enforcement measures, such as attendance officers and the school census—aided by new child labor laws and fewer accepted exceptions to attendance—ratcheted up, such that primary school attendance appears to have been largely enforced. By 1940, some 75% of 5- to 19-year-olds attended school. As historian C. H. Edson put it, "Schooling had replaced work as the 'career' of youth."[75] Educator Ellwood Cubberley, approving of the common school triumphant, noted in 1909, "Each year the child is coming to belong more and more to the state, and less and less to the parent; [soon the] plea in defense that 'the child is my child' will not be accepted any longer."[76]

Within this context, then, parental choices reflected the agency that remained within this newly emerging framework—a wider societal effort to regulate the conduct of youth. The boundary of choices shifted; state and local governments, with compulsory schooling as a wedge to gain entrance, began inserting themselves into spheres previously left to parents. Truant officers were the eyes and ears of the state as it expanded a public claim on child welfare, health, labor, and delinquency. Vaccinations, for example, became required for schooling. State interests in maintaining order, public health, labor force development, national identity, and so on, advanced through the government's access to more of the nation's youth, who were in school for longer periods, and in the now dominant publicly managed schools. Parental school choices for their children narrowed as government mandated their time, good behavior, vaccinations, and compliance to professional educators. As historian Tracy Steffes sums up,

> Attendance enforcement . . . expanded public surveillance of children and households and invited school officials into intimate family decisions about children's health, welfare, and labor that were once wholly private family matters. Compulsory attendance laws also served as a mechanism through which other state policies could be applied indirectly to children.[77]

The school soon became a principal site for negotiating the balance between state and family prerogatives.[78]

Parents, of course, continued to exercise choice in various ways over the education of their children. Many parents resisted the heightened state role—mostly by evasion, which was at times the result of their frequent involuntary relocations. For many struggling immigrant families, though, children in school represented lost family income, as well as a threat to ethnic heritage and parental authority.[79] And children did not always serve as allies to their parents; for example, when Italian immigrant Pietro Coviello angrily rejected the local school's altered spelling of his son's surname, his son in turn resisted him, saying, "It's easier for everybody. . . . What difference does it make? . . . It's more American."[80] His son, Leonard Covello, eventually a prominent school principal, later concluded: "This was the accepted process of Americanization. We were becoming Americans by learning how to be ashamed of our parents."[81]

Yet many parents complied, strained by the struggle to survive and limited in their ability to resist. Only some were able to organize. Indeed, resistance often reflected class differences, as the better-heeled exercised more influence, a long-standing pattern, per historian William Cutler.[82] Others, aware of the increasing demands of the modern workplace, were able to see the potential benefit of additional schooling for their children. Seeking to build allies for their expanding professional purview, school leaders increasingly created, or attempted to co-opt, homeschool or parent associations, hoping to sway parents to make choices in line with the leaders' own agendas. Those parents who were active in these organizations often exercised their influence directly on the schools to which they were assigned, altering their school experience without changing schools. Finally, some parents early on exercised choice simply by moving voluntarily to a desirable school catchment area—a practice still very much in practice.[83]

But did parental compliance or parental demand drive the explosion in enrollments? Recent studies suggest that demand for more schooling made more of an impact than the efforts to force compliance. Indeed, compulsory schooling legislation seems to have had little independent impact on attendance trends. Several empirical analyses argue that these laws only minimally account for growth in attendance. While accurate statistics are difficult to find, high voluntary attendance at elementary school seems to have been common in many places by the last quarter of the nineteenth century. Rising attendance—particularly the explosion in high school enrollment—appears to correlate much more closely to other factors driving interest rather than pushing compliance. Compulsion was often viewed (and justified by those in favor) as part of building a larger social order, and focused particularly on those in distressed communities. Yet attendance trends overall were little affected. Economists Goldin and Katz attribute the expansion "largely to factors such as the substantial pecuniary returns to a year of school, increased family wealth, and greater school access. The constraints imposed on youth, employers, and local government by child labor and compulsory schooling laws were far less important."[84] To the degree this is true, the resistance that did take place may have reflected less an opposition to increased education, than an opposition to the increased role of the state in providing it (a tension to be discussed in part 2). Were the implied ethnic, religious, and class prejudices of imposed childrearing norms the greater perceived restraint on parental choice? Were those least able to resist those who most complied, or did they simply evade passively as other alternatives developed for those better positioned to choose?[85]

It is worth recalling that just after the Civil War, African Americans in the South lobbied for access to state-funded common schools, but also negotiated for employers to provide schools and rapidly opened hundreds of their own schools. Churches, especially those now operating independently as black institutions, played central roles in sustaining with funds and space, complementing day classes with evening and weekend Sabbath schools. Historian Herbert Gutman found that in 1866 African Americans supported at least half the schools in seven states, and at least a quarter in another five. In Georgia, nearly 250 schools had opened by 1867; freedmen supported ninety-six, and owned fifty-seven buildings. Two years later, in North Carolina, more than 1,500 Sabbath schools taught more than 107,000 students. Northern missionary groups and philanthropies offered critical support, and also experienced the freedmens' strong desire for independent control; "what they desire," reported a white missionary teacher, "is assistance without control." While the end of Reconstruction led many of these schools to close, dropping black enrollment between 1880 and 1890, the southern black illiteracy rate had dropped 25 percentage points in the two decades following emancipation.[86]

Amid varied legal access, extralegal obstructions, and the demands of poverty, more and more families sent their children to publicly supported, publicly run, and increasingly compulsory schools in the late nineteenth and early twentieth centuries. Yet another cohort of parents chose otherwise. Instead of resisting public school directives or organizing themselves, they chose instead to support another institutional option, and they were not an insignificant group. Across the fifteen largest US cities, they represented nearly a third of K–12 enrollments. They sought and supported an alternative mass school system—one more consistent with their values at home, more respectful of their cultural and linguistic backgrounds, and more aligned with their community norms and religious institutions.[87] In the rapidly expanding American common public schools, many parents, especially among the newly arriving southern and eastern European Catholics, simply saw pan-Protestant institutions run by native-born educators of northern and western European stock, usually from other parts of their city or town.[88] In the remaining Calvinist echoes of the McGuffey Readers; in the selections from the St. James Bible, and not the Douay; and in the use of Protestant hymns and daily school prayers, many Roman Catholic parents and church leaders saw a threat to their faith and ethnic identity. Buffeted in the aftermath of the Civil War by a dizzying array of social, economic, and political forces, Catholic religious leaders, long involved in schooling, viewed an urgent need for expanding their offerings of faith-based education. They shared with their common school advocates a strong faith in the power of schooling, but differed in their diagnosis of the nation's most pressing ills. The Catholic hierarchy in the United States sought to attack the "most ruinous movements of indifferentism, naturalism, and materialism" of the nineteenth century.[89] The common school risked exposing children to heresy; even including Catholic teachers within common schools would not provide the sufficient countercultural force promised by parish schooling. "Usually suspicious of the institutions of their new country," the hierarchy of the immigrants' church "was able to show them why they were

THE AMERICAN RIVER GANGES.
THE PRIESTS AND THE CHILDREN.—(See Page 992.)

FIGURE 3. Illustration for Eugene Lawrence, "The Priests and the Children," *Harper's Weekly*, September 30, 1871.

right to be."[90] At their Third Plenary Council of Baltimore in 1884, the bishops built upon prior declarations and sought a systematic, high-quality parochial school system in order to do proper battle with the moral challenges of a world in the upheaval of armed conflicts, industrialization, urbanization, and scientific advance.[91] In the present age, claimed the council, "the Church of God and the spirit of the world are in a certain wondrous and bitter conflict over the education of youth."[92] An assertive Catholic hierarchy pledged support for mass schooling—"a sound civilization must depend upon sound popular education"[93]—and also recognized that the state should not have a role in teaching religion. Yet, in a modernizing era "when error is so pretentious and aggressive," the Catholic leadership challenged the "false and pernicious notion" that any school should exclude religion:

> To shut religion out of the school, and keep it for home and the Church, is, logically, to train up a generation that will consider religion good for home and the Church, but not for the practical business of real life.[94]

Our normative challenge of "whose education is it?"—introduced last chapter—was well understood as a central concern.

Catholic assertions only fanned fears of Roman loyalties and papist interferences, captured in political cartoonist Thomas Nast's iconic portrayal of the Catholic attack on common schools.

Acknowledging that foreign allegiances could appear suspicious as US immigration hit historic highs—some eleven million Catholics arrived between 1890 and 1920—Catholic leaders affirmed their patriotism: "We have no flag but the stars and stripes," observed a New York City pastor.[95] In declaring their loyalty, however, they also asserted that "Americanism came in plural forms and not in the single pattern of a Protestant *paideia*."[96] Catholic schooling in turn retained its own plurality, reflecting internal splits about the degree of assimilation required. Some Catholic leaders had sought to work within common schools; Cincinnati's Bishop John Baptist Purcell served in the city's schools as an examiner in the 1840s.[97] Other schools became "American Catholic schools," modeled along the lines of the common public schools; still others were established as "ethnic parish schools," often emphasizing the cultural and linguistic heritages of the parish community. The ethnic parish schools, for many parents, bridged old and new worlds, both assisting assimilation and diminishing its need.[98]

Thus, despite the dramatically expanding public school systems—for example, New York City tripled its enrollment from 1890 to 1920, to more than nine hundred thousand students—US Catholic bishops declared in Baltimore that the development of a parochial system was a top priority—"every Catholic child in a Catholic school."[99] The council mandated a school for every parish within two years, if one did not yet exist; the bishops further mandated that Catholic parents send their children there with rare exception.[100] Addressing the education of the clergy as well as the need to establish what would become Catholic University, the council decreed a wide series of measures to upgrade quality across a Catholic education system spanning through college. Meeting in Baltimore, the bishops challenged the faithful not simply "to multiply our schools" but also "to perfect them."[101] Competition with public schools was understood:

> We repudiate the idea that the Catholic school need be in any respect inferior to any other school whatsoever. And if hitherto, in some places, our people have acted on the principle that it is better to have an imperfect Catholic school than to have none, let them now push their praiseworthy ambition still further, and not relax their efforts till their schools be elevated to the highest educational excellence.[102]

Lest the competition be purely on the grounds of educational quality and life on earth, however, the bishops implored parents not to withdraw their students prematurely, "but to give them all the time and all the advantages that they have the capacity to profit by, so that, in after life, their children may 'rise up and call them blessed.'"[103]

More earthly, social interests were also advanced by the network of locally controlled parish schools that the Catholic system largely became, as it left great discretion to each pastor and community.[104] Catholic parishes— "constituting oases of familiarity in the desert of Protestant hostility"[105]—often reflected the ethnic identities of their communities, providing precious cultural and linguistic ties to the Old World. Indeed, when parish clergy did not reflect their ethnic community, parishioners often forced the hand of bishops worried about lay support for building funds.[106] Exemplified by the Catholic German, Irish, and Polish communities in particular, lay immigrants played critical leadership roles in building the parish, its school, its social clubs, cultural societies, newspapers, and its myriad other activities in the community.[107] As a result, the parish school tended to affirm immigrant identity and agency in ways public schools could not—especially in the language of instruction, in the backgrounds of the teachers, and in the school's moral discipline.[108] As school systems grew rapidly, they increasingly centralized around more distant professional administrations, removing control from often unlettered, local immigrant leadership. For example, in New York City, opposition to the cronyism of entrenched local ward systems and the advocacy for good city government "was charged with class and religious antagonisms"; odd bedfellows existed across ward politics and local ethnic Catholic communities.[109] As historian Diane Ravitch recounts, in a key battle against the notorious Tammany Hall in New York City,

> [t]he city's social leadership barely contained its distaste for the common Irishmen who were powers in the city; even more basic to the good Anglo-Saxon stock of New York was its ingrained aversion to Catholicism. With Irish Catholics controlling Tammany Hall, and Tammany Hall controlling the city, reformers saw the [1894] election as a crusade to save the city.[110]

Yet the parish school often provided opportunities for ethnic leadership in building diverse social and educational institutions within local communities, exactly at the time when larger professional systems and organizations seemed to make that less possible in other spheres.[111]

As a result, from the late nineteenth to early twentieth centuries, a large private mass education system arose to challenge public school enrollments in a number of cities and towns, especially in the North.[112] By the turn of the twentieth century, parochial schools could be found in three out of five Catholic parishes; enrollment increased sixfold between 1880 and 1930, by which time US immigration had been severely restricted.[113] A low-cost, mission-driven teaching force often kept tuition within the range of the working class; the professionalization of Roman Catholic teaching and administration reflected similar patterns in the public system, though the parochial system lagged behind in building the supporting structures within higher education.[114] In the rise of Roman Catholic schools, both parochial and independent, an emergent system of parental choice operated across numerous cities, including Boston, Chicago, Cleveland, Buffalo, Baltimore, Pittsburgh, St. Louis, San Francisco, New Orleans, Detroit, and Milwaukee.[115] Cities varied in the size of this private sector; at the high end, one estimate put Catholic school enrollment at nearly half of total enrollment in Cleveland in 1880. From 1870 to 1930, "in the country's largest cities . . . Catholic schools enrolled just under a third of all children who attended school" and "accounted for 60 percent of the entire enrollment in the nonpublic sector."[116]

The impact could be seen nationally. In 1887, US Commissioner of Education Nathaniel Dawson found that public school enrollment, for the first time since records were kept, had slowed, and in some areas (especially the North) actually had decreased.[117] For Dawson, "this was a matter of the highest gravity"; Boston minister Joshua Young saw, potentially, "a fatal deterioration of the public schools," even in the birthplace of common schooling, and the start of "the History of their Decline and Fall."[118] Many public school educators saw the rise of parochial education in the late nineteenth century as a direct affront to the progressive and nation-building aspirations of the common schools, a threat to the assimilation they saw as critical to the nation's survival during the post-Reconstruction period of massive European immigration, especially from the presumably less developed and less republican cultures of southern and eastern Europe. As the nation expanded further westward, public schooling's power to unify so many social, regional, racial and cultural cleavages seemed directly challenged, especially as ethnic parish schools often emphasized foreign language instruction, cultural activities, and different textbooks. Certainly some opposition reflected the earlier midcentury rise of the Know-Nothings—a nativist, anti-immigrant political movement—and a virulent, enduring anti-Catholicism, including violent clashes and church bombings across the country. For most communities, which *were* predominantly Protestant, the common schools were a cross-sect compromise for the greater republic; establishing separate Catholic schools seemed an end run on such local democratic control, especially when prior eras saw many Catholic leaders cooperate in common school operations. For historian Robert Gross, a "divisive cyclical process" developed; "more Catholic parochial schools produced more anxiety among Protestants, fueling greater anti-Catholic sentiment and, in turn, louder calls among Catholics for their own schools."[119] Common school reformers, proudly developing the "one best system," viewed professionally run public schools as part of a wider set of modernizing reforms in an era of increasingly large and complex organizations. Consistent with centralizing municipal reforms, common school systems would counter local corrupt ward school bosses in Democratic machines the likes of New York City's Tweed; the unregulated parochial system would thwart such good government measures, which were paralleled in other human services, such as policing and sanitation. Finally, many educators opposed the rise of private schooling for clearly bread-and-butter terms. If some school leaders saw the rising church schools as a pragmatic escape valve for urban public systems struggling to accommodate the dramatic inflow of new students, many others feared job losses. Well into the twentieth century, even Catholics working as public school teachers worried that "the increase of parochial schools put them out of jobs"; sending their children to a parochial school would "bite the hand that feeds me."[120] For many immigrant families, public school teaching served as a critical part of their economic ascent; in a dozen cities, the Irish alone constituted 20% or more of the public school teacher corps.[121]

To paraphrase one of our core questions from the introduction: How would legitimate demands for accountability intersect with this mass "innovation" of a private system? Despite the often heated political and ideological debates, and the very real intergroup tensions, many localities appear to have found middle ground between the two systems, "peaceable adjustments" facilitating parental choices and respecting local group interests within evolving state parameters.[122] For historian Benjamin Justice, in New York State what was "most historically significant . . . was not the war of words over church and state policy but the myriad ways in which the locals kept the peace."[123] In a few instances, for example, educators sought to publicly fund Catholic schools—most notably in Lowell, Massachusetts, for twenty-one years; in the towns of Faribault and Stillwater, Minnesota, in the early 1890s; and in Poughkeepsie, New York, from 1873 to 1898.[124] Archbishop John Ireland arranged for the parochial schools in two towns within the St. Paul archdiocese to be converted to public schools, though with the same teachers and students as before conversion. Each town had two public schools: the converted Catholic school and the traditional public. Nuns taught the public school curriculum in the converted schools, with religious instruction after hours. Once known outside the archdiocese—Ireland described it in a talk to the National Education Association—it was quickly opposed both by Catholics who feared too much accommodation and by non-Catholics who saw a violation of church/state separation; the arrangement lasted only two years. Yet five area communities implemented similar arrangements (though avoiding the public attention Ireland had brought to the Faribault-Stillwater scheme).[125] Nationally, perhaps the best known of these arrangements was the Poughkeepsie plan, which endured across three decades.

Operating within the blurred public/private boundaries prevalent in the early nineteenth century, and with a low appetite for taxation, Poughkeepsie residents had since 1843 run their public schools on a slim budget, often renting a large portion of the space needed for classrooms. Across a fifty-year period, classrooms were rented in various churches, a theater, and even a coach factory. After the Civil War, many cities faced exploding enrollment growth, and overcrowding became a perennial challenge. Local budgets strained to keep up. In the spring of 1873, in the months ahead of the financial panic that struck the nation, pastor Fr. Patrick F. McSweeny announced that St. Peter's parish could no longer afford to run its schools, and that the eight hundred students attending would need to attend the town's local public schools. The influx would represent a 50% increase in public school enrollment, and the students would enter already congested schools. The local board suddenly faced an emergency situation. The pastor, though, had a solution tucked in his back vestment pocket—one used in other towns across some fourteen states: the school board could lease the parish buildings during the school day, for the bargain rate of one dollar a year, and then run public schools there for the parish's children. "Control and use of the building was to be vested exclusively in the board of education during school hours and in the church at all other times."[126] Normal expenses and repairs would be picked up by the board. While the board would staff the schools as it wished, the pastor made it clear that Catholic teachers and nuns should be hired as long as they met board requirements. No religious instruction would occur during school hours, though the two schools would remain single-sex. Children from other sections of the city would be allowed to attend. The parish school building could remain the hub of the parish community, while the district avoided new school construction or pricier rentals.[127]

The agreement held for twenty-five years. Neither the area Catholic Church nor school board apparently reported any formal local objections.[128] The arrangement inspired similar plans in other smaller towns, particularly those "renowned for their stinginess toward funding public schools," like Elmira, New York.[129] Some tensions apparently endured. Protestant ministers and the local American Protestant Association had objected to the plan, along with the dropping of Bible reading in the parish-located schools. Some conservative Catholics outside Poughkeepsie expressed their concerns as well, worried about too close an accommodation with public schooling, and reflective of the internal struggle within the US Catholic church. For historian Timothy Walch, however, "local criticism of the plan faded in the face of the communitywide goal of assimilating the foreign born into American society."[130] Yet after several decades in effect, in 1898, Poughkeepsie resident Edward Keyser complained to New York State Superintendent Charles Skinner, objecting to the four nuns teaching in Schools 11 and 12, who were dressed in religious garb and addressed as "Sister" by their students.[131] Skinner concurred with the appellant, and threatened the loss of state aid if the agreement was not terminated. Objecting to the rental of classrooms from "Baptist, Methodist, Universalist and Catholic denominations," Skinner insisted that towns "must own the property in which their schools are conducted." In addition, all schools must "discontinue in the public schoolroom the use of the distinguishing dress or garb of any religious order."[132] Noting that the "spirit of our institutions . . . call for a complete and total severance of Church and State," he stated:

> The public school system must be conducted in such a broad and catholic spirit that Jew and Protestant and Catholic alike shall find therein absolutely no cause for complaint as to the exercise, directly or indirectly, or any denominational influence.[133]

The sisters left School 12, which was then rented back to the city for $1,000 annually, and School 11 converted back to a parochial school.[134] As the state became more assertive and the public system expanded rapidly, the range for "peaceable adjustments" integrating public and private systems of mass education locally seemed more constrained. Parents would face a more formal demarcation between systems.[135]

As the children of earlier Catholic immigrants themselves became parents in the early twentieth century, their preferences also drove changes in schooling options. Increasingly, they sent their children to American Catholic parish schools over ethnic or national parish schools; "by the 1930s, native language and culture had become extra-curricular subjects in most parochial schools and dropped altogether at some."[136] For those Catholic parents sending their children to public schools, extracurricular or weekend programs became a means of what historian Jeffrey Mirel terms "patriotic pluralism," assimilating to US society via the public school, but bringing their native heritages to the American culture through their children and their own religious and cultural institutions.[137] Additionally, as some Catholics began to advance socially and economically, local parish schools developed retention issues for other reasons. One set of reasons involved social positioning; according to historian Robert Cross, "whether an Irish-American felt justified in looking askance at parochial schools frequently depended on his social position, which in turn was generally correlated with his escape from the ghetto."[138] Besides, many public systems had removed the more blatant forms of anti-Catholic bias from textbooks and daily practices. Districts began to employ Catholic teachers, and Catholic candidates made their way onto local school boards.[139]

Another reason involved perceptions of school quality. Parents across sectors increasingly viewed schooling as critical to advancement in the urban industrial world; the nun teaching in the parochial school, a "pious peasant girl just arrived in America," no longer appealed to those "outgrowing the immigrant state-of-mind."[140] The editor of *Dziennik Zwiazkowy*, a newspaper formed out of the Polish National Alliance in 1908, noted concerns about inferior parochial education, blaming a clergy that, "for its own selfish advantage, would like to force Polish children in the parochial schools even if these schools are inferior."[141] Years before, Archbishop Ireland reported parents' concerns that, while the nuns were adept at teaching young children, older students were being "sent forth by the Sisters from their schools less fitted for the battle of life" than their public school peers.[142] Parents clearly saw the schools—parochial or public—as a means of advancing their children's prospects. In that vein, a Lithuanian weekly worried that local priests spent too much time on catechism and prayer, and not enough on "general education . . . for those planning to attend high school and university."[143] Catholic parents often chose both public and private schools for their children, with some time spent at worksites along the way. Many urban Catholic families chose parochial schools during the elementary years, but turned to the expanding public system of "people's colleges," the high schools, in later years. Often this was driven by cost and geography; parish elementary schools were usually local, but even with clergy teaching, tuition stretched limited family resources.[144] For those working-class families earning $400 or less annually, the tuition burden could easily rise to 5% or more of gross income.[145] Parish primary schools struggled to keep costs within $8 per student, while public high schools—with science labs, gyms, pools, vocational education, cooking, manual training, and so on—spent roughly $100 per capita by the 1920s, in impressive structures meant to meet rising parental ambitions.[146]

For the choice of the parish elementary school to work for parents, however, they needed assurance the high schools would accept their children. Parents rightly complained when public schools accepted transfers at grade levels below that last attended at the parish, for example. Public high schools, which increasingly accepted successful public elementary graduates without entrance exams, retained the tests for years for students from parish schools; students often transferred to public school in late elementary to avoid testing. In cities with larger Catholic enrollments and wider enthusiasm for administrative efficiencies, public systems of accreditation of private elementary schools were put in place so as to allow high school entrance on the same terms as public elementary schools. Public accreditation and oversight across the dual systems grew in the early twentieth century to encompass "teacher certification, curriculum, accounting, student health, buildings, and many other policy areas."[147] Even textbooks converged across sectors. While parish textbooks certainly highlighted the exploits of American Catholics through history, both sector's textbooks promoted common themes of "patriotism, piety, deference, thrift, honesty, and diligence"; per historian Walch, "the overwhelming majority of Catholic schoolbooks were in complete thematic agreement with public school texts" by the late nineteenth century.[148]

Many Catholic educators saw increased regulation as a necessary step in raising quality, and others recognized the measures as essential to marketing their schools to increasingly ambitious parents. Catholic University professor Patrick McCormick, recognizing that adopting public standards was often not a choice for parish schools, understood them nonetheless "as a necessary means of subsistence, or as a consequence of competition for local patronage."[149] Buffalo's diocesan Superintendent Edmund Gibbons also saw the opportunity accreditation, exams and other standards provided for marketing Catholic schools: "We must advertise in this age of advertising. . . . We shall display our wares if we wish to draw customers.[150] Historian Howard Weisz noted that the drive to "emulate public schools came from parents, jealous of the educational advantages of others. . . . Pastors accepted changes that would help their schools compete, if they felt the changes did not endanger the religious nature of the schools."[151] Common standards enabled a more efficient and higher quality school market across private and public sectors.

In addition to standards, districts also strained to handle the student enrollment flow within and across systems. Working families often moved around, searching for work, lower rent, or both. Sociologist Le Roy Bowman, in 1925, observed that "one school, ten years ago 99 per cent Jewish . . . [is] now 99 per cent Italian."[152] Thousands of the children of these "permanent transients" changed schools every year in major cities, complicated by movement in and out of parochial schools.[153] A Rhode Island superintendent complained that students were "continually changing from public to private, and from private to public . . . just as the mood of the parent happens to be."[154] Administrators noted that transfers might happen multiple times in a single year; in New York City, this involved hundreds of thousands of students. As compulsory attendance laws proliferated, so did district challenges in coordinating across public and parochial sectors. Was a student playing hooky, a truant officer would ask, or were they truly enrolled in a nearby parochial school? States began requiring private school attendance records to substantiate compliance and facilitate transfers across systems;

most parochial schools obliged. The unified parallel attendance systems placed parish schools and the growing diocesan systems on the same plane as public schools, and provided staff-strapped parochial schools with assistance in managing attendance.[155]

Viewed from across both public and parochial systems, and despite clearer boundaries between sectors, an increase in cross-sector regulations facilitated the growth of this wider public/private school market. Shared parental concerns and local arrangements often shaped the dual system of schools in many northern cities in similar ways. The regulatory response further facilitated both the movement of students across sectors, and the movement of ideas, forms, and content. Without minimizing the differences in faith-based, tuition-requiring versus publicly operated institutions, an early "choice" system provided evidence of the many local "acceptable adjustments" and cross-sector regulations that both tolerated and facilitated the dual market's development.

Rebels with Causes: Sorting Out Schools since *Brown*

> What the Blandings wanted . . . was simple enough: a two-story house in quiet, modern good taste, . . . a good-sized living room with a fireplace, a dining room, pantry, and kitchen, a small lavatory, four bedrooms and accompanying baths . . . a roomy cellar . . . plenty of closets.
>
> —ERIC HODGINS, *Mr. Blandings Builds His Dream House*

After the desperation of the Great Depression and the savagery of World War II, millions of Americans eagerly returned to a focus on domestic dreams, driving a booming economy across fresh interstate highways into rapidly expanding suburbs, generously supported by expansive federal housing programs and years of pent-up demand. K–12 enrollments skyrocketed again in the postwar era, roughly doubling from 1945 to 1968, to nearly fifty-one million students. By 1950, the suburbs were exploding, growing ten times faster than center cities, driven by federally subsidized new housing, cheap gas, expanding roadways, and the lure of the "suburban ideal." By mid-decade, some nine million Americans had settled upon the fresh sod of these "crabgrass frontiers."[156] Distinct from their European counterparts in "walking city" traditions, the United States' upper and middle classes endured increasing commutes in order to live out a suburban ideal, leaving lower class neighbors back in the relative density, poverty and aging housing of center cities.[157] Critics like Lewis Mumford lamented that this new suburb "caricatured both the historic city and the archetypal suburban refuge"; neighbors of the same class, income, and age groups spent their days

witnessing the same television performances, eating the same tasteless pre-
fabricated foods, from the same freezers, conforming in every outward and
inward respect to a common mold . . . a low-grade uniform environment from
which escape is impossible.[158]

It was also an environment enthusiastically sought. As historian Kenneth
Jackson notes, those purchasing homes—and Long Island's Levittown alone
numbered more than 17,400 units—"were not terribly concerned about the
problems of the inner-city housing market or the snobbish views of Lewis
Mumford and other social critics."[159] They found safety, private space, and
good schools at a newly affordable price. Avid consumers bought new color
TVs in order to watch *Leave It to Beaver* in cookie-cutter Cape Cods, split-
levels, ranches, and modified colonials in Levittown subdivisions. After two
debilitating decades, pushed from burgeoning cities and pulled by the suburban ideal, these people had found, within reach, "a private haven in a heartless
world."[160]

To avoid viewing the 1950s through a nostalgic fog, seeing an era of placid,
commercialized conformity, the decade also experienced the characteristic
tensions of the next several decades—politically and culturally. Beyond the
adolescent rebellions typified by James Dean in *Rebel without a Cause*, Mar-
lon Brando in *The Wild One*, or Elvis in any of several hip-swinging films,
historian John Bodnar urges examination of the "unruly adults" advancing
disruptive causes during this "Levittown" decade.[161] Alfred Kinsey disturbed
notions of sexuality and gender; Hugh Hefner advanced a hedonist lifestyle far
from family commitments. Rosa Parks stood and sat for fundamental social
change; Jackie Robinson played across deeply ingrained racial boundaries.
They each suggested choices previously off-limits. Grace Metalious's *Peyton
Place*, a runaway best seller, telling tales of lust, injustice, and noncompli-
ance in middle America—"disrupt[ed] sentimental assumptions of female
desire and patriotic ones of American identity."[162] McCarthy waged holy war
on Communism, the United States waged war in Korea, the war-hero president lamented the "military-industrial complex," and the Soviets wounded
American technological pride. The Pledge of Allegiance added "under God"
and the dollar bill added "In God We Trust," lest collectivist, materialist social
orders gain the upper ideological hand.[163] This was an unsettled and unsettling
decade, no matter how many wood-framed private havens arose on cookie-
cutter lots, nor how many copies of Norman Vincent Peale's *Power of Positive
Thinking* flew off bookstore shelves. Within this tumult, the outlines of our
present educational pluralism were visible in the writings of Bestor and Friedman, as well as the decision *Brown*.

In 1955, the Progressive Education Association (PEA), a hallmark institution of an earlier generation's reforms, closed its doors with little fanfare. While its final president, Ohio University professor H. Gordon Hullfish, felt the PEA "[passed] on with its work done, its influence great," the *New York Times* opined that, after its heyday in the 1930s, the PEA's closure owed mostly to

> the disrepute, even contempt, in which the term "progressive" has been held in recent years. In many school systems it has been the educational kiss of death to be labeled a disciple of Dewey or a member of the association.[164]

As a prior era quietly faded amid the sounds of new school construction, school reform pivoted.[165] Cold War fears helped fuel an emphasis on raising academic standards to meet a foreign threat. A radical market-oriented educational policy reintroduced itself, if to little initial avail, as a counter to state-controlled collectivist thinking. A decades-long battle for educational access and justice reached a new legal and political pitch. The 1950s thus proved a launching period for school choice struggles still with us today.

In 1953, two years before Dean's *Rebel* hit theaters, University of Illinois professor Arthur Bestor sounded a shrill call for the restoration of intellectual purposes in schooling, decrying the "bustling educational cafeteria" in schools. The rhetoric would prove emblematic of an enduring genre of education critiques. Cold War tensions running high, Bestor saw an "iron curtain" being fashioned by "professional educationists"; on one side, the "slave-labor camps . . . [of] . . . classroom teachers," and on the other, "the free world of science and learning, menaced but not yet conquered." In order to save the country's intellectual life, the nation must break the "control of a new breed of educator who has no real place in—who does not respect and who is not respected by—the world of scientists, scholars, and professional men."[166]

One of those scholars, University of Chicago economist Milton Friedman, sought to free those teachers and their schools as well, not from vapid curricula, but from the "dead hand of bureaucracy." Consistent with "the current pause, perhaps reversal, in the trend toward collectivism," the time was ripe for reenvisioning a more limited role for government in schooling—in other words, more choice. Friedman acknowledged that public funding was justified by the shared ends of citizenship. Yet he saw no justification for government running the schools it financed. In full-throated support to the reformative powers of the market in education, he proposed a voucher scheme that would allow parents to take their allocation of school dollars to the institutions they chose.[167] The approach would lead to a greater mix of schools, and the resulting competition would "quicken the pace of progress in this area as it has in so many others. Government would serve its proper function of improving the operation of the invisible hand."[168] Friedman acknowledged that "the education of my child contributes to other people's welfare by promoting a stable and democratic society." Vouchers would simply advance this "neighborhood effect" more efficiently. Yet as these postprogressive seeds of curriculum and policy were planted, the neighborhood effects of another sort shaped school choices much more immediately.

Choosing Neighbors and Schools

School choices today reflect the social geography of schooling that emerged after World War II. Given the local nature of US school governance, who lives where shapes school demographics, funding patterns, and educational politics. All were altered as neighborhoods shifted in the post–World War II period, and today's school choice profile reflects the large and dramatic residential changes of the last half century.[169] Suburban youth would become the largest segment of K–12 students, having been a minority of attendees in the 1940s, as a majority of the overall population inhabited suburbs after 2000.[170] The political and cultural strength of this constituency would figure prominently in the evolution of school policy.[171] The last half century also saw a corresponding geographic redistribution of relative educational achievement. In 1940, cities outperformed suburbs academically; forty years later, suburban advantages became the dominant pattern, with a longitudinal rise in attainment across the board.[172]

Over a similar period, another shift dramatically altered the racial geography of the United States. The nation's African American population, in the massive, "vast," and "leaderless" Great Migration over the first three quarters of the century, shifted from a largely rural southern population to a densely segregated urban one. Nearly six million African Americans left the South for new lives north and west.[173] This "turning point" in US history "would transform urban America and recast the social and political order of every city it touched."[174] This exodus to freedom, deeply resonant in US history,

> would force the South to search its soul and finally to lay aside a feudal caste system. It grew out of the unmet promises made after the Civil War and, through the sheer weight of it, helped push the country toward the civil rights revolutions of the 1960s.[175]

Black school-age youth, over the course of a few decades, moved from "living in the impoverished Southern countryside" to living in "a largely urban one, concentrated in the nation's principal cities in largely segregated neigh-

borhoods."[176] Perhaps 10% of African Americans lived outside the South at
the start of the Great Migration, but nearly half did when it ended in the
1970s. Yet, as African Americans migrated north and west, housing policy
and practices from federal subsidies to local restrictive covenants closed off
most suburban residences to African Americans.[177] For example, in 1960, of
eighty-two thousand residents in the Levittown Long Island community, no
African Americans were to be found. The Levitt organization would not sell
to African Americans for two decades after World War II. In the words of
owner Henry Levitt, "We can solve a housing problem, or we can try to solve
a racial problem. But we cannot combine the two."[178] Within cities, housing
market restrictions encouraged the early twentieth-century growth of concentrated black sections such as Harlem in New York City. Only 28% of African
Americans in Manhattan lived there in 1910; nearly 90% did by 1940, and
with a black population more than fifteen times greater.[179] Real estate practices
reinforced this.[180] Most banks and lending institutions refused to sell African
Americans mortgages for properties that they *could* buy, reflecting rampant
Federal Housing Administration "redlining" practices that excluded loans
for communities with large black or minority populations. Thus, while their
white neighbors qualified for federal support via FHA-backed mortgages for
suburban plots and accumulated significant family wealth in the post–World
War II boom, urban black families, redlined out of such loans, were forced into
hyperdense urban communities and sold homes via exorbitant contracts—
essentially, all-or-nothing installment plans.[181] One missed payment and the
property could be repossessed by the owner, with no return of down payment
nor any equity gained from the period of payments. A seller argued in 1962,
"If anybody who is well established in this business in Chicago doesn't earn
$100,000 a year, he is loafing."[182] Contract sales represented a significant drain
on black family wealth; a study in Chicago estimated that a million dollars of
black wealth was lost daily from this practice in the 1950s.[183] In turn, neighborhoods bore the brunt of efforts to meet inflated costs:

> Husbands and wives both worked double shifts. They neglected basic main-
> tenance. They subdivided their apartments, crammed in extra tenants, and,
> when possible, charged their tenants hefty rents. Indeed, the genius of this
> system was that it forced black contract buyers to be their own exploiters.[184]

Add to this the exclusion of African Americans from most labor unions, and
this rapidly growing community faced serious constraints on their income,
location, and subsequent wealth accumulation—all during a period of strong
economic expansion.[185] As black communities bore the brunt of high-density
population rates, constrained city services, and limited access to economic

growth, whites saw evidence confirming pathological views of black communities, maladjusted from recent rural lives, mired in a "culture of poverty," and, later, simply left behind by deindustrializing cities.[186]

Brown: Crawling Past *Plessy*

In the post–World War II period, the United States struggled mightily with the third core question set out in the introduction: What role do we seek for our schools in building a more inclusive, equitable and integrated plural society? The indirect effects of suburbanization patterns, housing discrimination, and inequitable access to labor markets were to limit the residential locations, and thus the schools that parents could choose. In addition, direct school segregation policies—de jure and de facto, from student assignment policies to new building locations to the drawing of school district lines—further limited parental school options, shaping the profile we inherit today. Schools were not simply passive recipients of other social policies; as historian Ansley Erickson has argued, "aspects of school policy have helped construct segregation."[187] In Raleigh, North Carolina, officials relocated top schools to the white northwest side, and built no schools for middle-class African Americans outside the segregated southeastern section of the city; in Nashville, urban renewal tactics in public housing and school building worked "in tandem" in advancing segregation.[188] In the early 1950s in twenty-one states—southern, border and western—parents were either required (seventeen states) or able (four states) to choose officially segregated schools; some 40% of US public school students attended in these districts.[189] The choices for white and black parents also varied significantly in terms of school resources, by race and by region. In the South, black schools received 60% of the funding levels per pupil as the white schools of the region, themselves funded at 60% of the national average.[190] More than half the black schools in Clarendon County, South Carolina, in 1950, for example, were "ramshackle shanties in which one or two teachers had only the most rudimentary instructional materials."[191] Black students attended school in much larger classes, with limited facilities, including inadequate plumbing or electricity, and with far fewer curricular options. Parents objecting could be subject to swift retribution, including job loss, loan denial, and physical violence.

In many areas of the North, de facto school segregation via residency and district lines—supplemented by various within-district school policies and administrative practices, such as gerrymandered catchment areas, student assignment, transfer practices, and new school building location decisions—effectively drew racial boundaries across cities and towns. Highsmith and

Erickson document how officials in Flint, Michigan, nationally known for its popular community schools program, manipulated a variety of school, housing, and other policies to maintain a segregated city, pursuing a twin rationale of locally building community while racially separating neighborhoods.[192] Teacher placements reflected this segregation as well. For example, no black teachers worked in San Francisco's public schools between the 1870s and 1944; Philadelphia's first black teacher in a predominantly white school was assigned in 1947.[193] Across the country, school officials

> collaborated with local homebuilders and federal mortgage underwriters to create segregated neighborhood units, gerrymandered attendance districts when black families desegregated all-white residential areas, built temporary schoolhouses to avoid transferring white students to black schools, manipulated student transfer rules to keep schools homogeneous, and resorted to innumerable other methods to preserve and extend racial separation.[194]

Contemporaneous with the reform critiques of Bestor and Friedman, the Supreme Court addressed the legality of the available school choices in its 1954/55 *Brown v. Board of Education* decisions, in which the court combined five cases and some two hundred plaintiffs. Owing to the increased importance of education in modern life, and in light of social science evidence of psychological harm to black children, the court found in *Brown I* that "separate educational facilities are inherently unequal." Thus, de jure segregated schools violated the Fourteenth Amendment's "equal protection" clause. A year later, in *Brown II*, the nation's highest court urged school districts to operate schools in a nondiscriminatory manner, implementing *Brown I*'s principles "with all deliberate speed."[195] Neither decision provided much guidance to school districts. Reactions were swift, if largely restrained, across the nation; a Nashville *Tennessean* editorial noted that "southerners have learned to live with change. They can learn to live with this one."[196] Yet in the former Confederate states, notes Charles Clotfelter, the "predominant attitude was horror and hysterical jeremiad"; in the Deep South, and even within more moderate border states, the next decade largely saw "resistance and foot-dragging," a period of "token integration" at best.[197] The quip quickly arose after Brown that while African Americans sought "speed," whites preferred to "deliberate."

Even prior to the *Brown* decision, several southern states, anticipating the direction of the courts, developed alternatives to integrated public schools. Some states tried to buttress the "equal" side of "separate but equal." In the decade preceding *Brown*, several southern states raised spending on black schools faster than in white schools, decreasing the per capita spending gap that existed between them. South Carolina, for example, boosted black per capita spending from 30% of white per capita spending in 1940, to 60% by 1952; large discrepancies remained, however.[198]

Southern states also developed options under a general banner of "freedom of choice." Brown eliminated de jure segregation; it did not mandate *integration*. School choice seemed a route to maintain the status quo within legal bounds. Three years before *Brown*, Georgia proposed school vouchers and joined South Carolina, Mississippi, Alabama, and other southern states in considering strategies to abolish public schools entirely. Six southern states passed legislation allowing public schools to be closed and replaced with tuition grants for private school attendance.[199] Private, segregated schools seemed an attractive choice to many even before *Brown* came down, and private school enrollment reached its peak in 1960, when southern rates of private schooling began to converge with those of other regions. Additionally, "choice" resonated well in the Cold War of the 1950s. To paraphrase historian Jim Carl, Jim Crow met the Cold War in much of the resistance to *Brown* because "freedom of choice was a patriotic alternative to a civil rights movement tinged by communism"; tuition grants provided "a way out of the growing collectivism of public schools."[200] Such grants also preserved segregation without mandates. In New Orleans, the Louisiana Financial Assistance Commission distributed more than fifteen thousand tuition vouchers between 1962 and 1966; none of the participating schools accepted the vouchers from both African Americans and whites. In the final year, 94% of the funds went to white parents.[201] "Freedom of choice" plans relied on a broad set of local influences, intimidations, legal maneuvering, and traditions to maintain "freely chosen" segregated schools. Parents were given the choice of schools, in the confidence that whites would not choose to attend black schools, and few vice versa. Stanley Trent, a young black rural student in Virginia at the time, recalled being asked by his parents which school he wanted to attend under a new "freedom of choice" plan. He replied, "'I don't want to go to no white school.' . . . My father signed the form. . . . We returned outside and continued to shoot some hoops."[202]

Parental choice and even local control was far from sacrosanct, however; when residential segregation or preference did not suffice to prevent integration, southern states turned to pupil assignment laws that gave wide discretion to local school boards.[203] All eleven southern states adopted pupil assignment laws after *Brown*, generally modeling their legislation on the laws of Alabama and North Carolina. District boards were given the authority to assign students—so as to require individuals to file their challenges per district, slowing any pushback. Boards had broad leeway if needed, and could assign students based on myriad, "race-neutral" criteria.[204] A black student who wished to transfer to a white school would need to visit the school, fill out application forms, take tests, move through hearings, appeal adverse decisions, and so on. In Richmond, Virginia, the Pupil Placement Board relied heavily on school attendance zones, given that most schools had been built squarely in either all-black or all-white neighborhoods. Feeder systems then channeled black and white students into corresponding middle and high schools. The board handled any discrepant transfer requests that might counteract the zones or feeders.[205]

For much of the first decade after *Brown*, the courts tended to require that all administrative remedies be exhausted prior to providing any relief; by the time other legal remedies occurred, many districts had changed demographically in dramatic ways.[206] Between *Brown* and when the Fourth Circuit ruled against its assignment practices, Richmond shifted from a majority white district to majority black. By 1970, when even the freedom of choice policies ended by court order, fewer than 30% of Richmond students were white.[207]

Some in the South took an even more aggressive route than choice plans or assignment policies, part of a wave of "massive resistance" to desegregation after *Brown*. White violence and intimidation surged. Litigation swelled, in part supported by state funding. The Ku Klux Klan and White Citizens' Councils gained membership rapidly.[208] In March, 1956, 101 members of the US House and Senate from across the South, led in part by South Carolina's US Senator Strom Thurmond, signed a "Declaration of Constitutional Principles," more broadly known as the Southern Manifesto. In *Brown*, it said, the court had affronted states' rights and substituted "naked power for established law . . . destroying the amicable relations between the white and Negro races," a "dangerous and explosive situation created by this decision and inflamed by outside meddlers."[209] Led by Senator Harry Byrd, Virginia authorized the closure of any public school required to desegregate; Norfolk, Charlottesville, Warren County, and Prince Edward County each shut their schools, with many black students left unschooled for years—Prince Edward County's public schools remained closed for five years. "We may observe with much sadness and irony that, outside of Africa," lamented Attorney General Robert F. Kennedy at the time, ". . . the only places on earth known not to provide free public education are Communist China, North Vietnam, Sarawak, Singapore, British Honduras—and Prince Edward County, Virginia."[210] Mississippi and Louisiana declared it illegal for children to attend mixed-race schools; in Georgia, it became a felony for any state or local official to spend public money on desegregated schools. In the now iconic 1957 encounter in Little Rock, Arkansas, President Dwight Eisenhower reluctantly sent some 1,100 troops to allow nine black students to attend Central High School. The troops stayed for the school year, but then Little Rock closed all its high schools for the following school year, stranding 3,665 students and some two hundred teachers, after firing forty-three teachers seen as sympathetic to desegregation. Remaining teachers were required to remain loyal and quiet. Arkansas governor Orval Faubus attempted, unsuccessfully, to privatize the entire system, including leasing public buildings to private firms. Nearly all white students received some education, with nearly half attending private schools during the "lost year" of 1958/59. Roughly half the black students received no education that year. Forced by the courts to reopen the schools, and under police protection, a total of six black students attended high school in 1959/60, and none attended the city's white junior high or elementary schools. By 1963, the once exclusively white junior and senior high schools were still less than 1% black.[211]

Aided by the impact of television, the reaction of moderates and opponents to the extreme measures of "massive resistance" diminished their appeal, and efforts of token integration proceeded. The images of troops protecting black children from the epithets and violence of white adults turned many away from the stridency.[212] For most of the southern and border region, states resisted through various "choice" plans, as well as through litigation, voter suppression, local organizing, regional advocacy, and (most critically, perhaps) pupil assignment policies—all meant to sustain segregation in ways immune to *Brown*.[213] School choice, while fervently saluted under the banner of freedom, and useful in maintaining segregated enrollments, quickly took a back seat to pupil assignment or closure when it threatened to advance integration. In the end, reams of post-*Brown* litigation increasingly narrowed school district maneuverability around the decision, thus legally expanding school choices for all parents; but the first decade post-*Brown* saw little actual desegregation take place. For the eleven southern states, only 1.2% of African Americans attended schools with whites just prior to the Civil Rights Act. Historian James Patterson has noted that, notwithstanding the Supreme Court's *Brown* decision, "virtually all southern black children who had entered the first grade in 1954 and who remained in southern school graduated from all-black schools twelve years later."[214]

The Bus Stops Here: The Pull of the Magnet School

Parental choices in schooling shifted considerably over the volatile next decade, bookended first by historic civil rights legislation as residents rioted in impoverished urban centers, and then by Nixon's resignation from office, as troops exited from a deeply divisive Vietnam War. By the 1980s, a new social geography of school choices had evolved, leaving behind a somewhat frayed social and policy fabric. Both the variety of educational options and the variety within school bodies changed dramatically, all amid continued and accelerated shifts in the legal latitude of school choice options.[215]

"Change between 1954 and 1964 had been glacial; progress in the next decade, especially 1969 and 1973," argues historian James Patterson, "had been staggeringly rapid."[216] The 1964 Civil Rights Act required that all districts receiving federal funds administer their educational programs without racial discrimination—in classrooms, in student projects, in supplemental services, in hiring, in facility use, and in parent participation. A year later, the federal government moved to cut off funding for those not desegregating, and additionally required "freedom of choice" plans. In 1966, further regulations insisted on actual integration, beyond choice plans and ostensibly open processes. Results needed to be obtained, and compliance was swift. As Gary Orfield noted, desegregation had doubled by 1964 and nearly tripled by 1965; by fall 1966 the percentage of African Americans attending school beyond all-black institutions had jumped 1,400%.[217] Between 1968 and 1973, the Supreme Court moved beyond *Brown* to require that some integration actually take place. Through its *Green*, *Swann*, and *Keyes* decisions, the court mandated results, including via forced student busing, North and South.[218] But if *Green* had accelerated the impact of *Brown*, *Milliken* put on the brakes. In the 1974 *Milliken* decision, the court limited the scope of mandated busing to cities found guilty of school segregation practices; unless suburbs were found explicitly to have done the same, busing schemes would not be required to cross urban-suburban boundaries. The suburbs would be spared busing; the cities would struggle mightily over the next three decades.[219]

The social geography across city-suburban boundaries had not remained constant since *Brown*; many cities had seen considerable white flight well before court-ordered busing began.[220] In Los Angeles, for example, more than 1,500 people gathered at a Beverly Hills High School emergency meeting as early as 1963 when initial talk of integration remedies to address inequitable school quality swirled around the city.[221] By the time LA's court-ordered desegregation plan rolled out years later in 1978, the demographics had shifted dramatically: nearly eighty thousand white students left between 1966 and 1970; between 1960 and 1980, white enrollment dropped 68%. Surrounding suburban enrollment and private school matriculation jumped; Orange County's population grew nearly threefold in the same period, with K–12 enrollment having risen dramatically between 1961 and 1967.[222] Certainly, white flight did not arise solely in response to court-ordered desegregation and busing; flight took place in cities like New York not subject to either. In Richmond, Virginia, for example, the percentage of white enrollment began to drop as early as 1929. Yet it accelerated after *Brown*, and even more so after busing began in 1971.[223]

Within this tumultuous context of the late 1960s and early 1970s, some sought new voluntary remedies for segregation, beyond open choice plans but short of forced busing. In the fall of 1968, at McCarver Elementary in Tacoma, Washington, an enduring new form of school choice took shape: an "'exemplary' magnet-type elementary school open to all district students."[224] The magnet school approach grew out of a larger, multiyear effort at voluntary desegregation in Tacoma, with significant public leadership, institutional and individual, as early as 1961 from the school superintendent.[225] In 1963, the first year that race-specific enrollment figures were gathered, the Tacoma Teachers Association and the Association of School Administrators appointed a committee to study de facto school segregation. Though Tacoma's black population was only around 7%, McCarver school, then a junior high, was nearly 90% African American.[226] By 1965, the local NAACP branch pressed for federal investigation. The next year, the district implemented an "optional enrollment program" for students in the McCarver junior high, allowing students to transfer to any district school or into McCarver, "provided such transfers reduce the degree of de facto segregation."[227] This then became a limited version of what would eventually be called a "controlled choice" program.[228] The program allowed central city, McCarver-area students to transfer voluntarily to schools outside their zone—sixth graders to any district junior high, and ninth graders to any Tacoma high school. Students outside the central city were encouraged to transfer to McCarver, as long as de facto segregation would be reduced. The plan expanded to cover four central-city school areas the following year; 191 students transferred under the plan, 61% minority and the balance white.[229]

As the idea of optional enrollment gained ground, McCarver converted into a model magnet elementary school in 1968, implementing innovations such as team teaching, with student groups adjusted based on interests and achievement; common staff planning periods; specialists in art, music, and PE; nongraded curricula series; individualized math and reading; a nontraditional Friday activities program; and "new emphasis on the use of self-directing multimedia equipment and materials."[230] While families in the school's local area got preference, students from across the district could apply. Supported by the board, superintendent Dr. Angelo Giaudrone included the creation of McCarver magnet school as part of the district's new "five-point program" to reduce de facto segregation. A year later, two predominantly white elementary schools, Wainright and Jefferson, joined McCarver to form a triad of such innovative magnets, aiming to reduce de facto segregation by drawing parents out of their segregated residential areas by the magnetic pull of such exemplary, well-resourced schools. Consistent with board support for the "exemplary," the Tacoma Association of Classroom Teachers publicly requested "a cooperative effort with the District in development of programs designed to eliminate and prevent *de facto* segregation, rather than to rely upon remedial and compensatory education."[231] The then assistant superintendent Alex Sergienko recalled that "suddenly we envisioned McCarver as a school of excellence—good enough to pull in white students from the more affluent neighborhoods."[232] Successfully gaining a Title III grant in the summer of 1968 and recruiting aggressively, the school opened with a minority enrollment down 27 percentage points, and with two hundred white students from across the area, including well-heeled suburbs.[233] Disturbances that summer, after Martin Luther King's assassination, brought further urgency to these local initiatives. A state evaluation three years later—and a federal report seven years later—found the efforts successful, ending de facto segregation at McCarver, integrating Wainright and Jefferson, supporting cross-racial friendships, reducing "racial isolation" in the district, maintaining public support, and avoiding the turmoil of other parts of the country.[234]

Chicago had opened its first magnet school, Robert A. Black Magnet Elementary, in 1968, the same year as Tacoma's McCarver.[235] The following year another magnet opened in Boston and soon hundreds were established across the country. The fourteen districts with magnets in 1976/77 jumped to 138 districts just five years later, skewing toward larger districts; by 1981/82, more than a thousand operated nationally—a figure that would quadruple over subsequent decades. At the start of the 1980s, the average district with magnets already enrolled over 5% of their students in magnets, and in nearly 70% of those districts, almost 14% of K–12 students were enrolled.[236] A decade later, the total number of magnets doubled, enrolling 15% of students in the districts in which they operated, which tended to be disproportionately minority and poor; over 60% of magnet school students nationally were nonwhite.[237] Magnet schools provided a less controversial approach to desegregation, offered a wide range of subject matter specializations from aerospace to math and science to performing arts, and generally cost roughly an additional $100 per student annually.[238] For decades, magnets have provided the dominant form of public urban school choice.

Magnet schools also allowed a "soft paternalism" approach to promoting racial integration, part of some courts' use of choice within desegregation cases.[239] Senator Pat Moynihan, a key supporter of magnets, recalled in the early 1970s when "something of a constitutional crisis was emerging in this land," when, with *Brown* already on the books for fifteen years, courts began ordering busing to end "all vestiges" of segregation, "root and branch."[240] Magnets offered a partial and "voluntary" means for countering the legacy of institutional segregation in the South and neighborhood segregation in the North. Moynihan noted:

> Magnet schools in the City of Buffalo, as in the City of Rochester, were devices to bring people from different neighborhoods to the same school, a problem as real in terms of segregation as ever the dual systems of the South had been.[241]

Agreeing that communities needed financial support in making such dramatic transformations, Congress approved federal funding for school districts undergoing desegregation, voluntary or otherwise, including for the first time magnet schools and programs. The support for magnets, argued Moynihan as he sought increased funding in 1987, especially in cities struggling with busing, "helped to bring about a level of integration and community support that was unthinkable ten years previous."[242] While some resisted the very premise of magnets—why not make all schools of "magnet" quality?—and others saw a "desegregation dodge," many sought a strategy that might avoid the strife that cities like Boston experienced over forced busing.[243] A number of courts included magnets within their orders in the 1970s, and allowed the continued use of voluntary programs that were attracting a greater racial mix in San Francisco, Denver, and Minneapolis. Boston, which had already created three magnets just after Tacoma's, set new precedence when a court-appointed group established School District Nine, a magnet district of eighteen city schools, with "special themes such as progressive 'open' schooling, arts, literacy, math/science, technology, or back-to-basics."[244] Each site could draw a quarter of its students locally and the balance from across the city, as long as the schools remained within 5% of the city's overall racial mix.[245] Having rejected a proposed fifty-five-school magnet system, an "intra-city voluntary transfer program" instead of busing, the judge felt nonetheless that the more moderate magnet approach would be the "crux and magic" of the plan, and an "enormous safety valve" for the anti-busing rage.[246] After Boston's "magnet district," the next fifteen years saw a tripling of enrollments in magnet programs around the country, especially in the largest urban districts.[247] What was a "command and control" approach to desegregation in the 1970s and 1980s slowly became a "market incentives" approach with a prominent role for magnets.[248] Many cities seemed to return to an approach Tacoma took several decades earlier.

Despite their growth into the mid-1990s, magnet schools began to face legal and financial headwinds. In Kansas City, Missouri, the court-ordered desegregation plan converted most of the district's schools into magnets, and not just in the hopes of drawing students from across the city, but also from across suburban boundaries. The appellate court upheld the plan, but in 1995, the Supreme Court—in an echo of the earlier *Milliken* decision—determined that crossing the suburban line fell outside the mandated desegregation remedy. The same year, Sarah Wessmann, a white Boston ninth grader denied admission to Boston Latin, challenged the reservation of seats by ethnicity in the city's selective admissions magnet schools. She won, and her case "became a crucial stepping stone in the assaults on the use of racial categories in school and college admissions."[249] Evaluations of magnet programs by the US Department of Education across three decades trace the shift away from desegregation goals signaled by these cases. In 1983, over 60% of magnets studied were "fully desegregated"; in 1996, only 42% evidently operated under desegregation guidelines; by 2003, over 40% of program studies indicated rising segregation.[250]

Beyond legal restraints, magnets also faced challenges in federal support from a new competitor: charter schools. Federal appropriations for magnets have stayed essentially flat since the late 1980s; charter dollars skyrocketed in the late 1990s to twice the magnet levels by the early 2000s, supplemented by significant philanthropic support.[251] At state levels, school finance litigation generally failed to remedy the significant funding disparities that many larger cities, and their magnets, faced—even as such litigation lowered its goals from equalizing district funding to establishing basic adequacy levels. Even a novel voucher scheme proffered by lawyers John Coons, William Clune, and Stephen Sugarman—"fundamentally different" than Friedman's, rooted in principles of both subsidiarity and equal opportunity, and reflecting the "revulsion for gross variations in per pupil expenditure from school district to school district"—did not gain sufficient traction in addressing school finance inequities.[252] In an intriguing argument, Coons and colleagues suggested several "power equalizing" schemes for vouchers that would better support the US tradition of "local control."

> The existing financing mechanisms are not truly systems of local control; rather they are a system of naked privilege for those localities which are created by the state with superior power. Local control in the sense of entities with parity of power to perform their assigned task of education has never existed.[253]

Yet the prior trend prevailed. "The progression of school finance suits has thus paralleled the progression of desegregation suits," claim legal scholars Ryan and Heise, "in that both reforms have preserved the boundaries between urban and suburban districts."[254] Further, in the 2006 *Meredith* decision, the Supreme Court raised the threshold for the use of race in advancing integration, requiring "strict scrutiny" standards that required most districts to find more indirect means for integrating their schools. Limited legally from their original desegregation aims, restrained financially by unequal funding schemes, and facing new competition in charters, magnets faced a less clear future by the mid-2000s.

Experimental Visions: Liberating Schools

Magnets had expanded quickly amid a wider experimentation with alternatives in K–12 schooling—some driven by civil rights efforts, others by free school visionaries, and some by blends of both. The story of other racially mixed school choices begins in the early 1960s, when activists set up alternative schools in Boston, Chicago, New York, Cleveland, and elsewhere during school boycotts protesting segregated schools in the North. In 1961, in McComb, Mississippi, more than one hundred students at Burglund High School walked out after their principal suspended a student for participating in a sit-in; they were arrested as they prayed on the steps of city hall. The Student Nonviolent Coordinating Committee (SNCC) quickly staffed up "Non-Violent High," teaching the students black literature, history, and art; the teachers, including activist Bob Moses, got six months in prison for contributing to the delinquency of minors. But the model of alternative schooling inspired many, including SNCC field secretary Charles Cobb, who saw a need to support such youth engagement in civil rights work. In late 1963, he proposed setting up a network of free, alternative summer schools in Mississippi for the following summer. Combining a remedial academic program with youth leadership development, the Freedom Schools would "challenge the student's curiosity about the world, introduce him to his particularly 'Negro' cultural background, and teach him basic literacy skills in one integrated program."[255] Part of the larger 1964 Freedom Summer efforts organized under the umbrella Council of Federated Organizations (COFO), forty-one Freedom Schools operated with some one thousand volunteers, risking heat and opposition to work with more than two thousand students across Mississippi.[256]

While the formal network of schools lasted only a few years, historian Jon Hale documents the long tail of influence on those involved, many dedicating their lives to generating more "liberating" educational alternatives. Some, like Cobb, saw an opportunity not solely to improve and desegregate the public schools, but to establish new institutional choices: "Education in Mississippi is an institution which can be validly replaced, as much of the educational institutions in the state are not recognized around the country anyway."[257] Reflecting the broader frustration and scars from years of desegregation efforts, activist Bob Moses suggested a new choice: African Americans' own schools, an option W. E. B. DuBois had surfaced back in 1935 and which was later developed in the Black Panther Party Liberation Schools and Afrocentric schools (discussed further in part 2). At the 1964 Democratic National Convention in Atlantic City, Moses asked:

> Why can't we set up our own schools? Because when you come right down to it, why integrate their schools? What is it that you will learn in their schools? Many of the Negroes can learn it, but what can they do with it? What they really need to learn is how to be organized to work on the society to change it.[258]

The larger challenge represented by the Freedom Schools was not lost on historian Howard Zinn, who taught at one of the schools. Upon his return to Boston he reflected that "the challenge to the social structure of Mississippi was obvious from the start. Its challenge to American education as a whole is more subtle"; the summer schools provided a "provocative suggestion that an entire school system can be created in any community outside the official order, and critical of its suppositions."[259] Reflecting a spirit that animated many of the era's free and alternative schools, Zinn asked:

> Is there, in the floating, prosperous, nervous American social order of the sixties, a national equivalent to the excitement of the civil rights movement, one strong enough in its pull to create a motivation for learning that even the enticements of monetary success cannot match?[260]

From roughly the mid-'60s to the present, this "more subtle" and "provocative" challenge continued to take root, across shifting political soils, as a myriad of wide-ranging K–12 schooling innovations broke out across the United States. A heterogeneous set of "movements" with distinct emphases and phases, they represented a background drumbeat of reform across half a century, a foundational challenge to the idea of the "one best system" of lore. Arguably, current school choice developments reflect only the latest manifestation of this enduring trend toward more differentiated schooling options for a republic of consumers. The post–World War II period had accustomed our society to increased brand variety, the privatization of public spaces, the coproduction of public services, and the experience of well-paced social and technological diversification across various aspects of life.[261] Some of these movements, such as the formation of magnets, continue into the present; indeed, some now call for increasing support for magnets in light of resegregation concerns.[262] Others, such as the free school and "community-control" movements, could not sustain themselves as such, though they contributed to socializing the core challenge.[263] Some, such as charters, represent a more recent accommodation in an era of conservative revival, suburban local control, economic concentration, corporate philanthropy, and entrepreneurial enthusiasm.[264]

Back in the 1960s—with urban centers churning, the Vietnam War raging, countercultural storms afoot, and baby boomers bumping K–12 enrollment to new highs—educators, parents, and others sought creative alternatives to systems already challenged in their racial divisions and pedagogical visions. Inspired by works such as A. S. Neill's *Summerhill* and Paul Goodman's *Growing Up Absurd*, and animated by twin (at times, competing) forces of rising social activism and the search for personal liberation, hundreds of "free schools" sprouted across the country, particularly from 1967 to 1973.[265] Two-thirds of the free schools of 1971 had formed within the prior two years.[266] While more exact estimates remain elusive, at least two hundred and maybe as many as over two thousand free schools existed across a decade and a half.[267] Nonpublic, small alternative schools, free schools represented a radical institutional critique of the sociocultural order and a route for liberating their students from the soul-stultifying lives of an oppressive, hierarchical society dominated by faceless, antidemocratic bureaucracies.[268] Students had great freedom within the school day; at Summerhill, an iconic model free school in England, lessons were optional and students had great "freedom to be themselves."[269] An antiauthoritarian, experimental, and liberating spirit drove many to follow Neill's dictum that "to impose anything by authority is wrong. The child should not do anything until he comes to the opinion—his own opinion—that it should be done. The curse of humanity is the external compulsion."[270] For free school leader John Holt, schools needed to liberate themselves from "turning people into commodities," from "the business of testing, grading, labeling, sorting, deciding who goes where and who gets what."[271] Newsletters, publications, centers, and conferences sprang up. *Summerhill* sold a million copies by 1968, and two years later more than one thousand people attended the Conference on Alternatives in Education at Zaca Lake in California.[272]

The free school movement proved stunningly brief; new free schools, newsletter subscriptions, and conferences plummeted by the mid-1970s. Many individual schools lasted only a few years, and by the end of the decade, few remnants of the movement existed.[273] Herbert Kohl burned out from the Other Ways school in Berkeley by 1971 and, despite a spate of new books in free and alternative education, felt that the energy and excitement had disappeared by 1973; those with whom he had worked were "licking their wounds and doing other work or [were] planning to continue but in more modest, less romantic ways."[274] For many, the challenges of messy, participatory democratic governance proved too daunting. For others, tight funding never relented; tuition and grants could not maintain even small sites. A brief effort to establish the New Nation Seed Fund to raise money for alternative schools, backed by key leaders of the field, apparently went nowhere.[275] The movement itself suffered from its own divisions, notably called out by Jonathan Kozol in 1972, who critiqued the many schools he labeled escapist retreats for the privileged, "all-white rural Free Schools" for those "escaping from the turmoil and the human desperation of the cities."[276] Most free schools seemed a world apart from the Freedom Schools.[277]

Even for their brevity, the free and Freedom School movements had continued the "provocative suggestion" Zinn noted. While some sought simply to exit an oppressive system, others sought to model what public schooling might become. Activist Charles Lawrence wanted his urban Boston free school to serve as "a vanguard for public education, a model for how public schools might look."[278] In pushing radical solutions to pressing social issues, in developing very small schools in a landscape of larger ones, in locating their schools in churches and nontraditional sites, in advancing distinctive pedagogies at odds with traditional classrooms, in creating explicitly mission-driven schools, and in staffing those schools in alternative ways—free and Freedom Schools provided visible examples of schooling outside the "one best system." They also served notice of the significant thresholds—operational, political, legal, and social—that would need to be reached in order to ultimately shift that system in any significant way.

Toward Plural Public Education

The fate of free and Freedom Schools underlined the challenge in sustaining school alternatives, as a larger effort to incorporate varied "alternative" programs and schools within public systems continued to grow.[279] A 1974 survey of three hundred–plus alternative schools found that over 80% were newer than five years old, most enrolled fewer than two hundred students, and most students were urban.[280] Students often worked in small study groups on topics of interest, including pressing social issues, taking their work into the community at Fernwood School in Oregon, perhaps the first of public alternative programs.[281] In Philadelphia, lottery-selected students at the Parkway Program, "the 'granddaddy' of the *school without walls* concept," broke into four units of two hundred, with ten teachers and ten interns each, running more than 250 courses and cooperating with ninety institutions.[282] Each internal school unit developed its own curriculum, ran town meetings, sought out community support, and provided daily tutorial groups, all toward building "self-reliant, self-defining and self-directed" individuals.[283] The program hosted many visitors and received considerable coverage, from *Time, Life,* and the *Saturday Review* to academic journals.[284] Some districts established small, experimental schools within existing schools, as at Pioneer Two in Ann

Arbor, Michigan, providing "an unstructured, open environment, involving pupils in the planning and operation of the school and maintaining a high degree of individualization." Ungraded schools emerged, such as the Brown School in Louisville, where students and faculty organized around learning domains.[285] John Dewey High in Brooklyn had no grade levels, no tracking, no Carnegie units or standard class schedule; students learned at their own pace, and could select the pace of sequential skill programs such as foreign language or algebra.[286] Several districts nurtured systems with multiple alter native schools, notably so in Minneapolis; Portland (Oregon); Seattle; Quincy (Illinois); and Berkeley. Boston and New York opened a dozen "minischools" of 100 to 125 students each; Haaren High School in Midtown Manhattan was restructured into fourteen theme-based minischools offering a mix of specialized and standard courses.[287] Anthony Alvarado began experimenting with innovative new schools across District Four in Manhattan, including Deborah Meier's Central Park East, which became a national model.[288] Boston instituted its Flexible Campus Program, stimulating distinctive programming at each of the city's high schools; students typically attended a half day of classes, and a half day at an "off-campus learning experience." Outside large cities, some regional alternative schools developed, with participating districts sharing costs and personnel.[289]

The curricular and pedagogical innovations of the public alternative schools gained perhaps their most public voice through a Carnegie Foundation– funded study by Charles Silberman, published in 1970 as *Crisis in the Classroom*.[290] A journalist then at *Fortune* magazine, Silberman found most schools to be grim, joyless places, filled with petty rules and oppressive to children. School culture shared in a diffused mindlessness from which the society also suffered, with little evident attention by educators to "think seriously or deeply about the purposes or consequences of education."[291] In a serialized version in the *Atlantic Monthly* entitled "Murder in the Classroom," Silberman observed that "the banality and triviality of the curriculum in most schools has to be experienced to be believed."[292] He recommended the Parkway Program and other alternative schools, among other measures, as modeling the elements needed for greater student engagement.

Reflecting perhaps the growing public sensitivity to educational issues— including parents' dissatisfaction with the schools their children attended— corporations and foundations supported several experiments in the sector.[293] Standard Oil contributed to Harlem Prep, McGraw-Hill contributed to mini-school Harambee Prep, Pfizer assisted Wingate Prep, all in New York City; the Urban Research Corporation provided key funding to start Chicago's Metro; and the Ford Foundation helped establish the Parkway Program in

Philadelphia. Carnegie and Ford Foundations funded research studies, such as Silberman's, and (with UNESCO) the Center for New Schools. Certainly federal dollars played an influential role, from ESEA funds (Title I and III), Office of Economic Opportunity grants, and, of course, through the Experimental Schools Program and the National Alternative Schools Program, initiated in 1970/71. National commissions and conferences combined with increased state involvement to create a growing national presence for alternative schooling. Some welcomed the support, while others saw the co-opting hand of the system, especially as state education agencies entered what sociologist Gary Natriello labeled the "second response phase" to the alternative schools movement.[294] Some activists feared the deadening hand of professionalism, a visionless expansion of technical processes, and an institutionalization within public schooling by which "the human qualities constituting the life-blood of alternative education [would be] trampled underfoot."[295] Might the creative, humane spirit of alternative educational visions become too standardized, too uniform under the banner of "professional" practices, dimming the passions of teachers and students alike? Nonetheless, moving past initial resistance, many states began to actively encourage alternative programs and schools, and proliferation followed. Newsletters, such as the *New Schools Exchange Newsletter* and *Changing Schools*, sprouted up mid-decade; centers like the Teacher Drop-Out Center at the University of Massachusetts Amherst and the Educational Alternatives Project at Indiana University connected activists and programs. By the mid-1970s, there were likely already five thousand to ten thousand public alternative programs operating across the United States. They enjoyed significant public approval: a 1973 poll found that most adults and even more educators supported alternatives for "students who are not interested in, or are bored with, the usual kind of education."[296]

As alternative schools became institutionalized within public systems, Mario Fantini played a key role. Fantini, formerly a program officer at the Ford Foundation, had cut his school reform teeth during the Ocean Hill–Brownsville controversy in Brooklyn and also served as liaison to the Parkway Program. Then dean of education at the State University of New York, he acknowledged the contribution of free schoolers and others, and now advocated for "plural education" within public systems, or "public schools of choice." But he argued that legitimizing these alternatives within the public system required recognizing the lessons to be learned from the prior decade or so of experience with free schools, Freedom Schools, and other alternatives. If educators wished to gain traction for creative alternatives to standard schooling, then they would need to appeal to "mainstream parents, students and teachers . . . the political gatekeepers of educational reform within our public schools."[297] What had the last decade taught? For starters, reformers had an image problem, claimed Fantini, a perception of being too "fringe" for the middle class, who was most interested in assuring success in college or other future learning. The bulk of alternative programs "came from urban settings with minority children or with the counter-culture folk," Fantini states; further,

> educational programs for blacks are seldom perceived as models for whites. The attitude is almost the same . . . for "long-haired hippie-type youth." . . . "If this is what you're calling alternatives, fine for them but not for us."[298]

Many parents and educators saw alternative approaches as a sharp rebuke to their practices; labels of "open" and "humanistic" only implied that those opposing these approaches were closed and inhuman. Many conservatives objected to what they saw as challenges to "traditional" religion, families, markets, and patriotism, seeing in "progressive education" a disrespect for their core beliefs, "a suspect system of sneering modern values."[299] These "other school reformers," as Adam Laats has argued, did not simply resist others' alternatives; they advanced their own view of schooling's role:

> If teachers assume that truth is something students must discover on their own, gullible and romantic young people will tend to choose rashly. Instead, teachers and schools must take responsibility to pass along the inherited wisdom of millennia of civilization. Schools must transmit truth, not merely act as facilitators for the bumbling inquiries of immature minds.[300]

Further, some minority communities resisted alternatives as an end run on inequity; "we want what the whites have—not something different."[301] Given the increased association of many alternative programs with compensatory efforts, "accepting an alternative would be admitting that something was wrong with [minority communities]—a verdict already rendered by white society."[302] Finally, reformers needed to understand that some alternative approaches—Ivan Illich and Everett Reimer's "deschooling" or the Summerhill model—would be "the most difficult to legitimize under a public school framework and will likely remain outside," as "emerging ground rules" require that the full complement of educational objectives be pursued.[303] Public alternatives could not choose only the intellectual, or just the spiritual, or solely some portion of required content areas; the public held them accountable for the full range of learning objectives. For some in the alternative schools movement—particularly those from the free schools—the prospect of joining the system, even with financial stability, was a bridge too far. Yet for others, Fantini's argument for "plural education" helpfully guided the movement into a rhetorical mainstream, "the American pluralistic tradition, along with religious pluralism and a free-enterprise economic ideology."[304] Allowing parental and teacher choices among public schools would also *individualize* education politics, avoiding the too-prevalent group-oriented strife of the era.

Fantini viewed an urgency to the matter. He saw countervailing winds to the creation of innovative, visionary, and educationally substantive options within public systems. For "while we are trying to come to grips with pluralism in education," he stated, "another trend is gaining momentum before our very eyes."[305] Seeing the emergence of a back-to-basics movement, a "no-nonsense return to the 3 R's," part of a larger conservative backlash to the '60s, he worried that the "call for more uniformity" and a "law and order policy within the schools" would simply lead to "more standardization," including

> strict adherence to standardized measures of achievement, ability grouping by IQ, non-promotion policies, lowering the compulsory school attendance age, placing more police guards in school. . . . It would convey a notion of child growth and development in which there were "winners and losers"—and with the latter receiving the verdict that the problem was theirs, not the schools.[306]

Presciently sensing many of the trends that would bind school choices in the late 1970s and the 1980s, he warned that the nation faced a "crossroads," with

> one road leading to variety in education and to a concept of growth in which each child is provided an environment that best supports his or her learning style and personal development, in which there are no student failures, only program failures. The other road establishes one right way, with clear norms, with learners competing for the right to be considered "winners," with the losers relegated to an underclass status.[307]

From Plural Visions to Bounded Choices

American Federation of Teachers (AFT) union president Al Shanker, speaking toward the end of the Reagan presidency, described a similar crossroads for school reform in the United States. Since the administration's report on education, *A Nation at Risk*, the first path of reforms had "constituted a much-needed corrective to the softness of schools in the late '60s and throughout the '70s."[308] Tougher standards were needed. Yet the reforms rested on many "naïve assumptions," claimed Shanker, overconfident in the power of stating standards and of mandating improved quality, as if "being educated is something like taking a pill."[309] This "first wave" of tougher standards might help students for whom the system already worked, Shanker argued, but would still ignore about 80 percent of students. Echoing Fantini's fears of the mid-

1970s, Shanker lamented in 1988 that there was "one remedy, one pill, one way of reaching kids."[310] Reformers had come and gone across two centuries and schools still looked the same. The problem with the first path for Shanker was its one-size-fits-all, all-at-once approach, which ignored how schools actually improve: "It hasn't changed because we're trying to change everybody at the same time," and if you try "to change a whole system at once, you won't do it, or you'll water it down so much it's meaningless." Imposed mandates guaranteed failure, especially for the majority of students for whom school does not work well.

Echoing sentiments from across three decades, Shanker argued for a *second* reform movement, "a bottom-up approach to reform," a "fragile" and "very different" wave from the first. He saw this second wave emerging in a handful of schools where groups of educators were experimenting creatively. This "radical and tiny movement" included a handful or two of districts, and networks like Sizer's Coalition of Essential Schools, of which Meier's schools were a part, and John Goodlad's group.[311] The essential challenge was the scale of the movement, driving this second wave to thousands of districts: "Can we put in a new policy mechanism that will give teachers and parents the right to 'opt for' a new type of school . . . ?"[312] Could that be done without waiting for all the conditions to be optimal, for everyone to accept a certain single direction? Reform fatigue dating back to the 1960s seemed evident in the question.

Inspired also by a recent visit to an experimental, teacher-team led school in Germany, Shanker then proposed what became known as "charters"—a term he used in a subsequent *New York Times* column, based on Ray Budde's resurrected proposal from the 1970s.[313] Groups of teachers—six or more— would propose a new school, a "way of reaching the kids that are now not being reached." The students served would have to reflect the overall school population, and if within a school, the other teachers would have to approve its existence. If approved by a panel of the board, along with the union and possibly outsiders, it would be left alone to operate autonomously within the district "for five to ten years," barring any "precipitous drop in certain indicators" or no one wishing to work or learn there. Shanker envisioned experimental schools within schools to start, spinning off on their own if successful. They would get their own budget and their share of the per capita student spending, and have flexibility in spending it. Such schools would include faculty decision-making, ways to break teacher isolation, coaching more than lecturing, cooperative learning, peer teaching, integrated learning technologies, and the development of creative, critical thinkers. They would avoid the harmful interstudent competition, public humiliation, "some of the standardized tests," and "doing what most adults can't do, which is to sit still for five or six hours a day listening to somebody talk."[314] The school would make its goals publicly known, as well as how it intended to measure them and be held accountable. But it would also admit that it was "engaged in a search . . . a lot like trying to find a cure for the common cold. . . . Anybody who promises anything else is like the people who are selling all sorts of cures for incurable diseases out there."[315]

The approach need not await ideal conditions, nor everyone's participation. Shanker declared it had a "great advantage": "There is hardly a school in this country where you can't find six or seven or eight or nine teachers who will sit together and come up with ideas that are quite different, and who will make this work." Linking his proposal to the "increasingly popular magnet school concept" that he supported, the union president noted that most magnets were new or entirely converted schools. He saw the proposal as an approach for changing *existing* schools, which may have thousands of students and a large faculty, and only change very slowly. "So here is a way in which you could turn parts of that [existing] school into a magnet." Charters would allow current sites to "magnetize" themselves among those willing to do so, and might even save on administrative costs, with "a team of teachers shaping each other up."[316] Such teacher-led reform would spur a much more scalable school reform movement, argued Shanker, enhancing the choices parents would enjoy.

Some were unimpressed. William Kristol, chief of staff to Reagan's secretary of education William Bennett, said that while the department "didn't have problems" with the proposal, "we think there is lots of evidence that traditional methods are working."[317] But the proposal landed on extremely fertile ground in Minnesota, assisted by foundation and business community support. Minnesota had already passed landmark interdistrict open enrollment legislation three years earlier, expanding parental choices across the state.[318] The Minnesota Foundation invited Shanker to its fall seminar, along with Joe Nathan, later head of the Center for School Change at the University of Minnesota. Nathan and Ted Kolderie of the think tank Citizens League then played key roles in developing and adapting Shanker's and Budde's ideas, serving as effective disseminators of the idea nationally.[319] The Citizens League published an influential report in support of "Chartered Schools" just seven months after Shanker's talk, and provided key support to state legislation that passed three years later.[320]

The legislation soon shifted, though, away from Shanker's proposal for "magnetizing" through teacher teams from within public schools, toward something more like Minnesota's groundbreaking legislation for "outcomes-based schools."[321] As the reform spread, it departed from the approach Shanker had articulated. California Democrats, battling a proposal for school vouchers, borrowed directly from Minnesota, passing a charter law the following year. California state senator Gary K. Hart viewed charters as "a creative alternative within public education," and a useful political parry to vouchers. But according to the Minnesota law, "one or more licensed teachers" could be authorized to form a school, as a "cooperative" or "nonprofit." Licensed teachers had to be the majority of the school's board of directors. In California, the guidelines became less specific: "any one or more persons" could petition for a charter, though at least 10% of the district's teachers or half at any one school would need to sign the petition. A district with just half the teachers' signatures could convert the entire district into charters. Private funding was specifically allowed. The Democratic Leadership Council soon placed this evolving charter model center stage in presidential candidate Bill Clinton's policy book, part of their wider effort at "reinventing government." Once he was elected in 1992, the Clinton administration developed the proposal further.[322] A federal charter start-up grant program, proposed just after Minnesota's law, eventually was included in the ESEA reauthorization of 1994, jumping quickly to over $200 million, surpassing magnet school support dramatically by the end of the decade. By 1993, Shanker labeled the transformed notion of charter a "mechanical gimmick," one of "the quick fixes that won't fix anything."[323]

Federal Support Shifts from Magnets to Charters

The 1990s proved the pivotal decade. Policy analyst Bryan Hassel describes the diffusion of charter laws as "nothing short of phenomenal," with 20% of states adopting in four years, 50% of states in six.[324] Thirty-nine states had school choice laws on the books within fifteen years of the Minnesota passage. Consistent with the larger historical trends after World War II, recent analysis suggests that adoption odds increased "under Republican gubernatorial control with lower classroom spending levels, a longer record of education finance litigation, and a higher concentration of private schools."[325] By 2014, all but eight states had charter laws on the books, and all but ten had charter schools operating. Dispersion, though, was quite uneven: nearly 60% of all charter schools operated in just six states.[326]

By the time No Child Left Behind (NCLB)—the key guiding federal education legislation of the last fifteen years—passed with bipartisan support in 2001, charter schools had already been established in most states. Federal policy then set parental choice options within a comprehensive test-driven accountability framework, intertwining parental school choice with new federal student performance mandates; students in failing schools would have the

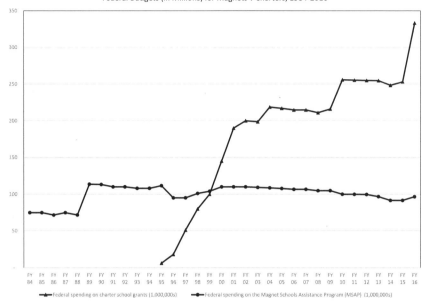

FIGURE 4. Federal Budgets for Magnets versus Charters, 1984–2016.

The figure is a recreated and expanded version of "Figure 1: Annual Federal School Programs," in E. Frankenberg and G. Siegel-Hawley, "Choosing Diversity: School Choice and Racial Integration in the Age of Obama," Stanford Journal on Civil Rights and Civil Liberties 6, no. 2, 244. The data was regenerated and expanded into more recent years.

The following sources were used for verification and expansion of the graph, accessed May 23, 2018:

US Department of Education, "Magnet Schools Assistance Program," *Biennial Evaluation Report, Fiscal Years 1993–1994* (U.S. Government Printing Office: 1995—393-379/30326), https://www2.ed.gov/pubs/Biennial/132.html.

For FY1995: *The Budget Message of the President*, February 6, 1995, https://www.gpo.gov/fdsys/pkg/BUDGET-1996-BUD/pdf/BUDGET-1996-BUD.pdf.

Averaging FY1994 with FY1996 for FY1995 magnet figure: US Department of Education, "FY 1998 Budget Summary," https://www2.ed.gov/offices/OUS/Budget98/BudgetSum/index.html.

FY1996 forward: Figures drawn from US Department of Education fiscal year budget summary reports, from the following URLs:

https://www2.ed.gov/offices/OUS/Budget98/BudgetSum/index.html
https://www2.ed.gov/offices/OUS/Budget99/BudgetSum/pages/sum-a.html#Magnet%20Schools%20Assistance
https://www2.ed.gov/offices/OUS/Budget01/BudgetSumm/sum-a.html#magnet
https://ed.gov/about/overview/budget/budget03/summary/section-ii/edlite-A.html#15
https://www2.ed.gov/about/overview/budget/budget05/summary/edlite-section2a.html#magnet
https://www2.ed.gov/about/overview/budget/budget07/summary/edlite-section2a.html#magnet
https://www2.ed.gov/about/overview/budget/budget08/summary/edlite-section2a.html#magnet
https://www2.ed.gov/about/overview/budget/budget09/summary/edlite-section2a.html#magnet
https://www2.ed.gov/about/overview/budget/budget11/summary/edlite-section3a.html#expanding
https://www2.ed.gov/programs/magnet/funding.html
https://www2.ed.gov/about/overview/budget/budget13/summary/13summary.pdf;
https://www2.ed.gov/about/overview/budget/budget14/summary/14summary.pdf
https://www2.ed.gov/about/overview/budget/budget16/summary/16summary.pdf
https://www2.ed.gov/about/overview/budget/budget17/summary/17summary.pdf

option of attending another school, including a charter, were one available. Charter students increased fourfold over the decade, while overall enrollment rose only 4%.[327] Later in the decade, federal legislation spurred rapid expansion of state charter provisions by leveraging $4 billion in stimulus funding as states struggled through the nation's greatest economic crisis since the Great Depression. Inside a massive $800 billion package, the American Recovery and Reinvestment Act of 2009 (ARRA), Secretary of Education Arne Duncan inserted a small text for a "state incentive fund," later named the Race to the Top (RTTT) part of the act's State Fiscal Stabilization Fund, resulting in a state request for proposal (RFP) process designed by Duncan's special advisor Jon Schnur. Desperate for funding and politically vulnerable if they ignored it, forty-one governors responded to the RTTT's RFP over the summer of 2009, adjusting state laws to lift charter caps, signing on to national standards and national assessment consortia, and committing to yet-to-be-created tests— and to institute data systems and evaluation schemes linked to them. Though supporters argued these provisions would enhance parental choice options and their quality, little understanding existed about what all this would actually mean.[328] As a political observer noted, "The secretary arguably got more states to buy his brand of change in 18 months than any other U.S. school chief had in the Cabinet-level Education Department's 29-year history."[329]

As we write, however, states are working to understand the implications of the recent federal legislation that supersedes NCLB—the Every Student Succeeds Act of 2015—and shifts considerable policy inertia back to the states. Pushback from the political right and left on the perceived privatization of public schooling, excessive test-driven accountability, and federal overreach into state and local control yielded a significant policy pivot over the last several years.[330] While this recent shift in the federal-state-local balancing act, along with changes in aspects of the accountability framework noted above, remains a work in progress, how should we understand the dramatic rise of charter schools and other "choice" policies of the previous two decades? What drove such a rapid shift in the school choices for some parents?

Certainly, recent school choice policy changes reflect wider societal shifts of the period, as well as continuing tendencies noted earlier. Charters reflect a conservative, entrepreneurial era's faith in market-based approaches, the dominance of suburban traditions of local control, and our mainstream society's discomfort in addressing systemic racial and class tensions openly. As historian David Labaree has argued, social issues are "educationalized" so as to avoid facing contentious and complex root causes while paying homage to a deeply rooted individualist ethic.[331] After the social tumult and cultural division of prior decades, market mechanisms promise a consumer nation a neutral arbiter, with schools the place for gritty strivers to flourish. In lieu of hard social decisions around structural poverty and enduring segregation, school choice offers a satisfying appearance of innovative effort at no additional public cost. Parents poorly served by current public schools, tired of pushing against unresponsive bureaucracies and frustrated by stalled social movements, see charters as a more attainable choice than a reformed public system. The US private labor force—dramatically deunionized over the past several decades, with flat or falling family incomes—has taken note of the growing numbers of unionized public school teachers in government-run institutions. The coproduction of public services expanded across numerous sectors, including corrections and national security; more broadly, small nimble start-ups were glorified as gateways to unprecedented innovations.[332] Charters nicely matched this historical confluence. Finally, expediency often triumphs as well. As political scientist Dorothy Shipps has noted, market-based policy reforms require much less civic mobilizing than educational reform efforts aimed at empowering stakeholders or directly addressing core teaching/learning issues.[333] Witness the relatively greater resistance to Common Core and testing than even to charter schools in recent public debates.

Some recent developments, though, stand out among these trends and tensions. One in particular is the growing presence of what Hess and Henig term "muscular philanthropy"—large orchestrated foundation efforts to instigate significant reforms in US education; and, relatedly, what Anthony Picciano coined the "education-industrial complex," defined as "networks of ideological, technophile, and for-profit entities that seek to promote their beliefs, ideas, products, and services in furtherance of their own goals and objectives."[334] These networks form an interrelated ecology of corporate, governmental, media, policy, nonprofit, and foundation resources; the profile and integration of this "new education philanthropy" in recent school reform activity and policy—including its roles in driving the ecology's new shape—draw few historical parallels. Certainly philanthropy has long influenced the field of education and the resulting aspects of school choice. Private giving has shaped many K–12 institutions over centuries; for example, the Carnegie Foundation's philanthropy left lasting legacies on faculty retirement accounts, libraries, and so on; more recently, the Ford Foundation played a powerful role in the 1960s and 1970s. Yet recent events underline three possibly distinctive historical developments affecting school choice: (1) the influence of philanthropy on government policy and programming; (2) its role in the wider fields of media and advocacy; and (3) its explicit development of a parallel infrastructure for the whole K–12 enterprise. While each has antecedents, the systematic scope and intensity seem unusual, if not entirely unprecedented, and certainly underexplored in the research.[335]

The "new" education philanthropy has established its influence within federal, state, and local government bodies, both elected and unelected, in an intriguing array of strategic investments. Most noted have been, for example, the former Gates Foundation employees who assumed senior positions within the US Department of Education under the Obama administration, particularly around Race to the Top, charters, and educational technology. Margot Rogers, Arne Duncan's first chief of staff, served as special assistant to the director of education at Gates, managing "the development of the foundation's five-year education strategy"; Joanne Weiss, who managed the RTTT fund, and later became Duncan's second chief of staff, had been COO at a major Gates grantee, the NewSchools Venture Fund, an investment fund focused heavily on charters and educational technology start-ups; and Jim Shelton, assistant deputy secretary for innovation and improvement, who managed the Investing in Innovation Fund (i3; authorized in the same stimulus package as RTTT), came from having just managed Gates Foundation education work in the northeast the previous five years.[336] Yet beyond direct government entanglement, Gates and others have systematically invested in the organizations affecting public discourse on school choice issues, from professional associations to policy think tanks to media outlets. For example, the organizations testifying to Congress most frequently on teacher-quality issues in 2010 received nearly $14 million in support from Gates and Broad. The new education philanthropy has also invested directly in public issue campaigns, from the 2007 presidential campaign, in which Gates and Broad invested $60 million to bring attention to their education reform agenda; to Learn-NY, a Gates-bankrolled campaign to erase term limits for Michael Bloomberg, the New York City mayor highly supportive of their work; to NBC News' Education Nation, a series of public events and programming focused on reforms backed by new education philanthropies; to Waiting for "Superman", backed by Gates and Broad, a Paramount Pictures documentary presenting an emotional appeal for the opportunities charters promised desperate families. In 2009, Gates directly entered media production, partnering with Viacom, a large media conglomerate, to form Get Schooled, a tax-exempt entity. Soon headed by a former senior education program officer at Gates, it aimed to "weave education-theme story lines into existing shows or to create new shows centered on education."[337] Finally, significant investments over the last two decades have shaped an alternative infrastructure for the education profession. Organizations including Teach for America, KIPP (Knowledge Is Power Program), Education Pioneers, and many others now structure an alternative profession, from preservice preparation to leadership preparation to policy research to public leadership to educational technology and consulting enterprises. Weiss noted that national standards would facilitate national market formation, justifying greater investment in education enterprises, especially in testing, data management, curriculum, and remedial services—what Patricia Burch has termed "the new education privatization."[338] Weiss has also stated the benefits of the larger markets created by common academic standards: "The adoption of common standards and shared assessments means that education entrepreneurs will enjoy national markets where the best products can be taken to scale."[339] In advance of RTTT, the Education Industry Association excitedly noted that "education is rapidly becoming a $1 trillion industry, representing 10% of America's GNP and second in size only to the healthcare industry."[340] While each of these developments has some precedence, the scope of the sustained and loosely coordinated strategy seems unprecedented, and partially explains the fervor of the backlash. Normative judgments and performance evaluations differ, certainly. Yet while some urban parents see an increase in choices (at least in theory), many local education professionals appear to have lost autonomy, owing to a shift toward federal, state, and philanthropic entities. While recent federal legislative battles have enhanced state authority, actual parental choices and the national policy discourse seem heavily influenced by the philanthropically driven educational system of nonprofit and for-profit providers, advocates, and enablers. (This is not to assess the net outcomes on performance or the developing system's capacity for deep innovation.) Yet a major new intentional influence on parents' schooling choices emerged over the last two decades from an alternative education infrastructure of philanthropically guided private institutions. This private, unelected, sustained, national, and publicly unaccountable system's influence on publicly funded schooling seems, in this sense, historically unprecedented.[341]

Within this evolving public/private infrastructure and configuration of school choices, as in earlier eras, parents exercised the agency they could, both in shaping the options available and in getting their children to the schools they desired—at times, in creative subversion to the system's design. Certainly, as noted above, families with the financial means often chose residency based on perceived school quality and the community's social status, navigating shifting systemic barriers of class and race. In the late 1950s, Ann and Jim Braithewaite, a professional African American couple, took two years and some three hundred phone calls to find their suburban home outside Philadelphia, and avoided standing in front of their picture window for "some time."[342] Quaker neighbors stayed with them the first night they moved in. Yet many black professionals, in pushing past racial barriers, also sought to exit lower-income black communities. Living in integrated settings "may have been as much a means of achieving social distance from the black working class," argues historian Andrew Wiese, "as securing social intimacy with middle-class whites."[343] Millions of other parents opted out of public schools no matter where they lived, and educated their children at home. Many viewed any professionally controlled public schooling for their children—especially within a rapidly diversifying secular society under an increasingly powerful state—as excessive loss of parental control.[344] Some parents seized upon policy changes to support the schooling they desired. When Wisconsin established the Milwaukee Parental Choice Program in 1990, the parents, staff, and directors of the closing Bruce-Guadalupe Community School merged with a local community center and accepted school vouchers. It survives to the present.[345] Many other parents worked the public options they had, leveraging whatever social capital advantages and informal information networks they could muster in navigating the system, including placement within targeted public school programs. Middle-class white families sought affordable school quality, and perhaps a modicum of diversity—but only so much.[346] Programs within the same school often reflected persistent segregations; general education versus gifted and talented (G&T) provides one example.[347] As one parent expressed, the choice of program allowed for a rather bounded version of the common school:

> I just want [my children] to be surrounded by kids that are somewhat like them, or at least half of the kids. I think living in New York gives them a good view on what the world is like and different types of people and they see all kinds. But I didn't want them being at school with people that weren't coming from like-minded families.[348]

Parents have also sought expanded choices by organizing themselves collectively, bringing pressure on individual schools, entire systems, and related social agencies through public campaigns, civil disobedience, action research, teacher training, volunteering in schools, and lobbying governments. From the Logan Square Neighborhood Association in Chicago, to Padres & Jóvenes Unidos in Denver, to the Northwest Bronx Community and Clergy Coalition in New York City, parents organized at neighborhood, municipal and state levels to affect policy and practices. In the Mississippi Delta, hundreds of African American parents gathered to strategize a campaign for state funding increases; in San Jose, California, parents joined others in designing and supporting new autonomous schools responsive to the Latino community.[349]

The United States continues to wrestle with the ghosts of *Brown*, Bestor, and Friedman in the differing profiles of school choices it provides. Struggling with government-mandated, mission-modeled, and "market-driven" approaches since World War II, dramatic differences in educational resources, quality and experiences remain. Arthur Bestor, whose father led the Chautauqua Institution for decades, deplored the lack of academic rigor in the "educational wastelands" of US schooling in the 1950s, a product of "regressive education" and the "anti-intellectual stance" of so many educators.[350] Milton Friedman worried less about the rigor and more about the rigor mortis of government-run schooling, proposing a school voucher scheme of "public financing but private operators." Writing just as *Brown* came down, he noted that the proposal "has recently been suggested in several southern states as a means of evading the . . . ruling against segregation"—and "I deplore segregation and racial prejudice." Yet he stuck with the market-based proposal, arguing that it offered a means of getting past the dichotomous choice of either "forced nonsegregation" or "forced segregation." As long as that was the choice, "only drastic change is possible; one must go from one extreme to the other." He saw privately operated schools as providing space for more incremental change. Choice would allow "exclusively white schools, exclusively colored schools, and mixed schools." For those opposing "segregation and racial prejudice,"

> the appropriate activity . . . is to try to persuade others of their views; if and as they succeed, the mixed schools will grow at the expense of the nonmixed, and a gradual transition will take place.[351]

By our present era, parental choice appears to have defaulted to a preference for such persuasion. Existing options reflect decades of frustrating struggles rooted in segregated residential patterns, when local control held fast within suburban boundaries and the collective political will rarely coalesced to level the disparate contexts of individual choices. Market-driven reforms to increase parental options—particularly charters—applied principally within urban rings that often experienced lower funding and less local control in governance.[352] Because federal magnet funding required explicit desegregation goals and remained flat in real terms, and integration ambitions faded amid narrowed legal bounds, charters filled a vacuum, promising quality through market mechanisms operating within constrained funding and narrow curricular bounds. Voucher programs and scholarship tax credits have gained momentum recently as well, including important legal victories. Consistent with charters, they require no new funding; they also demur on integration and leverage the ongoing appeal of coproduced public services.

Through six decades, the nation has continued its educational experimentation across progressive and conservative eras. Early on, civil rights and counterculture leaders sought to advance personal and collective transformations, reflecting the United States's long-standing mix of rebellion, utopianism, and unfulfilled democratic aspirations. In more recent years, educational entrepreneurs mimicked a Silicon Valley culture, launching educational start-ups as end runs on public bureaucracies, seeking to increase individual human capital performance within an insecure and competitive world. As a result, for some families, schooling choices expanded just as pedagogical visions and equity aspirations narrowed. For many, though—such as those living in the leafy legacies of Levittown—residential location still trumps all other ways to choose a school.

We turn now to explore more directly the arguments surrounding current parental choices.

PART 2

The Value of Choice: A Normative Assessment

One of the main distinctions between a democratic regime and an author-itarian one is that a democracy is meant to reflect and protect the human capacity to choose. In a democracy, the protection of a sphere free of public intervention—where a person can act without public consequence—is seen at least as an aspect, if not the very core, of liberty.

The choice of an educational context for one's children is seen by many as an important dimension of liberty. Parenting is often practiced as a vehicle for extending one's identity and core values onto others and into the future, and parents are commonly seen as having a right to express their cultural, religious, moral, or intellectual preferences and affiliations through their parenting deci-sions.[1] Like all rights, this one has its limits. Two main issues contest the right of parents to freely choose the education of their children. First, the rights that the children themselves hold, especially when those stand in contrast with the expression of the parent's right (as some suggest is the case when parents offer their children strict religious education only, or other forms of education that might limit their future opportunities[2]). Second, parents' rights to educate their children are limited by the state's reasonable jurisdiction over the enact-ment of shared social values, as in the case when parents' enacted preferences would undermine a key social goal such as equality or human dignity. These principled concerns, as well as some practical limitations, are characteristic of the long history of school choice in the United States as described in this vol-ume thus far. Contemporary iterations of school choice practices (introduced in the section above, "From Plural Visions to Bounded Choices") center on another player beyond the family and the government: namely, "the market," or business interests. We therefore devote some of the discussion in this part to the social and institutional considerations arising from the interplay between individual and family, state and government in all their various layers, and the market—an interplay evident from the first days of the republic, and raising a unique set of normative challenges in its current iteration.

As we note earlier in the book, the debate about school choice cuts across the political spectrum. Advocates of school choice include defenders of small government and nonintervention as well as egalitarians whose main focus is social justice.[3] Principled support for school choice is thus based on a variety of ideological commitments, including preference for smaller government, less investment in public education, and more reliance on market strategies and private sector innovation to improve the quality of schools. The coalition of poor, working-class, and minority advocates of school choice with conservative and libertarian advocates suggests there are different justifications for the call to introduce greater school choice into the public education system.

The choice sector relies on many of these justifications in advancing policies that support its expansion. For instance, as we discussed in detail earlier, in 2014 nearly 6,500 charter schools operated in the United States, up from 4,662 in 2008/9; they served some 2.5 million children, or just over 5% of all students.[4] Their share of students may be small but has grown rapidly, and choice is regularly presented as a key policy in the progress of education reform. It is one of the sole bipartisan issues, with strong support from both political parties and in all recent administrations. Philanthropic and business efforts to expand choice abound in recent decades, informing the contours of policy and the choices available to parents.

Current school choice policies in the United States are often presented as based on rights—the right of parents to control their children's education, and the right of parents and children to have access to equitable opportunities. The introduction of school choice is meant to realize these rights by providing a variety of options for families to choose from, and by giving families who have had limited access to high-quality schools the opportunity to send their children to stronger schools.

However, the normative arguments for and against school choice extend well beyond talk of rights. As conservative scholar Frederick Hess has stated, "If the goal is to get low-income children out of terrible urban school systems and into high-quality private schools where they can learn safely and increase their odds of getting high-school diplomas," then well-designed school choice policies can best accomplish that.[5] Alternatively, if the goal is to improve students' scores on standardized tests, the results enjoyed by choice programs are more dubious. Such programs become more questionable when the broader goals are college admission and completion, as well as civic development. The design and evaluation of school choice programs is thus tightly linked to the particular goals and justifications for these programs. In other words, the specific choices made available to parents are not just a result of "supporting school choice." Rather, school choice programs are designed with specific goals and justifications in mind by policy makers who are committed to a particular view of education (rather than more broadly to providing choice to parents). At the same time, assessing whether a particular choice policy has been successful must be based on understanding the issue it was designed to address or the goals it was designed to advance.

The following sections present key arguments in the school choice debate, and offer some policy guidelines in response to both empirical evidence and normative arguments on the issue, and in light of the historical analysis. We organize our discussion by keeping in mind that education serves both public and private aims, and that it is also positional—namely, people are "ranked" according to their educational credentials, so it matters not only what one person's educational outcomes are but significantly also how they stand in comparison to others.

To understand the role each of these aspects plays, the arguments are presented separately in each section. First is the argument from free market or "more choice" advocates, focusing more on the role of education as a private matter—one that each family needs to figure out for its members. We then move to the counterarguments on the same issue offered by public school proponents.

To foreshadow, the discussion begins by addressing the basic question: Whose education is it? In other words, how should decisions be made about how and where to educate children? This question—which, as we've seen, is as old as the republic—also touches on the issue of the aims of education: processes of decision-making about schools and education indicate the way society sees its collective goals. While many school choice advocates see parents as the best judges of their children's needs and interests in schooling as well as the specific aims of their own children's schooling, and couple this freedom to decide with a vision of an open education "marketplace," proponents of public schools worry that prioritizing parental preference can undermine some of their children's interests as well as supplant shared aims with narrow self-interests.

The next section focuses on issues surrounding accountability for schools in the context of choice, and the innovation that choice schools are meant to enable. With the historical case of the development of Catholic schools in mind, we ask, can particular designs of choice in schooling advance educational innovation, by opening up less-regulated institutions and having parents select the best ones? And does such innovation and deregulation come at any cost to democratic accountability of the schools toward the families and the communities they serve? The section begins with those who argue for choice as advancing innovation, followed by public school advocates' arguments regarding the harms of choice to accountability.

Finally, the third section, "Equal Access to Quality Education, or Another Layer of Separation?," investigates issues of recognition, inclusion, and exclusion—issues that undergird the developments in the last few decades that we discussed in part 1. Do more and newer choices provide greater recognition to different cultural groups? The section begins with those who argue that they do. And do these choices stand in contradiction to school integration and its promise of greater equality? The second part of this section follows the arguments raised by public school advocates concerned that choice promotes greater segregation and inequality.

Whose Education Is It? Private Interests and the Public Role of Schools

PRIVATE OPTIONS FOR EDUCATION CONSUMERS

Advocates of market-based school choice are calling for policies that will address what they see as a cumbersome institution held back by bureaucratic forces and union interests. Monopoly, bureaucracy, and stagnation are identified as consequences of the enormous size of the schooling system, the strength of teachers' unions, and the difficulties of measuring and reforming instructional methods. School choice is seen as a way to free families and education providers from complex regulations, to circumvent the layers of administration and red tape, and to create free competition that would improve educational quality. The difficulty of the large public school, and school system, has adapting to the preferences and needs of communities and individuals is presented as a structural limitation of a governmental or public service, one that can only be cured by privatizing the service—allowing smaller and more responsive entities to serve the changing needs of their customers.

Conservative and libertarian advocates often raise arguments for a greater parental role in educational decisions, assuming that personal choice within a free market structure is far superior to government imposition and the regulation of private decisions. This kind of freedom to choose one's own path is ardently defended in the domain of family life: it is easy to assume that the government should not intervene in one's decisions about how they lead their private and family life. Both conservative and libertarian thinkers insist that their own judgment about such decisions should not be replaced by the judgment of a government official who knows nothing about a parent's values, preferences, or goals, and is not familiar with the child's unique skills, needs, and interests. Extending the same vision into the school choice debate suggests that the way someone raises their children—including how they choose to educate them—is a private decision, which should not be guided or limited by the government. The use of school vouchers is the clearest realization of this vision, because it provides parents with the funds to pay for the education of their children in any institution they may prefer.

In fact, the vision of free choice in voucher policies and other choice designs is not as free as it seems, because parents can choose only from the options available to them in their vicinity. In allowing the market to develop these choices (meaning, by approving private, religious, and other school options rather than providing one or more public options), the government lends its power to the myriad private businesses, faith organizations, and others that are seen as offering more options to individuals than what the government might offer. Privately operated institutions, or ones where the business sector has a greater influence, are presented by contemporary school choice advocates as nimbler, more innovative, and more efficiently run than public ones. Freedom of choice for individuals is thus seen as dependent on the availability of options that in turn are offered by the private sector. In the realm of education, as in other fields, choice advocates criticize regulation as intruding on personal freedom (in telling parents which school their children must attend) and as harming the development of effective practices (in telling teachers and schools how to operate), in addition to introducing schools to higher operating costs and failing to make a satisfying impact. According to free market advocates, government-provided and -regulated schools are more costly and less efficient. The claim is recurrent: back in the mid-nineteenth century, in announcing a new building, school head Charles Hammond declared the new addition further proof that academies privately managed resources with greater efficiency.[6] Breaking the current near monopoly of the government in the education field—close to 90% of US students attend public schools, as has been the case for much of the nation's history—is suggested to potentially bring about a number of benefits. First, it would return the decision-making power about educational paths to parents, who they say are best suited to know what is best for their children.[7] Parents have long been required by both regulation and circumstance to send their children to a given neighborhood school, no matter how unsuitable it might be or how unresponsive to their individual needs and concerns. Parents' rights advocates claim that breaking the boundaries of catchment areas and providing parents with a broader array of opportunities to select an appropriate school for their particular children regardless of address is an important step in minimizing the intrusion of government into the realm of family life. At the same time, it is suggested that greater choice for parents would incentivize schools to compete and thus to improve their practices, their responsiveness to parental expectations and students' needs, and their overall achievement.

These contemporary market arguments for educational choice—which are often intertwined with the parental authority argument—originated in the United States with Milton Friedman's 1955 essay on vouchers.[8] The thrust of Friedman's argument, as noted in the previous chapter, was that giving parents the freedom to choose appropriate schools for their children would allow them to exercise their parental rights, while simultaneously promoting a deregulated marketplace of options. These various schools, having to compete for vouchers, would work tirelessly to improve in order to attract new clients, rather than being mired in the stagnation of having a captive audience. In 1990 Chubb and Moe took a similar approach, proclaiming that "reformers would do well to entertain the notion that choice is a panacea. . . . It has the capacity all by itself to bring about the kind of transformation that, for years, reformers have been seeking to engineer in myriad other ways."[9]

This optimistic vision relies on the assumption that the education realm can indeed be restructured, both in terms of regulation and in terms of incentive structures, to operate as a competition-driven free market. Notably, a free market vision is hard to implement when it is unclear what is the product of the effort—Is it grades? Effective schools? Educated well-rounded students? Moreover, the mere existence of public schools, even if they are but one option among many, limits the applicability of this vision. As long as some students are assigned to district schools independent of the school's performance, it is hard to see how market forces can truly be in play. (Other deviations from the market model in education are discussed below.) Subsequently, some advocates of school choice have called for a fuller implementation of the market model in education, arguing that preliminary results show that competition works, and insisting that "if every dollar spent on a student followed him when he changed schools—a state of affairs that exists nowhere in this country today—the verdict on choice-inspired competition would likely be quite different."[10]

For many advocates of deregulation and market competition, the mere availability of choice signifies success. Providing parents with options and with the opportunity to have their voices heard through the selection they make is in itself seen as a better circumstance than the geographically limited process of school assignment in most district schools. Others caution that having additional options is just one aspect of a true market, and that other factors have to be present—incentive mechanisms, clearer forms of deregulation, and so on—in order for a true market to emerge with all its attendant benefits.

Small-government and parental-authority advocates call for an expansion of choice within the schooling system not only as part of a free market approach but also as justifiable by reference to personal freedom and limiting government power. Allowing a philanthropist or an entrepreneur to create a school or a charter network might inject new spirit into old and maybe tired institutions, as well as permit parents to select from a new array of options not available to them under the "one best system." This may include minority parents who prefer to separate their children into a community of shared language, culture, or background—an option not available through zoning and catchment areas regulated by local and state government. These schools might excel because opening the education "market" to multiple providers through charters and other means can support improvement by competition. For instance, members of a West Philadelphia community could establish the Harambee Institute, an African American K–8 charter school, where their children could focus on a specialized curriculum and a school culture that emphasized specific traditions, values, and goals.[11] The assumption is that this new option is attractive to some parents who opt for it, while also providing an incentive to other schools to reconsider their curricular offerings as they compete for the same students. Thus this self-separated community can make use of a deregulated market to develop institutions and content they are committed to and to take ownership of the education of their youth.

When concerns about actual outcomes are raised by critics (as discussed below), advocates of the free market often argue that any failures are a result of inadequate forms and levels of deregulation. Many scholars—both advocates and opponents of school choice—warn that the necessary conditions for the functioning of an effective market do not take place in the realm of schooling. Researchers on both sides agree that open access to information and the rational consideration of options in the decision-making process are harder to achieve in the education field than they are in others. But significantly, advocates of school choice add that, in the domain of school choice, the necessary market conditions for success—in particular, the fuller form of deregulation that allows for an open provider field to develop—have not been achieved. These advocates attribute many of the shortcomings of current school choice programs to the persistence of public options in schooling and to the regulatory complexity of the market rather than to any issues internal to the choice environment. This is why, they suggest, school choice has not yet fulfilled its promise of freedom and improvement.

It is worth noting that while many libertarians embrace school choice as a way to protect the parental domain of decision-making over education, others see current forms of school choice as incompatible with the libertarian vision: "Libertarians support markets because and to the extent that they are (1) Voluntary (rather than coercive), (2) Decentralized (rather than centralized), (3) Competitive (rather than monopolistic), (4) Positive-sum (rather than zero-sum or negative-sum)."[12] Given that education is compulsory and at least to some extent retains centralized and even monopolistic traits through its public provision and regulation, it seems that the libertarian case for markets in education is weakened. Finally, the case for personal freedom on which the market-driven vision of libertarianism relies is complicated by the possibility of tensions between parental liberty and children's liberty. Thus, if a libertarian would argue for vouchers on the premise that parents should be allowed to choose a school for their children—including religious schools or other schools that educate for comprehensive belief or values—the result can clearly be a restriction of the liberty of their children who are made to attend these schools and possibly be indoctrinated into this vision. The tensions between parents' rights and children's rights are beyond the scope of the current discussion, but it is worth noting that it presents an additional challenge to the libertarian argument for school choice.

SCHOOLS FOR THE PUBLIC, BY THE PUBLIC

The public nature of schools is an important democratic asset—one that is diminished by the introduction of competition, market forces, and deregulation into the education field. Critics of school choice worry that if schools participate in competition for the hearts and wallets of consumers (rather than serving the public and maintaining a shared civic space), educators and schools will not be able to serve broader social aims, such as democratic citizenship or equal opportunity. In addition, some critics are concerned that market forces by their very nature generate winners and losers, and thus are altogether unsuitable for a domain like education that is supposed to level the playing field for all, and where children and their basic needs are at stake.

For many educational thinkers, the public role of education is its most important dimension, and the preparation for participating in the public sphere is the key justification for using public funds to support the education system.[13] More than providing individuals with an opportunity for personal growth and for the achievement of personal educational and professional goals, schools are democratic public institutions whose goal is to create the conditions for civic equality. They do so largely by providing the public with a shared context in which to develop their sense of themselves as members of a larger community. The civic and public role of education is seen as central to the well-being of society and as an important contributor to the well-being of its citizens. Consequently, some scholars of school choice insist that education must take place within the public system—in other words, that school choice must be provided only within the realm of public regulation and provision, in contexts such as (properly regulated) public charter schools, magnet schools, inter- and intradistrict choice.[14] Those who study public schools and analyze the conditions for their success (as well as their impact and their legitimacy) note that individuals and families learn to engage with one another and with public institutions through public schools, thus enhancing their own skills as civic actors and influencing the policies of the schools that serve them.[15]

The introduction of choice is seen by some public school advocates as threatening the benefits accrued through public schooling in a number of ways. First, in relation to charters, while charter schools are in some senses public schools—in that they rely on public funds for their operation—they are still exempt from some of the regulatory power of the state (to an extent determined by their specific charter). As a result, they may be unable or disinclined to develop some of the public and civic aspects that have long been the hallmark of public schools. Granted, the current policy regime with its focus on standardized tests in measurable areas has pushed many public schools to limit their offerings in civic studies and other related areas, and to focus more of their instructional time on tested subjects. However, as public institutions and as a result of their long traditions in this area, charters are still promoting a commitment to citizenship and to being public-minded; whereas choice schools, which are driven by market forces, often see their role as directly tied to improving tests results, and thus would be less inclined to devote much time to other civic and public matters (beyond that of academic opportunity to underserved youth—often a key aspect of their mission). The market justification for the introduction of charter and other choice schools focuses attention on individual achievement rather than the common good, and as a result, schools' interest in devoting much time to these matters is inherently limited.[16] Public services are increasingly coproduced by the government and private entities; in the case of schools, charter operators are private entities that benefit from philanthropy as well as business investments, and are sometimes driven by profit goals. In this context, the ends to which institutions are devoted will be matters of design and regulation, the recognized and implicit interests of public and private entities that shape and provide the educational service, and the market and other interests of the parent-consumer. The recognition of the public and common good as an educational aim (which is inherent to public schools) will be promoted in choice schools only to the extent that the government bodies, as coproducers of the service, promote it.

While the charter school movement began in part as an effort, at least in part, to better respond to the needs of marginalized students through local, responsive schools, these community-based efforts were "appropriated and reengineered by philanthropic, corporate, hedge-fund and real estate interests."[17] As discussed in the historical chapter before, real estate interests have long been part of the evolving school choice landscape in the United States; however, the influence of large, coordinated, and increasingly international corporate philanthropic efforts seems distinctive, as are the influence of hedge funds and other investment groups.

In addition to the general requirement for public schools to cultivate civic affiliation and public-mindedness, public schools are seen as important vehicles for the development of respect and tolerance across different communities within the population, especially by creating lasting encounters among diverse populations. This goal has clearly eroded with the expansion of choice, as well as with the increasing homogenization of neighborhoods—especially along racial and socioeconomic lines—and the subsequent reduction in student diversity in public schools. Choice can break politically determined geographical boundaries in ways that either promote or impede integration, as made clear in part 1. Neighborhood and catchment-area school zones are often separated along racial and class-based lines,[18] and thus public schools rarely resemble Mann's vision of a common school or its more recent iteration as a "great sphere" to which children arrive from a diverse set of circumstances, background, and values.[19] Nonetheless, in contrast to their magnet predecessors, charter schools are still less diverse and more racially isolated than the public schools their students would otherwise have attended. Overall, charter schools tend to serve more African American students than respective public schools in the same district, fewer Hispanic (especially ESL) students, and fewer students with special needs.[20] Thus, while public schools do not serve the "great sphere" goal well enough, they are still serving it better than choice schools.

CAN PARENTS BE EFFECTIVE EDUCATION CONSUMERS?

Yes, Parents Are the Best Choosers

A key justification for school choice is the preference many parents express to control the values to which their children are exposed in schools. This is sometimes discussed in the context of religious beliefs, as when schools teach evolution as part of the required biology curriculum and face objections from parents who fear that exposure to the theory of evolution would undermine their children's beliefs, and possibly therefore their adherence to the religious views their parents would like them to follow. In some cases, other aspects of the curriculum are challenged on similar grounds.[21] While we will not discuss in this book the tension between the public school curriculum and the beliefs and values held by some religious families,[22] it is important to consider the fact that certain choice mechanisms such as vouchers allow parents to send their children to schools that would educate them according to their religious beliefs—something they might not be able to afford otherwise. That there are parents (Laats's "other school reformers" cited earlier) who seek choice in order to avoid damage from a perceived anti-religious "progressive" secularism complicates that issue across sectors.[23]

The justification for choice as a way to support parental authority stems from J. S. Mill's suggestion that parents should be responsible for the type of education that their children receive: "Hardly any one indeed will deny that it is one of the most sacred duties of the parents (or, as law and usage now stand, the father), after summoning a human being into the world, to give to that being an education fitting him to perform his part well in life towards others and towards himself."[24] Based on Mill's argument and subsequent work, parental authority is argued to be central for citizens in a democratic society for two key reasons. Politically, if the state is the sole authority over the type of education that children receive—where they go to school, what they learn there, who teaches them—and the state is also the provider of education through setting up and operating the public education system, then a child's mind may be molded in a way that befits the state's political preferences. As a result, the legitimacy of the state might be compromised, since the consent of the citizens may be given to it as a result of its molding their views.[25] If an alternative structure is set up whereby the free market provides education in varied forms and types, then the marketplace of ideas would remain vibrant and the freedom of thought would be more safely preserved—allowing society to develop new ideas and perspectives and continue its progress, and allowing citizens to consider their allegiance to the state more openly.

In addition, proponents of parental choice in education suggest that it is important to preserve parental authority because children are primarily charges of their parents, and unless parents take some extreme action that compromises their right to control the decisions about their children's lives, the state has no right to intervene and undermine those preferences. Beyond the argument for a parental right to make decisions about the education of their children, some suggest that, pragmatically speaking, parents know their children best and therefore can protect their particular best interests most effectively. This argument can stem from a "sentimental conception of the family" whereby parents always have their children's best interests in mind,[26] or from a pragmatist or efficiency-based view that sees parents as the most effective and direct advocates on behalf of their children.

No, Parents Cannot Always Be Effective Choosers

Despite the fact that parents often know their children well and have their best interest in mind, there are some strong arguments against leaving the choice of schooling for children to their discretion. The main concerns about allowing parents to make this decision focus on the fact that there are known limitations on our ability to choose rationally, coupled with structural and social practices that limit parents' ability to make the best choices. Moreover, parental choice is not always a mechanism that supports the aims of both children and society, which need to be served by schools if they are seen as public institutions.

The choice of a school is widely known as a particularly difficult one to make, especially in an environment of multiple and diverse choices. The reason that this is an especially hard choice is that the reasons for choosing a particular option are wide ranging, and include one's personal values (and their family's values) as well as their priorities about schools—what is most important in a school? Different people rank differently the importance of average performance on tests, religious affiliation, safety, geographic location, and so on; choosers often also account for their neighbors' and friends' decisions as part of the selection process. Additionally, to choose a school, parents would need to account for their child' abilities, needs, and interests, and related considerations—all of which needs to be calculated in relation to each of the available and diverse options. Making a decision with so many relevant factors is difficult and taxing.

As a result, for individuals to make informed choices, they need to garner enough information, to assess it properly in light of their preferences, and to make decisions in complex social contexts. An argument against deferring to personal choice and judgment in these areas is that the process of individual decision-making is hampered by both external and internal limitations. Because individuals are limited in their access to information and in their ability to process it, they might reach decisions that do not align with their ultimate expectations and aspirations. Moreover, when all these choices are aggregated, they often do not promote public goals, including both practical ones like efficiency, and normative or ideal ones like equality or integration.

To go into this argument in a bit more detail, in school choice as in other areas of decision-making, two main conditions are required: access to reliable information, and the capacity to make a good decision (often summarized as "autonomy and rationality"). Unfortunately, both conditions are not always available to parents, families who participate in school choice programs (or to others).[27]

First, regarding access to reliable information, studies performed using a variety of methods indicate the many barriers parents face when trying to understand the choices available to them. Predictably, parents who are not native speakers of English, or who have limited literacy in English, have access to fewer resources and to information of lower quality when attempting to figure out their children's educational options. Latino Spanish-speaking families, for example, have been shown to have fewer tools to engage in the choice process; many districts do not provide enough information in Spanish, making their choice process even more limited.[28] Along with these technical barriers, many parents face time constraints and other limitations on access to clear information, including difficulty deciphering the details and identifying those that are salient for their needs and interests. In addition, social class plays an important role in access to quality information. As numerous studies have shown, information networks generally and those related to school options specifically are divided along race and class lines, creating more opportunities for easy access to accurate information to white and middle-class parents as compared to their minority and poor counterparts.[29] There is also evidence that certain "choice schools"—especially charter schools—are working to make information more readily available to families of students they prefer to enroll, in terms of English proficiency, a more stable neighborhood, or other characteristics that make certain students potentially easier to teach.

Moreover, the assumption that, when given access to relevant information, individuals will be able to assess and use it effectively to advance their goals is put into question by numerous studies on decision-making. The capacity to decide rationally—even when rationality is defined most narrowly as correlation between ends and means, or the congruence between the aims one is trying to promote and the means one chooses to promote those aims—is significantly limited by the bounded nature of human rationality. While a few decades of studies of the decision-making process have shown this to be the case for individuals making decisions in various contexts, the context of school choice complicates the matter in three important ways.

First, even if a parent learns of a bad circumstance at her child's school, she hesitates to move him to a new one. Not only would a new school likely mean her child would be taught a different curriculum, but her child would be pulled away from his friends and everything familiar to him.

Second, parents' personal preferences and views about what a high-quality school looks like do not always align with formal views of school quality. Formally, school quality these days is tied almost exclusively to test scores, while parents continue to value different qualities in a school, including its distance from their house, the stability and accessibility of the staff, a sense of connection to other families served by the school, and a subjective sense of safety in and around the school.

Moreover, studies of parents in school choice contexts reminds us that the "rational" choices as embedded in policy may not actually recognize elements within the rational choices of those targeted—for example, the relative importance of proximity vis-à-vis official markers of quality—or the value evident in areas of schooling about which the policy does not generate data.

Compounding these difficulties is the fact that the decision ultimately affects the child more than it does the parent; hence, the party making the decision—with all the challenges that characterize it—is impacting another person's future more than their own. The extent to which this is legitimate hinges upon the value we attach to parental authority over children's autonomy.

Finally, as has been suggested in the earlier section, "Schools for the Public, by the Public" the consequences of a child's schooling go well beyond fulfilling his parents' preferences. A child must be protected from limiting or damaging decisions that his parents may make about his schooling. This can happen through making sure that all children are educated, without intervening with the specifics of where and how this education takes place. But society too has a high stake here, as its political and economic future depends on an educated citizenry. For these reasons, leaving parents solely in charge of decisions about the schooling of their children may be unwarranted—they might not have the tools or the context to make an informed choice, and they might make a choice that would harm or limit either their child or (in the aggregate) society in the future. As noted in the previous part, New England leaders worried about just that when establishing the Old Deluder Satan Act back in the seventeenth century, requiring larger towns to provide teachers.

Labs for Innovation, or Unaccountable "Ghost Districts"?

CHOICE THROUGH PRIVATIZATION SUPPORTS INNOVATION

A key argument for granting charters to new schools, and for developing this form of choice as a major public policy, is that charter schools would not be constrained by the complex bureaucratic requirements that make regular public schools slow to change. Part 1 describes some of the historical context to this argument; the first magnets in Tacoma, for example, touted several pedagogical innovations they were able to implement. As a result, it is assumed that charter schools are well suited to try different approaches, revise curricular and pedagogical decisions as needed, and overall be responsive to the needs of their students. In light of these characteristics, charter schools are seen by many advocates as "labs for innovations," trying on small-scale ideas and approaches that, if successful, can later be endorsed by other charter and traditional public schools.

The "laboratories for innovation" language has been introduced and endorsed by both Democratic and Republican administrations, and is presented as a significant reasoning for the introduction of school choice. The notion that unfettering schools from the bonds of state and federal requirements would allow them to experiment; try different pedagogic, curricular, and administrative approaches; and come up with more innovative ways to tackle persistent problems schools face, has prompted the call from the Obama administration for reducing or eliminating caps on the number of charters that states issue. In his first major speech on education, in March 2009, President Barack Obama indicated that promoting innovation and excellence in schools depends in part on eliminating the caps on charter schools—in place at the time in twenty-six states—and thus allowing for experimentation and new ideas to evolve.[30]

Clearly, charter schools are unencumbered by some of the complex bureaucratic structures that are typical of large traditional districts. They are exempt from some requirements and limitations placed on public schools, including the use of given and scripted curricula where these are in place, some admissions requirements, and—significantly—the hiring and firing procedures for teachers that are guided in many states and cities by union contracts. For many choice advocates overall (not just in the context of the charter school movement), the unions represent a key obstacle to effective education reform; for them, the ability of charters to operate without allowing their teachers to unionize represents a significant advantage. The assumption in this regard is that, absent unions, school leadership can hire and fire solely on the basis of the quality of instruction teachers provide, or according to "value-added" measures, and therefore can ensure higher quality teaching than districts that are limited by union contracts that prioritize seniority and make it difficult to fire unsuccessful teachers.

Moreover, charters can operate on a different calendar from traditional districts. Many charter schools—both single institutions and those part of charter management organizations (CMOs)—operate their schools for longer hours each day (often 7:30 a.m. to 5:00 p.m.), a longer school week that includes Saturday, and a longer school year with a shorter summer vacation. This flexibility is possible due to the freedom of employment practices these operations enjoy. Clearly, the profile of the teachers in these organizations is different as a result. Many of them are younger in both age and experience, and are driven and committed to the "no excuses" charter mentality.

Charter schools begin to expand some of the lessons they have learned not only as they scale up their operations but also as public schools strive to learn from their successes. A recent report from Mathematica, "Learning from Charter School Management Organizations: Strategies for Student Behavior and Teacher Coaching" encourages traditional public schools to implement successful strategies used in the more successful CMOs it has identified.[31] Despite recognizing that the two types of schools operate on different scales and in different bureaucratic and other environments, the report claims that "some districts are already experimenting with strategies similar to the practices of high-performing CMOs, and these new initiatives could inform future policy and practice."[32] These are early indications of the usage of charter schools—and especially the more successful CMOs—as labs for innovation.[33] Their successes are replicated not only by scaling up their own operations,[34] but also by efforts to emulate them in traditional public schools and in other charters.

Next we consider two critiques of the "labs for innovation" argument— first, the practical limits of innovation, and second, the limitations of account- ability in this model.

THE LIMITS OF INNOVATION

Supporters of traditional public schools point to the fact that many "inno- vative" charters and other schools are committed to improving educational outcomes as those are understood in the most traditional sense—namely, raising students' scores on standardized tests, and through the most tradi- tional instructional means. Initially, in the early years of the charter school movement, most charters were begun by grassroots organizations set up by local parents, teachers, or community leaders. Whether they were traditional district schools that converted to charters, or new schools that applied for and received a charter to open a new space, they mostly operated as stand-alones in local settings. The vision of a lab of innovation was central to the type of school that often was set up by a highly committed group and was intensely responsive to the needs of the community it served.

Since 2000, the network approach to charter schools, or the view that charter management organizations can better operate charters and provide better outcomes than stand-alone schools, has largely replaced the single- school approach. While the majority of charters are still freestanding, the share of CMO-operated schools is rapidly growing. These nonprofit or for-profit entities directly manage public charter schools and are generally viewed as a way to meld the benefits of school districts—such as lower operational costs, centralized bureaucracies, ability to scale up ideas, collaboration among similar schools, and support structures—with the autonomy and entrepreneurial drive of the charter sector.[35]

CMOs are viewed as a way to manage various administrative needs that single schools often find quite challenging, and they have been established to manage groups of charter schools in order to intensify their impact on the public school system and to alleviate some of the common challenges faced by stand-alone charter schools. Both state funding and private philanthropy are available to CMOs, thus offering greater buying power to meet operational needs. In addition, the daily operations and the processes related to admission, teacher training, student evaluation and other needs can better be managed by these umbrella organizations for all the schools in their network. Some of the schools start as CMO schools, and others start as stand-alone and later join a network as they scale up or face the complex requirements of running a school.[36] As a result, it is hard to have a clear, full picture of the number of CMO-managed charter schools versus the number of stand-alone charter schools, but it seems clear that the tide is moving in the direction of CMOs.

In the late 1990s and early 2000s, the major philanthropies funding charter schools invested heavily in CMOs and similar organizations, spending an estimated total of $500 million between 1999 and 2009. Most large donors and foundations no longer fund stand-alone schools.[37] As Don Shalvey of the Gates Foundation (formerly the head of Aspire, a CMO) said in 2011, "CMOs are widely believed to have a better chance of being successful than stand-alone charter schools, because they have the infrastructure and resources to replicate good practices and take advantage of economies of scale."[38] Their investments have been targeted to specific urban school districts, such as Los Angeles and New York City, which have been considered difficult, if not impossible, to reform; philanthropic support has favored that subset of cities, though, under state or mayoral control, minimizing the role of traditional local governance.[39] With these additional funds from Gates, Walton, Broad, and other philanthropic foundations, added to the public monies supporting these schools, about one hundred thousand students in 350 schools have been educated to varying degrees of success.

In recent years, the generally positive reputations of CMOs among some policy makers have led policy leaders, including former secretary of education Arne Duncan, to call for greater replication of high-performing charter schools via CMOs, especially as a strategy for turning around or replacing chronically low-performing public schools. While some critics have suggested that such scaling up would overextend CMOs and lead to the opening of low-quality charters, others insist that the higher-performing CMOs are ready to scale up their operations. For example, at the annual meeting of the National Alliance for Public Charter Schools in Minneapolis in June 2012, the main focus of discussion was "scaling up" and the capacity of existing schools to expand their models.[40]

The trend is therefore moving in the direction of CMO-operated charters, with some concerns that the ills of districts—such as they are—will be replicated under this new model. The expansion of charters is based on the effort of some charter operators and funders to scale up their models, exiting the "labs for innovations" phase and aiming to benefit greater numbers of students with their models. But even as the "labs of innovation" argument has passed its prime, CMOs grow to imitate district structures—their bureaucratic structures, management algorithms, and institutional culture. Formerly nimble organizations turn into "ghost districts"—district-like organizational structures that replicate traditional districts even as they are funded and coordinated by a mix of public and private moneys and rules—which do not, by and large, represent a marked improvement over traditional districts in their practices, bureaucratic structures, or measured outcomes.

One aspect of the charter approach that cannot—and probably should not—be replicated in the public schools sector is staff attrition. Few teachers survive for very long in working environments that require high levels of focus and engagement for most of one's waking hours (teachers are often required to be available to offer homework help after the long school days and into the night). For example, in New York City's 136 charter schools in 2012, one-third of teachers and one-fifth of principals left every year.[41] These staffing problems—which are often the result of early burnout arising from the start-up mentality of these organizations and the high demands placed on staff—point to some of the complexity in sustaining and scaling up charter operations. The high teacher turnover is problematic not only because it indicates poor working conditions for teachers, but also significantly because it undermines the stability and continuity necessary for student success. Personal connection to teachers, the relations between the family and the staff in school, and most of all the presence of an experienced, seasoned teacher are predictive of student success. Draining young teachers of their energy too quickly drives them away from the profession before they have had the chance to become the excellent teachers many of them can become, and contributes (among various other factors) to the teacher shortages that many districts are experiencing in recent years.

Perhaps the most discouraging aspect of the effort to scale up successful charter schools is their adherence to the narrow vision of education as an outcome on standardized tests, an issue that does not attract much attention in the vast literature on charter schools.[42] It is important to note that the analysis of CMOs and charter success or failure focuses on their students' achievements on standardized tests, and the bulk of the effort by these schools is devoted to improving test scores. As their brief history covered in part 1 indicates, charter schools were broadly supported at first not only because of the belief in market forces, the power of competition, and the desire for minimized government intervention in education. Charters started also as a way to equalize access to quality education, especially in support of improved access for poor students, students of color, English language learners, and students in urban districts. Charters today largely operate in urban districts and serve marginalized groups, providing alternatives to students who did not have them before. But the alternative that charters offer is oftentimes, at best, a better executed version of the same narrow, limited format that was offered in the underfunded district schools from which their students come. While suburban and affluent students benefit from rich curricular and extracurricular offerings in both public and private schools—with multiple opportunities to excel in the arts, a wide variety of athletics programs, a broad curriculum with access to labs and other resources—most underserved students are exposed to a narrower curriculum meant to overcome measured gaps in literacy and math; that is true in both district and choice schools in underserved urban and rural areas. In many "no excuses" charter schools, the mission and practice demand a focus on standardized forms of achievement in math and reading. While some CMO schools offer AP classes and certain extracurricular activities in their effort to improve college admission rates, the majority of their long school day is devoted to rote practice, and is aimed at improving students' skills to perform better on the state- and federally required standardized tests. The outcomes of these assessments are the main measure by which the CMOs and charters are themselves evaluated, and therefore are possibly of even greater importance in these schools than they are in public schools.[43]

Consequently, most charter schools at their best offer underserved students a safer environment and a more feasible opportunity to excel on standardized tests—no small achievements—but still a narrow, uninspiring, basic curriculum and harsh pedagogical and behavior management practices. One hears an echo of the early nineteenth-century Lancasterian or monitorial system—now pilloried as an example of harsh, rote pedagogy—which scaled rapidly, viewed by many as an efficient solution in resource-strapped communities at the time. Yet, compared with the more open, broad, and engaging curricular offerings, as well the more collaborative and engaged pedagogical practices common in suburban and private schools, the innovations developed in charter schools can seem unsatisfying. Let us turn, then, to consider the final argument in support of charter schools: the equalization of access to quality education.

LIMITS OF ACCOUNTABILITY THROUGH PRIVATE CHOICE

The demand for greater accountability animates much of the contemporary school choice movement. According to its logic, families are essentially trapped in public schools to which their children are assigned, and therefore the schools have no incentive to respond to families' requests or preferences. Conversely, when a family chooses a school, that school is more directly accountable to them. This has been disputed by scholars and advocates who suggest that "choice schools" are not responsive to parents but instead offer a stark "take it or leave it" choice. Others raise concerns about low levels of financial and other forms of accountability among choice (especially charter) schools.[44]

In holding democratic institutions accountable, three aspects are discussed in the literature: accountability through transparency, accountability through participation, and accountability through sanctioning.[45] While we cannot discuss the broader suitability of each of these forms of accountability to the context of the education system as a whole, we would like to briefly address the ways in which choice in schooling affects each type of accountability by schools to the families they serve.

ACCOUNTABILITY THROUGH TRANSPARENCY

Accountability through transparency is based on the demand that decisions and structures be made visible to the people and communities they serve, and that the services provided are rendered in such a way as to allow recipients to understand the practices that lead to the decision. Accountability through transparency emphasizes the importance of accessible and reliable information. In the realm of schooling, this is the most central form of accountability on which reform policies have focused during the standards movement reforms. The approach, of course, has considerable history; for example, in the early twentieth century, concerned educators in some states established school report cards, published all county test scores side-by-side by subject area, and stepped up supervisory visits.[46] More recently, the shorthand version of the accountability process would suggest that standardized tests are used to inform students, parents, and teachers about what was learned; they are used to inform future instruction, programs, and policies that can mend what was not well taught or well learned; and with the proper policies in place, they can allow parents to abandon a school that does not satisfy achievement expectations and to move a student to a better-performing school.[47] Within this conceptual framework of accountability through transparency, the choice movement provides a mechanism for the "consumers" to hold their "service providers" accountable. This process has a few steps. First, standardized tests are introduced so that a shared measure of quality can be established. Next, the results of these tests, aggregated by school (and also disaggregated by given groups) are made available to the public through various media. Third, the public is given an opportunity to choose a school according to the information that is available to them. This opportunity is available in a continuous way, so that if a family is unhappy with their choice or if their circumstances (or the school's performance) change, they can decide to transfer their child to a different school. Choice is thus a process that is founded on accountability and promotes it, with its anchor being the transparent information available to parents as they go through the process of making their decision.

Information about schools is clearly not limited to their test scores, and parents may have a legitimate interest in other aspects of the school's functioning, such as its pedagogical and disciplinary practices, finances, or its processes of governance and decision-making. In public schools, such transparency operates through an elected school board or other related bodies, which are required to operate in transparent ways and to provide the public with access to their records and procedures (the latter relates also to opening paths for participation, as discussed later). Private as well as charter schools are exempt from releasing their financial information, and their governing boards are not always open to the public and therefore tend not to be transparent in their decision-making processes.

Transparency can therefore serve only a limited role in providing school accountability that informs choice; information about testing is not necessarily the most salient information for all parents. Many families care as much or more about other aspects of schools, such as location, safety, student-body makeup, and course and extracurricular offerings. Moreover, there are many hurdles to making information accessible to the constituents who could use it. Parents and others may require the information in different languages; the information may be presented in jargon or technical terms that are hard for nonprofessionals to follow; and so on.[48] Similarly, parents with lower education levels and households that do not include a stay-at-home parent may face further limitations in the amount of time they can devote to sifting through the information and their ability to access it, depending on how it is presented and what one needs to do to acquire the needed information. For some, the cost of information acquisition may be prohibitive.[49]

ACCOUNTABILITY THROUGH PARTICIPATION

Accountability through participation is one of the most widely accepted forms of accountability for institutions and organizations that provide services to democratic citizens. In essence, this is a form of accountability that invites citizens who receive services from a democratic institution to participate in decision-making processes that affect them. Orr and Rogers argue that inclusive engagement is important to public schools because it makes for better decision-making. They write:

> Public engagement for public education is a part of the democratic ideal that all people should have a voice and that a diversity of voices make for better public input and policy outcomes. The premise of democracy is that sufficient understanding can take shape only if everyone is at the table.[50]

Historically, citizens—including parents—who benefited from the services of public schools could hold them accountable through two main forms of participation. They could participate in the daily processes of decision making at the school level by taking part in homeschool associations or parent-teacher associations, or through other structures that invite parents and sometimes other community members to take part in certain domains of the school. In addition, public schools enable parents to participate in the overall management of the district through electing local representatives to the school board, and subsequently participating in community school board meetings or otherwise making their opinions known to their elected representatives.

As one of us (Johanek) has written, "Evident in our history have been persistent efforts to position the school as a civic agent beyond the classroom walls, with schools playing diverse roles as 'public work' civic educators within their wider communities."[51] While participation in school board elections has often been low,[52] the availability of boards both as a symbolic form of participation and as a structured context for processing disagreement as they arise is important for maintaining this form of accountability through participation.

ACCOUNTABILITY THROUGH SANCTIONING

A third form of accountability is maintaining a capacity to sanction. This is an enforcement mechanism that provides oversight as to the fulfillment of norms and expectations from the institution. In cases where these norms are transgressed, the service recipients should have recourse—a way to either demand punishment of the service provider, or to enforce ways to ensure that this kind of transgression is not repeated. In institutions like schools that provide needed services, the main form of sanctioning available to families is what Albert O. Hirschman called simply "exit."[53] For Hirschman, exit, or the move to another provider, is primarily a market mechanism that dissatisfied customers use after (or instead of) trying to persuade the institution to respond to their concerns. School choice in this context is a way for parents to abandon a school whose services they deem insufficient or inadequate for their child, and "take their business"—their child, and the funding the state provides for their education—to another school.

Sanctioning is limited in the current design of choice by the fact that, in many cases, schools are able to choose the students more than students and families are able to choose their school. This reversal of roles is a result of two mechanisms that are baked into the current system of choice. First, given that schools are mostly ordered by level of performance on a limited set of measures (namely, standardized tests), schools in a given area are quite clearly ordered according to their level of desirability to parents—among the schools that are available and accessible to their child, school X is the "best," school Y is the "second best," and so on. Consequently, more students apply to school X than it can accommodate, and the administrators of that school can select who they will admit (some schools select randomly among applicants when they are oversubscribed).

Another mechanism that allows schools to sanction students—rather than vice versa—and thus corrupting this particular form of accountability, is by "counseling out" or pushing out students that are more challenging to educate (usually once their per-student funding has been received). Charter schools and schools accepting vouchers, despite being funded by public tax dollars, are commonly exempt from taking on students with more significant disabilities. In addition, they commonly reject or eject students whose parents are not sufficiently involved, students with challenging behaviors, or students who are regularly absent or who fail classes, to name a few. They do so in an effort to create a productive learning environment; but in the process they refuse to serve some students, thus limiting their accountability to only a part of the community. They also create more challenging learning and teaching conditions in the public schools that are required to admit the students rejected from choice schools.

ACCOUNTABILITY THROUGH RESISTANCE

Another possible way for the public to oversee school accountability measures, along with or instead of the previous ones, takes the form of ensuring

the availability of avenues for resistance to policy decisions taken on the public's behalf.[54] An example of such resistance could be seen in Philadelphia in
2013/14, during the process of replacing public schools with CMO charter
schools. For parents in the Muñoz Marín School, this move was worrisome
because they saw their local public school as a pillar of their community,
even if it did not achieve the kind of performance on standardized tests that
were expected of it. The resistance of the parents consisted directly in maintaining their current single option rather than switching to a "choice school"
model—they preferred their zoned public school that all their children were
required to attend over a "choice" charter school that would be open to their
children along with others. Keeping schools accountable by refusing choices,
by demanding the existing set of limited choices, is sometimes an important
aspect of the democratic process as well.[55]

In this section we have suggested that accountability is understood too
narrowly in contemporary education debates to provide significant democratic legitimacy to arguments about school choice. The limits of the public's
ability to keep choice schools accountable renders them problematic from
a democratic standpoint. We turn now to another democratic demand of
schools, which advocates of school choice offer as a significant contribution
that choice offers—namely, equal access.

Equal Access to Quality Education, or Another Layer of Separation?

CHOICE PROVIDES EQUAL ACCESS TO QUALITY EDUCATION

School choice has always been available to affluent, engaged, or well-informed
families, from residential decisions that provide access to successful public
schools and to a host of private and parochial school options. One of the
strong arguments for broader availability of school choice is that parents who
are poor, minority, immigrant, and otherwise disenfranchised should have
similar access to decisions about their children's education. Most important,
they should benefit from opportunities to attend more successful schools.
Unsatisfactory instruction and lack of access to educational opportunities
affect some children more than others. Most of these children live in urban
areas (some similar issues affect rural communities, but the introduction of
school choice there has been more complicated). Many of them are members
of racial and ethnic minorities. Many live in poverty—a fact that affects the
resources available to them both at home (in the form of nutrition, health care,
and other basic needs that affect learning and well-being) and in their schools

(because of lower levels of local funding). Some advocates support school choice because so many poor, mostly minority students are concentrated in unsafe schools that lack some basic necessities. Advocates on behalf of these children have indicated "how those problems fall more heavily on minority and disadvantaged communities, noting a civil rights argument for access to a quality education through school choice."[56] They sometimes call for policies that would "take back" the system and rearrange it to better serve the children who are most underserved by the current structure.

Advocates for poor and minority students who support school choice as a solution to the ails of urban schools call for the establishment of an equalized opportunity set, one that will both level the playing field and will increase and improve opportunities available to poor students as compared to current dismal conditions in some urban schools. One argument from equality or equal opportunity is that since affluent parents enjoy school choice through residential selection and private school enrollment, all other families should have the benefit of similar options.[57] Like other arguments for school choice, this line of argument too relies on support for parental authority in educational decision-making, as well as a belief in the power of the market to promote well-being.

It is not only advocacy but legislation as well that has come to recognize the argument based on equal access. The No Child Left Behind Act was partially justified as a policy that could help equalize educational opportunity by opening school choice options. In the section on the law devoted to the achievement gap, secretary of education Margaret Spellings stated: "For the first time ever, we are looking ourselves in the mirror and holding ourselves accountable for educating every child. That means all children, no matter their race or income level or zip code."[58]

The opportunity provided to poor and minority families to choose a school for their children through the introduction of vouchers, magnets, or charter schools can offer not only access to more varied and attractive schooling options than were available to them in traditional districts, but also access to schools that are specially designed to attend to specific interests, abilities, and needs. Advocates suggest that these schools can better serve the unique needs of specific communities by targeting them and serving them as a separate group. Thus charter schools are supported by advocates for the poor as creating a way out of inadequate public schools, providing children from underserved communities with educational opportunities they do not have otherwise. This argument is separate from—and sometimes serves as a substitute for—the demand for desegregation. In its place comes a demand for equalizing both the opportunity to choose and the resources for the schools parents choose that their children attend. In other words, while some advocates maintain a demand for regulation that would help desegregate schools especially in terms of the racial makeup of their students, others are embracing choice but calling for regulation that would equalize the opportunities afforded to children and families in their different schools.

Some studies (such as the ones conducted in Charlotte-Mecklenburg, North Carolina, after the repeal of the *Swann* decision[59]) reveal that, after the busing requirement was rescinded by the courts, schools resegregated by race and ethnicity; the resegregation of schools led to decreased opportunities for children from poor and minority families. Once poor and minority students were attending separate schools, their overall levels of achievement dropped. Generally, when school choice is offered to families, schools tend to become more stratified by social class and race.[60] These outcomes are unacceptable for advocates on both sides of the policy discussion. Still, some see the benefit of open choice and market forces as outweighing these problems of implementation, while others believe that separate schools can benefit the children attending them as well as their communities.

For some equality advocates, self-separation is a way to offer cultural content that is not otherwise available to children in minority communities, to develop self-respect and cohesion of their cultural community, and to have access to schools that have desirable qualities—safety, certain content, accessibility—also not otherwise available. The opportunity for parents to express their authority over the education of their children and to provide them with communal, cultural and other beliefs and practices strengthens the case for charters, including self-separated charters that focus on specific communities. Charter schools have the freedom to focus, for instance, on a specific linguistic community and provide not only remedial support in English language acquisition (as is offered in many schools), but also immersion in the language and cultural traditions of students and their families, a curriculum that would respond to their identities and experiences (for example, the experience of migration), and a more responsive environment that considers their particular resources and struggles. Whereas traditional schools are by design focused on a geographic area and serve all children from that area who attend their local public school, charters are able to target their efforts to specific communities and therefore can better serve the specific interests and needs of the members of the community on which they focus.

Charters, if implemented particularly in underserved locations—as they most often are—can provide greater educational opportunities to low-income and minority children. Charter schools have been shown by some studies to improve the motivation as well as the educational outcomes of selected students.[61] Comparative studies show some gains to charter school students over comparable public school students in some testing measures.[62] Longitudinal studies find gains in attainment for charter high schools.[63] However, some claim that the methods used in many of these studies fail to provide a clear or full picture of the impact of charter schools, and especially that they fail to clarify the causality of the impacts.[64] Overall, access to different schools is seen by some advocates as a clear benefit for families who otherwise would have no choice but to attend a low-performing public school; and, in some large urban areas, many families are sending their children to choice schools.

CHOICE CREATES ANOTHER LAYER OF INEQUALITY AND SEPARATION

Through its history, and with growing urgency in recent decades, the school choice debate has focused on improving the quality of education through providing parents with the opportunity to select their children's school. The questions surrounding the quality of schooling—how to define and assess it, how to provide, increase or equalize access to quality schooling—continue to serve as a lightning rod in the discussion of school choice. Many advocates of increased choice argue that through choice parents can pressure all schools to improve their quality so as to attract more and stronger families to select them. Three main critiques against this argument will be considered here in turn—namely, (1) that charters and other choice schools do not in fact provide higher-quality education, (2) that they do not provide equal access to the education they offer, and (3) that even if the former two critiques were to be resolved or dismissed, the price paid in resegregation of schools is too high a price for the possible gains that choice generates.

HIGHER-QUALITY EDUCATION?

A number of studies have attempted to gauge the effect of charters on academic success. In recent years a consensus is emerging that, overall, charters do not provide better educational outcomes than comparable public schools. In 2009, a study of charter school performance in fifteen states and the District of Columbia by the Center for Research on Education Outcomes (CREDO) found that 17% of charter schools outperformed local district schools, 46% performed similarly, and 37% performed worse than local district schools.[65] In 2013 CREDO published a follow-up study with some new important results, including a strong finding that charter schools' relative performance tends to be stable over time, and therefore weak charters remain so even as they mature (contrary to common belief that the mediocre effects of charters are a result of the concentration of new schools in the sample, and that as they age, charters do and will improve).[66] Similarly, an Institute for Educational Science study found that charter schools are no more or less successful than traditional public schools in improving student achievement or progress.[67] Recently, Mathematica analyzed student outcomes in twenty-two select CMOs and found that ten of them exceeded the results of their sending districts, eight had comparable results, and four had worse student outcomes than their districts. Given the significant additional funds available to these schools, their admissions and attrition standards, and the greater amount of instructional time they provide their students, these results have been seen by many as weaker than expected. The CREDO study also showed that replication is a very complex art, and that, as CMOs form, their flagship schools' achievements are rarely replicated as the network expands; the new sites still regularly perform well, but generally students attending a charter school that was part of a CMO network showed mixed results.[68]

Similar results are found when comparing other types of choice schools with traditional, or district-managed, public schools. In a four-year study of district-run schools' performance as compared to schools managed by nonprofits as well as for-profit companies (notably Edison Schools) in Philadelphia, the researchers found that the former outpaced the latter on most measures of achievement; and in any case the externally managed schools did no better than those that remained under district stewardships.[69]

That said, the research suggests that, in general, in terms of the quality of education provided, it matters little if a school is a traditional public school or a charter school. High-, middle-, and low-quality schooling can be found in about equal proportions in both of these forms, and quality is thus not a key outcome of the governance form of a school but rather of its specific practices.

It should be reiterated that the focus in all these analyses is the educational achievement as indicated by scores on standardized tests or related measures of comparative achievement. As noted above, this is not sufficient information for parents, or for researchers, by which to assess the quality of a school.

EQUAL ACCESS TO QUALITY EDUCATION?

Public policies—laws, regulations, funding structure—create the specific options from which parents can make decisions about their children's education. Outside their choice of schooling for their children, affluent parents are spending a growing share of their income on their children's educational activities; that share represents not just multiples of more dollars, but also a larger percentage of much higher disposable income.[70] In the selection of schools, more-affluent parents make a decision based on formal measures (such as test scores) and on personal fit through their residential decisions, choice of a private school, and other available options. The lower a family is located on the income scale, the fewer options it has to invest in out-of-school educational activities, because of limited disposable income and limited availability; and the more limited their choice set becomes in selecting a school, as moving is often not an option, tuition is beyond reach, and other good options are often scarce. Charter schools were meant to counter this reality by providing solid educational options to parents who had few if any alternatives beyond their assigned neighborhood schools, which were sometimes seen as underperforming.

Overall, as we have seen, some of the key choices available to parents today (including charters) do not offer a better-quality education than traditional public schools. But it is possible that the more successful charters are good enough to justify their proliferation, and that their models can be scaled up and expanded, thus providing high-quality education to many children. One of the critics of the charter movement, Diane Ravitch, has challenged the KIPP (Knowledge Is Power Program) network to take over an entire (interested) distressed district and provide education to all the children within it. Her challenge points to the concern that many charter critics raise, namely, that KIPP and other charter networks cherry-pick families and children who are easier to educate from within the communities they serve. While such networks tend to open schools in distressed, poor, and underserved areas, it is clear that there are differences in preparation, inclinations, abilities, and family engagement within these communities (as in any other community). The concern is that, if charter schools identify and "skim" the children within this community who are easier to educate, have greater abilities, are more motivated, or have more supportive families, then all this ultimately achieves is to create an additional layer of inequality. Poor children (many of whom are members of minority communities) have long been schooled separately from more-affluent and middle-class children (many of them white) because of the "Nixon compromise" discussed in the first part of this book, as well as residential separation, student assignment policies, transportation systems, and other official and unofficial policies, and have long been provided with lower-quality educational opportunities. Thanks to the charter movement, the more capable poor children are now separated from the children in their communities who have a harder time in schools because of various factors, and a new layer of unequal access exists.

The problem with this new layer of unequal access is not only the final demise of the common school, which is regrettable in itself; it is also the fact that the children who face greater challenges—the poorer children, children of parents who are too overwhelmed or for other reasons are largely disengaged from their children's schooling, children who are homeless and highly mobile, those who have little access to the English language, poor children with disabilities and those with behavioral issues—all of them are bundled together and left at the local, underfunded public school. Experiences in other countries with long-standing choice policies reinforce this concern; in Chile, for example, after voucher-based schemes were introduced, educational gaps grew significantly.[71] Poor children's ability to benefit from productive peer effects is further reduced by the loss of more successful peers to charter schools, and their ability to enjoy the benefits of a more engaged community of parents is diminished as well. This issue is raised in the context of admissions practices at many charter schools, where access includes hurdles that are not present in traditional districts. Parents need to seek out information and resources, to apply to multiple schools in a sometimes grueling and complex process that can take a full year. They sometimes need to be interviewed and sign engagement contracts; some charters require tests while others require clean behavior sheets. Some charters are allowed to exclude English language learners and students with disabilities, and others seem to unofficially turn them away. The ideal of equal access is rarely realized in the current complicated landscape of school choice.

In addition, attrition is a significant limitation on access to quality education in charters. This is an important consideration, given that the 2013 CREDO study identified KIPP (along with Uncommon Schools) as exemplars of "supernetworks" that, overall, provide underserved groups of students with greater opportunities. The CREDO report says, "It is gratifying to see that the balance of impact for these groups of students [students of color or in poverty] was positive for the most part. . . . These CMO advantages outpace the equivalent gains that their students would have realized in TPS [traditional public schools] and also, for may[many] categories do better than the independent charter schools."[72] Some recent studies raise reasons for concern in this regard. In a 2011 study of the KIPP network,[73] Gary Miron and colleagues find that while KIPP schools enroll more African American students than their sending districts, they enroll fewer Hispanic students (for whom ESL instruction is expensive, making it harder to achieve the desired academic results). KIPP schools also served far fewer students with disabilities (more on this important issue below). Most notable for the current debate, though, is their high level of attrition. Attrition rates for poor children (identified as those eligible for free and reduced-price lunch) are equal between KIPP and sending schools, but overall student attrition is much higher in the KIPP schools. Most strikingly, between grades 6 and 8 (most KIPP schools are middle schools, though they span the K–12 range in some areas), 40% of their male African American students drop out and the cohort shrinks by 30%. Possibly because of zero-tolerance policies and the high demands of time and involvement, and maybe because of other reasons as well, many students cannot or choose not to stay in KIPP schools (and other charter schools); many go back to their sending schools, where the peer group is smaller and weaker on some measures than it was before.

Significantly, students with mild to severe disabilities represent one of the most severely underserved groups of students by charter schools. The title of a 2012 federal report on the topic says it plainly: "Charter Schools: Additional Federal Attention Needed to Help Protect Access to Students with Disabilities."[74] As the report clarifies, charter schools overall serve a smaller percentage of special needs students as compared to traditional public schools (8% and 11%, respectively). In some districts the share is even smaller, possibly as a result of inappropriate admissions practices. Children with special needs are not always welcome as participants in choice programs; various schools are exempt from taking them in or from developing appropriate programs for them as the Individuals with Disabilities Education Act (IDEA) requires; oversubscribed schools, which are often the more successful schools in choice structures, tend to avoid admitting children with identified special needs. As a result, some children with special needs are left outside the choice landscape, thus limiting the implementation of mainstreaming and inclusion programs. This is a general deficiency of choice programs, and in the current context it represents a problem for poor minority students who are identified as having special needs. In Philadelphia, where universal high school choice allows all students to apply for a citywide array of high schools, most children with special needs enroll in neighborhood (or nonselective) schools, and only 4% attend "special admission" or the most selective ones. As a result, selective schools have around 3% of their students identified as eligible for special education services, while some nonselective neighborhood schools have over 25% of their students requiring special services. This could be a result of the fact that the most selective schools are oversubscribed and can choose to admit students who are easier, and cheaper, to educate; it could also be the case that these schools are not required to provide all special education services, and therefore students requiring these services are reluctant to apply.

As is clear from this brief description, charter schools do not provide equal access to children who have special needs. Despite the promising possibilities of either tailoring charter schools to children with certain special needs (a charter for children on the autistic spectrum, for example), or a charter that finds innovative ways to practice inclusion and responsive pedagogy, little has been done in this regard. Moreover, many charters fail to develop adequate services for prospective students with special needs, and therefore effectively do not provide them with access to the education they provide.

The claim that charters provide equal access to quality education is thus substantially challenged on both of its aspects—the quality of education charters provide is not overall higher, as measured by standardized test scores (let alone broader or more substantive measures), and the access to their services is not truly equal. Let us consider a final dimension of this line of argument: that the tendency of charters to be more separated by race and class than their sending districts is justified because of the superior services they offer, or that the choice provided to parents in the education of their children offsets the costs in terms of creating new layers of separation.

NEW LAYERS OF SEPARATION

The introduction of choice into large urban districts—including opening new charters, converting existing schools into charter and other choice schools, and the introduction of vouchers to parents in various cities and states—provides an opportunity for parents to select schools that fit their preferences and the needs of their children. For many families, this means choosing schools that cater to other families "like them" in terms of socioeconomic class, racial and ethnic origin, home language, and similar attributes.

The issue of quality education through choice is thus not only tied to grades on standardized tests. A quality education can also mean one that is more suitable to a particular child or a specific community, one that provides access to cultural, linguistic, and other pedagogic and curricular opportunities less often available in the traditional public school. Equal access can thus be made available through opening more, stronger schools as well as through controlling the makeup of the student body and responding to the interests and needs of the community served. One recalls from the early 1970s the efforts of Mexican American parents in towns like Brownfield, Texas, struggling to establish bilingual/bicultural schools that would celebrate their cultures and not focus on what "was wrong with the Chicano child."[75] This goes back to diversity and self-separation in the populations that specific charters serve. It seems clear that without active regulation of admissions practices—a regulation that faces many challenges in a market environment such as the charter movement presents—schools will often not remain integrated, and that charter schools and other forms of choice exacerbate these tendencies.[76]

As Elizabeth Anderson reminds us, "Segregation of social groups is a principal cause of group inequality."[77] It also seems that some charters which target specific linguistic, ethnic, and other communities are best suited to serve the needs and preferences of a largely homogenous student body (as related to the relevant trait such as home language or ethnic background). The price for this kind of tailored educational environment is paid in the minimization of diversity, and subsequently in the limited opportunities for learning that arise from interaction with people who are different (linguistically, ethnically, etc.). As a result, students may have fewer opportunities to learn to become more respectful and tolerant of difference—a key lesson of democratic citizenship.

To the extent that specific charters can better respond to a given community and provide unique ways of learning that match the preferences and needs of the population served, it may be suggested that the homogenization of the student body—and the subsequent cost in access to diversity and tolerance—is a price that a democratic society should be willing to pay. Thus Robert Pondiscio, a senior fellow at the conservative Thomas B. Fordham Institute, states, "I see nothing wrong with charters functioning as a poor man's private school. I see much that's right about that."[78]

Encounters with diverse groups can take place through curricular and extracurricular opportunities even in a relatively homogenous school. Moreover, many public schools are effectively homogenous as well, as a result of residential separation, and therefore the homogenization of charter schools should not be singled out as a problem that they alone should be required to solve.

However, many charter schools focus on a given community—for example, African American youth in a specific urban center—but do not attempt to provide them with a responsive or relevant form of schooling couched in their historical or cultural context (contrary to an intentional focus on relevant content and values, along with academic excellence, offered by community-based charter and other schools). Rather, many such schools (especially those run by CMOs whose governance structure is all but local) provide effectively segregated schools with a scripted or ready-made curriculum and stringent pedagogy focused on tackling achievement on standardized tests. While these academic opportunities are important, the price paid in loss of diversity is harder to justify. Why is that so? First and foremost, if the focus is on forms of knowledge that are shared across groups rather than specific to the students in the school, as literacy and numeracy required for standardized tests generally are, the key justifiable reason for separating children from different communities disappears. In addition, some studies suggest (though this is still debated in the research community) that the peer-group effect is a predictor of academic success.[79] If the focus of study is academic success by traditional measures, it seems clear from existing research that poor children, who face greater challenges in their academic work because of external pressures and lack of learning opportunities in their home environments, would do better in a mixed-classroom environment through interaction with more advantaged peers as compared to a targeted, homogenous environment. Therefore, even if the goal is solely that of success on traditional academic measures—including gaining proficiency levels on standardized tests and closing achievement gaps—a mixed environment has at least as much promise as a separated one.

Moreover, beyond the separation of racial and ethnic groups that is the result of geographic separation as well as school choice, choice mechanisms often exacerbate these forms of separation by adding to them the separation of different types of members of underserved groups; that is, separating poor families with more capacities such as some extra income, more time or more involvement in schools from those with less. This is the vision quoted above about the "poor man's private school." This vision aims to offer more opportunities to those who will take them, while leaving those who cannot or will not—and their children—with even more limited opportunities.

From a democratic perspective, the loss in interaction, in familiarity with members of other groups, and in opportunities to develop the tolerance and respect that are the hallmarks of a vibrant public sphere, is significant enough that a clear gain in crucial other domains would be required to justify it. Absent such gains, the loss may be too significant for a democratic society to bear—and studies of charter schools do not reveal such gains.

Therefore, some critics are concerned with charter schools' effects as they reshape the education "market," especially in regards to the complicated matter of integration and separation, specifically by race. Market forces seem at least in some cases to work against racial integration. They provide pathways for communities to organize their children in separate educational enclaves, thus often creating limited opportunities for poor and minority children, both in terms of peer effects and in terms of networking and developing social capital. However, not all forms of segregation are alike. In some cases, minority parents and communities choose to self-separate into culturally cohesive, mission-centered, empowering school environments that provide their children with an opportunity for cultural self-expression as well as with a greater opportunity for educational achievement.[80] Such self-separation is especially justified when parents sense that their assigned schools fail to serve their children well. In some integrated public schools, the realistic opportunity to succeed is unevenly distributed across racial lines and therefore self-separation is seen by parents as a possible solution.[81] This could be the case when communities purposefully create schools (like the Harambee Institute in Philadelphia mentioned earlier) that attract and represent mostly children from a minority ethnic, linguistic or racial group. Some Latino/a schools and some Afrocentric schools show a lot of promise in educating self-separated groups of children.

But most forms of effective segregation—segregation that is not legally mandated—including most forms of racial self-separation, are not voluntary in any strong sense of the term. Oftentimes the differing expectations of families, along with residential segregation and the importance of school proximity, create racially segregated schools that were not intended to be so.[82] It seems that "racial segregation patterns [in charter schools] are the result of White flight and Black and Native American students self-segregating into charter schools that are more racially isolated than the district schools they exit."[83] In such instances too, when the racial segregation of schools could be described as a result less of intentional organizing (though catchment areas and recruitment patterns still play into the outcome) and more of an ongoing process of aggregate personal choices along with social and historical conditions, negative consequences have been documented, such as reduction in achievement among poor and minority students in effectively resegregated schools.

However, in certain cases there are possible positive results to the relatively homogenous makeup of the ensuing school community. Again, this was the impetus behind the early grassroots efforts of self-separation. In the 1970s and '80s, the notion of schools that are culturally self-separated took hold in some urban African American communities, which started schools based on characteristics such as heritage, language, histories, and values. They contended that "Afrocentric education is important for building Black students' self-esteem through awareness of African culture and contributions, and to develop their sense of responsibility to a larger community."[84] While oftentimes the mission of the schools as well as their curriculum and pedagogy focus on African themes, they also maintain a strong commitment to student success in traditional senses, aiming to prepare their graduates for college and the job market. Similarly, some schools serving Latino/a students focus on the resources in their community, including the Spanish language, in the process of strengthening the educational offering for this mostly underserved community. Other forms of self-separation as a way of improving opportunities to members of marginalized groups abound both within and beyond the regulatory context of school choice.[85]

Some argue that students in racially self-separated schools develop a greater knowledge of their place in history, a greater sense of belonging, and as a result have improved life choices as compared to children in some racially integrated schools, given class differences and persisting racial prejudice. Michael Merry has argued that the culturally coherent education which self-separated schools can provide (as long as they are established without coercion) may assist minority children in countering the negative stereotypes and discrimination they face in the larger society.[86] In this way they can produce positive outcomes in the form of greater educational attainment and achievement, and greater self-confidence and sense of efficacy as a member of a minority group within the larger society. All these can promote both individuals' and minority groups' positive presence in the public sphere, expressing their views and preferences on a more equal level with other groups. In terms of academic achievement, some Afrocentric schools show good results—studies in Detroit, Chicago, and Cleveland showed that Afrocentric schools did better than district schools on NAEP (National Assessment of Education Progress, or "the nation's report card") and the states' standardized tests.[87] However, the sample size is quite small and may not be generalizable; in addition, students and families may self-select into these schools and thus have more favorable characteristics—specifically, more involved families—than their public school peers. Some researchers have concluded that any form of separation, including self-separation, can have negative effects on children. This claim focuses on the possible benefits of accruing mainstream or middle-class values, norms, and habits, as well as on the possibility of dialogue and understanding across boundaries. Although there are cultural resources available to all communities, isolating minority and poor students can put them at a disadvantage in terms of acquiring socially desirable skills as well as developing the social networks that promote employment and other opportunities.[88]

As we have noted throughout this discussion, many charter schools specifically target minority populations today, though their methods and ultimate goals differ. These students tend to live in poverty, mostly in urban areas, and to attend public schools that face budget challenges and subsequently struggle with educational achievement. Witnessing the largely inadequate educational opportunities for youth in these communities, some charter operators have used the current environment of choice to open schools that target children in urban, poor, and minority communities and aim to provide them with a stronger pathway to educational achievement. Seven out of ten African American charter school students attend schools that have few white students.[89] Like other charters, the KIPP network, which had 183 schools serving almost seventy thousand students in 2015, is dedicated to the success of children from underserved communities. They are different from culturally centered schools in their approach; for example, while Afrocentric schools attempt to replicate and emphasize values and practices of the local community, KIPP and other similar schools focus on skills for academic success as defined by the larger society. They practice pedagogical methods that are meant to replicate and instill common practices of middle-class families, from physical responses to a speaker (making eye contact, nodding) to aspiration and commitment to complete college.[90]

Still, some urban communities' advocates insist that self-separation, even if it originates in involuntary effective segregation, can serve urban youth well if it does not result in differentiated resources allocation. It is clear that there are two separate values here: self-determination and externally defined success (including college admittance, future income, etc.). While the two are by no means incompatible, it is important that school choice policies take them both into account and consider ways to advance them, to the extent that the communities in which the policy is implemented are supportive of both goals.

The separation across race and class lines that is evident in the schooling system overall, and is exacerbated by an expansion of choice, has some positive effects when initiated or addressed intentionally. Its social and political effects are a negative consequence for society overall and for the children who are prevented from benefiting from one another's points of view, experiences, and interests. At the personal level, the opportunity for some students—who would otherwise be neglected in underfunded and underperforming schools—to benefit from a more promising academic environment is significant. But this is often outweighed by the negative effects on the public schools they are no longer attending and the children who remain there. The interests, rights, and needs of all children are not properly addressed in the current landscape of school choice, and neither are the social and public aims of education. To make choice policy achieve its stated goals, a host of changes are required. For instance, admission practices should be monitored for their effects on those who are admitted and those who are not; retention and attrition patterns should be monitored and controlled to make sure that specific populations are not shortchanged; and other impacts—including patterns of ethnic and racial separation and impact on vulnerable populations, as well as financial burdens on sending districts—must be considered. In the following section, we turn to the need to consider public and private benefits in the ways in which school choice is designed.

CONCLUSION
Making Up Our Collective Mind

Where does all this leave us, these philosophical forays and historical jaunts? What does it all tell us about the current school choice debate?

To start, it flips the current debate on its head. School choice is not about introducing market forces or parental choice into schooling. We have had market-driven schooling throughout our history, and parental demands figure dominantly across three centuries.

Those choices, however, continue to be shaped by how we collectively choose to balance public and private interests for this unique positional good. As we noted in the introduction, how we design school choice options—including for whom—reveals how we have made up our minds regarding these questions:

1. Whose education is it? In what ways should parents, students, and/or the state decide? How should decisions be made about how and where to educate children?
2. How much innovation do we wish, and how much accountability? By what measures? How will we hold compulsory schooling accountable for both our public as well as private educational goals?
3. What role do we seek for our schools in building a more inclusive, equitable, and integrated plural society? How will our design of school choice advance or retard our collective progress?

Underlying these core questions is a quest to understand society's vision about the education of its next generation. How fair do we want our schooling to be? How democratically accountable? How responsive to private goals? How innovative and unique, and how common in the preparation of our citizenry? The design of our education system, including choices built into it, reflects our accumulated answers to these questions over time; examining our current schooling, do they correspond to the values we espouse today? That is the school choice debate we need to have now.

Many American parents have long had the opportunity to select a school for their children, and even to determine whether their children attend school. In that sense, choice dates back to the colonial era. Since that time, each era answers distinctly who has which choices, how, and where; that response reflects each era's resolution of the underlying questions of public and private ends. In the past decade or so, "choice" has begun to occupy a heightened role in reform efforts, and to draw growing amounts of attention, resources, and criticism. Reformers see school choice as the kind of structural change that can serve as a lever to pull ahead the entire system—in all fifty states, and fourteen thousand districts—out of perceived mediocrity and failure. It is an alluring vision to many, one that gives more power to individual parents at the same time that it maintains institutional control at the highest levels of government. Reformers see charters as a means to circumvent red tape, political obstacles, and labor resistance, especially in urban districts.

Today's debates and practices around school choice, as in the early republic or late nineteenth century, offer an intriguing glance into our present moment as a nation. Consider how we speak of the current era. Contemporary observers often characterize the era as one of expansion in school choice, of increased options in an expanding education market—an era that is arising, per the dominant story, in the wake of disillusionment with the consolidated, government-operated "one best system."[1] Yet during this present era of purportedly increased parental choices, those choices are constrained by more years of required schooling than even half a century ago. An increasingly common, required, and tested "academic" curriculum crowds out other curricular options. While certainly more districts today allow parents to select schools beyond those to which they might otherwise be assigned, this occurs within a system of expanded obligations in fewer institutions in fewer districts, and in a more thoroughly prescribed academic curriculum.[2] In other words, most parents today (outside the most affluent ones who can pay for private and less-regulated schooling) face more options that are relatively more similar to each other, and the information available to those parents about options is mostly related to each school's position on one scale of achievement: standardized test scores. Relatively little variety is available as to pedagogical style, curricular concentration, or teacher preparation. Further, the distribution of options is uneven; the policy structures surrounding school choice make the opportunities available to different families deeply unequal, often contributing to the opportunity gap in education. Families are not equally inclined to choose, nor are they equally able to formulate and pursue their schooling preferences.[3] As a result, more "choices"—especially when those are of varying quality—does not mean greater equality.

We are not alone in wrestling with these trade-offs. The US discussion correlates and contributes to a wider international context of varied approaches to parental choices in schooling. In some regions this conflates with debates on the role of private markets, and in some areas, choice operates within public systems. The relation of schooling to other family-serving institutions also varies considerably. Some of the global school choice notions are fueled by US ideas, and some are directly influenced by US companies and philanthropies that export their visions, structures, and models to other countries.[4] Yet each national context also testifies to the role of local actors and histories, distinctive familial/societal trade-offs, and culturally embedded social norms. In Chile, for example, where voucher-supported schools represent the largest sector—relative to either private or city-run schools—the role of market-based reforms occupies center stage in a deeply contested political context, with nervous edges dating back to the Pinochet dictatorship. Questions of parental school choices imply answers about national destiny, of equitable solidarity, and of preserving Chilean character and its expanded national economy. "For you, Milton Friedman wrote an interesting chapter," argues Cristian Cox, then dean of the education faculty at Catholic University of Chile. "For us, we had a general who imposed it [voucher-based reforms] as a grand experiment, and we're finally revisiting it!"[5] In Finland, parents can choose freely their children's schools, including any of the seventy-five independent schools around the country. Yet no private options exist; all are publicly funded schools, and the difference in quality among schools remains the smallest in the world.[6] All families can access health care and social services, schools receive equitable funding, colleges remain free, and only top students make it into teacher preparation programs. Further, parents can choose from among heavily subsidized clubs outside of schools for sports, music and art. This emphasis on equitable choices, argues Finnish scholar Pasi Sahlberg, grew out of a devastated economy half a century ago, a fractured history between Swedish and Russian dominance, and a pragmatic desire to survive by tapping all the talents a small population represented.[7] Each nation's choice design reflects larger national conversations and context; in each nation, parents embark on the process of selecting a school for their children within a unique economic, cultural and historical context.

Hence a key outcome of this historical and philosophical investigation is that public policy debates should begin from an understanding of the *shifting profile of choices* available to different families at a given time. These profiles reveal the more fundamental debate. Much of the debate today focuses osten-sibly on the rift between "neoliberals" or supporters of charters and other new forms of schooling who support the expansion of choice, and "progressives" or supporters of public education and would thus rather assign children to schools and provide more limited choice. Yet the portrayal of a clear ideo-logical or principled opposition between supporters and opponents of school choice is not supported by the historical and normative accounts of school choice in the United States. Presenting a clear opposition between zealous neoliberal, pro-business reformers on the one hand, and pro-union, anti-choice progressives on the other, does not fully capture the public views on the topic; nor does it properly portray the policy options available. Given the history of plural options and various forms of regulation since the dawn of the republic, the question that citizens and policy makers should ask themselves is not whether choice should be made (more) available, but rather what kind of balance we should strike between choice and regulation, relative to the balance of public and private aims we seek. In highlighting individual agency, "choice" obscures our need to make collective choices about the goals of education. A more informed debate would focus on the options available to families, distribution of these options across class and race, the opportunities children have to pursue a productive path, and how these options advance collective public ends.

Do charters, vouchers, and other contemporary forms of choice represent an expansion of choice for parents, or a reconfiguration that affords choice to some parents and not others? In other words, are we getting more choice now or not? And does it matter (normatively speaking)? If charters now open in communities once served by parish schools that they have replaced, does school choice expand? How much expansion includes diversification within and beyond institutional choices for some, and only a shift in institu-tional choices for others? To the extent that choice in recent years has been expanding, its growth is focused on the increased number of privately owned companies who participate in the education "market," and the increasing choice in education rather than specifically in schooling. Alternatives to traditional public schools are more accepted; but at the same time, some of their practices are more regulated because of the drifting of decision-making powers to the mayors, governors, and the federal government[8] and the effort to standardize and regulate schools. Choice within this context of school-ing has become narrowed by the extension of compulsory attendance laws, the introduction of required curricula (including the recent advent of the controversial Common Core State Standards), and requisite testing. As with other forms of choice in schooling, this limitation of freedom even within the context of a given school is unevenly distributed. Poor and minority children experience a more rigid learning environment while their affluent peers enjoy options such as elective courses, IB (International Baccalaureate), AP (Advanced Placement), college credit programs, and other forms of flexible and tailored learning within their assigned schools.

We have also bounded our discussion of school choice by limiting it to parental choice of schools, just as our education policies tend to converge with school policies. Yet parental choices in education have never been limited to choices of schools; today's vastly different educational landscape remains the unspoken elephant in the policy room. We live within an educational revolution in terms of new educating organizations, ubiquitous and increasingly sophisticated tools, and exceedingly more interconnected learners. Youth travel, starting in middle school, has become a global industry of $185 billion, representing 20% of all tourism; an industry leader predicted this will roughly double by 2020.[9] New educational apps surface daily; learning logarithms advance; students access the library of the world from their phones. The choices this learning revolution offers, however, skews along some painfully familiar lines. Wealthier families spend considerably more on supplemental educational activities—"books, computers, high-quality child care, summer camps, private schooling, and other enrichments"—and the gaps have been growing.[10] Those in the top two income quintiles spend three times as much in percentage terms as the lowest quintile, with large absolute differences resulting. By the mid-2000s, the absolute dollar gap had tripled from three decades prior; top quintile households spent seven times the dollar amount on "family enrichment activities" as those in the lowest quintile. As one result, children in wealthy families, in addition to four hundred more hours of literacy activities, also will experience "novel contexts"—activities "other than at home, school, or in the care of another parent or a day-care provider"—for 1,300 more hours prior to entering school than their peers of modest means.[11] In assessing school choice today, we are reminded of historian Lawrence Cremin's critique of the free/alternative school movement in the early 1970s; for all its supposed novelty, it remained as persistently "school-bound as the progressive education of an earlier time," not addressing the emerging roles of new media and markets.[12] "What if free schools (and all other schools for that matter) were to take seriously the radically new situation in which all education inescapably proceeds?"[13]

Yet the historical and normative discussion throughout this book has focused on choice in schooling, considered through the lens of families selecting a school and to a lesser extent groups and organizations offering choices to families. We did not address in detail many factors that are tied to choice or result from it—the civic action required to change choice policies, the interaction between choice and external parameters such as home values, and more. Along the way, we aimed to be attuned both to the overall set of institutional options available at a given time, and the often more limited options realistically available to some of families or students. From this analysis we hope it became clear that, in order to make choice policy achieve its stated goals of improvement, equity, and greater freedom, opponents of choice need to recognize its long history in the United States and parents' long-active role in shaping the educational options of their children. Proponents of choice need to recognize the problematic nature of some of its more recent directions, and be open to specific forms of regulation that are as much a part of the history of this nation as they are a normative requirement. Inasmuch as school buildings are monitored for safety, staff can and should be properly trained and qualified, and shared decisions should be made about admission and retention of students. Choice schools must recognize, for example, that if they "skim" the top students from a catchment area or dismiss problematic, low-achieving, or disabled students, the overall effect may be negative—especially for children who return to their public school, often midyear and with additional challenges as a result of the process.

Understanding the history of school choice and the philosophical considerations that inform these policies also demands recognition of the complex role that school choice continuously plays in the racial, religious, ethnic, and otherwise identity-based politics of the United States—in the past and today—in addition to its role as a marker of ideological commitments to civic-oriented, market-oriented, and other visions of democracy. The racial context has been particularly instructive in our discussion. Racial desegregation in the past has been a driver of school choice, as the discussion of magnets has shown; but choice also serves as a force that can limit and subvert racial equality, friendship, and mutual recognition, as the unfortunate history of charters and other choices in the South after *Brown* indicates. Certain choice policies allow parents and communities to move away from one another and avoid the kind of structured, prolonged, and constructive contact that integrated schools can enable. Acknowledging the historical and contemporary social contexts in which school choice (and related policies) operates is a necessary step in framing education as the type of good that it is, namely, both public and private.

As we noted up front and illustrated throughout, education is a unique kind of good in that it serves public and private purposes. Personal goals about success, the preservation of values, and the introduction of opportunities intersect and sometimes compete with public goals like equality, good citizenship, and mutual understanding. The free market is one mechanism to promote some of these goals; the centralized provision and regulation of schools by the government is another.

It seems clear to us that parents must have a say in the schooling of their children. It also seems clear from both the historical and the normative analyses that were offered here that parents cannot accomplish this task well on their own. There are multiple reasons for this: many individuals are limited in their capacity to access and use information effectively, because of a combination of personal skills (time, education, language) and barriers that make information acquisition prohibitively expensive (geographical distance, weak information networks, social barriers). In addition, children's interests are not always represented by their parents' choices in their complexity. While parents may choose strict religious education, children may have an interest in a broader world view; while parents may be biased against educating girls, both the girls and society at large may have a strong interest, as well as a right, in allowing them to pursue their education. Moreover, parents cannot be expected to make decisions about their children's education with a publicly minded perspective as their guiding value. In order to ensure that the public perspective is represented, the landscape of choices must be subjected to public oversight.

One of the reasons that such oversight is needed today more urgently than ever is the greater involvement of business and private interests in the development of choices available to parents. In a sense, private and business interests are opening as well as limiting the choices available to parents and to communities. Along with philanthropic investments, often driven at least in part by business interests, public policy is shaped outside the public's reach.[14]

Our present era features a particularly strong ideological commitment to idealized market mechanisms, across policy areas. Reflective of this dominant market ideology, school choice discussions fail to address a collective civic function persistent in the history of US schooling—one beyond the aggregation of individual needs or aspirations, beyond the shared benefits to society of well-developed individuals. Public schools have also served as a place for shared community work, shared learning, and shared problem-setting and resolution. This "public work" function of the community's citizen-owned educational utility has taken shape in a variety of ways across US history.[15] Schools have long served as forums for public issue debates, adult learning, citizenship development, community social life, and occasionally, research into local community challenges. The recent resurgence of "community schooling" reflects this long-standing collective impulse for the public's schools to serve civic functions beyond individual student preparation.[16]

Framing school reform entirely as a matter of parental choice obfuscates this persistent impulse for a public utility capable of assisting community resolution of common challenges. Schools occupy a unique space between families and the public square; they have often served as an institutional bridge between private and public interests. The private interests of parents in the education of their children draw them to participate in broader common discussions about shared needs and interests in the community. The current temper of discussion in our political institutions, however, would recommend a prolonged reinvigoration of public schools' capacity to shape a nonpartisan civic space—one that models our collective educational needs for public problem-solving. This requires a broader view of the rich historical and philosophical ambitions embedded in an institution that has long aspired to be much more than a service agency to individual clients.

In light of this argument, the increased role of the private sector in schooling gives us reason for pause. The private, corporate sector, including domestic and international funders, plays an unprecedented role in the management and funding of education, its related derivative support enterprises, and in the formation of public policy. Indeed, perhaps the most striking feature of the current charter sector has been the creation of a parallel private professional infrastructure the scope and scale of which US schooling has never known. The charter sector continues to develop an especially robust and well-resourced set of institutions to address new charters, along with related venture funding, operational supports, leadership development, teacher recruitment, policy advocacy, political lobbying, professional development, conferences, and communications strategies. Corporate direction—whether in the form of management organizations like CMOs and EMOs, or in organizational discipline or data analysis approaches—reaches into daily operations in ways unseen previously. The assertively anti-union approach alienated many, including Al Shanker, who parted ways early with what he saw as a takeover of the charter idea by "the education industry."[17] Over the last two decades, an ecosystem of institutions has consciously organized itself within that "industry"—with dominant players including the Gates, Broad, Walton, Dell, and Bloomberg Foundations; Teach for America; American Enterprise Institute; Democrats for Education Reform (DFER); Education Pioneers, and others—and with a degree of integration with government agencies and influence on policy that alternative or private systems never attained. The close linkage of and influence by the educational technology sector, and the explicit market-making intent of federal policy encouraging common national academic standards, for example, are new developments for US public schools. The expanding international reach of private reform organizations challenges the relative strength of local political entities globally; Teach for All, a twenty-three-million-dollar global organization growing out of Teach for America, now coordinates forty-six national partner organizations across six continents.[18]

Ironically, perhaps, our recent policy preference toward private, "market-based," and "for-profit" players may help explain some of the concurrent frustration with the disappointing levels of innovative school choice options. Any organization making an investment in a school model or tool seeks to amortize that investment across customers. Scale matters; indeed, scaling is critical to providing a sufficiently credible return on investment. To be market-driven means looking always for more market, and so specialized needs don't stack up very well. We should not presume that for-profit players will develop highly creative or even evidence-based pedagogical approaches if they do not see a market for those among parents, who are often quite hesitant to move beyond their own schooling experiences. Clean and orderly sells, which may be a critical advance in a specific market, but should not be confused with educationally rich approaches. If we choose to encourage more for-profit players, or even return-minded social impact philanthropists, we should not confuse their potential contributions (such as efficiency or innovation) with the development of pedagogical visions well beyond where the parental market is— or, more significant, with the need to develop public policy through a broader lens and with broader commitments and goals. Federal policy, such as in Race to the Top, has explicitly sought to expand the market available to investors so that they could scale. That many choose to operate in low-cost, pedagogically conservative ways is not an accident, but rather a built-in feature of such an approach. An EMO tries to cover overhead, software development, branding, training, and so on by scaling the student body and/or by diversifying services (e.g., providing consulting into districts), which many have increasingly developed in part to cover the risk of schools as a product line. As noted earlier, this was why more common national academic standards were so central to policy logic—a larger market had to be built. However, simply creating a market does not necessarily spur innovation, as some might claim. Still, some localities do innovate, developing their own educationally rich preferences that encourage local children thrive. The US tradition of strong local control enables this sort of tailoring to parents in a specific community. But responding to local context will likely frustrate any effort to scale.

Additionally, education markets seem to shift perilously closer to the entrepreneurial, unregulated state that recently was rethought and restrained in other, more mature markets such as the financial sector. It is clear that the influx of private-sector resources—including public attention and interest, leadership capacity, and material resources—into the education field has provided some significant support to chronically underfunded neighborhood schools (turned charters). However, it is also clear that the risks and benefits need to be distributed thoughtfully, and that systemic stability is a strong interest of the education system (which is not always supported by the relatively fickle business and private sector, where individual investors or benefactors can turn their attention to new projects at any time). The distribution of risks in this context means that there should be clear and regulated expectations regarding the risks to students and schools that are drained of resources as a result of the introduction of choice, through the skimming of easier-to-educate students (leaving students with special needs, English language learners, and other costlier students in neighborhood schools that lose much of their resources when their attendance declines).[19] Some safeguards including public accountability and financial liability should be used to help prevent the prospect of charter and other choice schools closing their gates on a moment's notice because of a business decision, leaving families scrambling for seats in other schools midyear, disrupting routines, and burdening already stretched public schools that must take all students in. The costs of reintegrating these students should not be personal and public alone; there should also be liability and accountability by the corporations that fail to offer the education they promise. It is now being recognized more broadly that markets with such lucrative private potential should not as a matter of course be "insured" by public bailout money if they fail, but rather prepare to ensure structural stability and funded backup options. Similarly, business opportunities in the large and currently open education market should not be thought of solely as philanthropic endeavors or alternatively as forays into uncharted territory. Rather, the risks and rewards should be considered more carefully as tied to the various actors and stakeholders in this shifting market.[20]

A perennially "uprooted" people, we in the United States continually reconstruct our republic, in part, through compulsory schooling. What sort of republic do we wish, and what burden do we wish for our schools? Will they build collective identity? Will they enhance our individual freedoms? Will they help us become more just, more equitable, more richly human? The architecture of school choice—supporting both public and private ends—sets the core beams of our democracy's schoolhouse. We live most publicly there. Inside, we make the minds of our future citizenry, framed decisively by how we make up our minds about our collective ends.

Notes

Please note: the epigraphs throughout part 1 are from the following sources:

Opening: Carl F. Kaestle, "Clio at the Table: Historical Perspectives and Policymaking in the Field of Education," in *Clio at the Table: Using History to Inform and Improve Education Policy*, ed. Kenneth K. Wong and Robert Rothman, History of Schools and Schooling (New York: Peter Lang, 2009), 293.

"Original Choices": Constitution Society, "Massachusetts Bay School Law (1642)," accessed July 21, 2014, http://www.constitution.org/primarysources/schoollaw1642.html. "It being one chief project of that old deluder, Satan, to keep men from the knowledge of the Scriptures . . . and to the end that learning may not be buried in the grave of our forefathers, in church and commonwealth. . . . It is therefore ordered that every township . . . appoint one within their town to teach all such children as shall resort to him to write and read." Constitution Society, "The Old Deluder Act (1647)," accessed July 21, 2014, http://www.constitution.org/primarysources/deluder .html.

"An Educational Ecology Emerges": quoted in Theodore R. Sizer, *The Age of the Academies*, Classics in Education (New York: Bureau of Publications, Teachers College, Columbia University, 1964), 127.

"Rebels with Causes": Eric Hodgins, *Mr. Blandings Builds His Dream House* (New York: Simon & Schuster, 1946), quoted in Kenneth T. Jackson, *Crabgrass Frontier: The Suburbanization of the United States* (New York: Oxford University Press, 1985), loc. 4567–71 of 9107, Kindle.

Introduction

1. See, for example, Duncan Green, "Education Wonkworld: The Final Salvo: Kevin Watkins Responds to Justin Sandefur on Public v Private," People, Spaces, Deliberation (blog), World Bank, August 13, 2012, http://blogs.worldbank.org/publicsphere/node/6068.

2. Paul C. Bishop, Arun Barman, Danielle Hale, Jessica Lautz, and Selma Lewis, "Profile of Home Buyers and Sellers" (Chicago: National Association of Realtors, 2009), 27; exhibit 2-10, 32, exhibit 2-11, 33; National Association of Realtors (NAR), "Survey: Most Parents Make Home-Buying Decisions around Their Kids," *Realtor Magazine*, May 22, 2014, http://realtormag.realtor .org/daily-news/2014/05/22/survey-most-parents-make-home-buying-decisions-around-their

-kids. While NAR figures are from 2009, 2018 figures seem consistent (25% versus 26% reporting quality of school as affecting purchase, higher among younger cohorts of buyers, with 40% of those 37 and younger citing school quality as factor in choice of neighborhood); *Home Buyer and Seller Generational Trends Report, 2018*, National Association of REALTORS Research Department, exhibit 2-7, https://www.nar.realtor/sites/default/files/documents/2018-home-buyers-and-sellers-generational-trends-03-14-2018.pdf, accessed July 11, 2018; roughly consistent is NCES data from 2012 reporting that nearly 20% of public school parents indicate they moved to their neighborhood for the school; it is worth noting some incongruence in terminology and data, in that most parents report "assigned" schooling as their first "choice," suggesting that further clarity on the evidence regarding choice is desirable; "nearly 20%" is 18.6%, from "Fast Facts—Public School Choice Programs," accessed July 11, 2018, https://nces.ed.gov/fastfacts/display.asp?id=6.

3. For the 27% figure, see S. Grady and S. Bielick, *Trends in the Use of School Choice: 1993 to 2007* (NCES 2010-004), National Center for Education Statistics, Institute of Education Sciences (Washington, DC: US Department of Education, 2010), v, https://nces.ed.gov/pubs2010/2010004 .pdf. The "more than thirteen million" figure was arrived at by taking 27% of total public school enrollment for 2014 from US Department of Education, National Center for Education Statistics, "Table 216.20: Number and Enrollment of Public Elementary and Secondary Schools, by School Level, Type, and Charter and Magnet Status: Selected Years, 1990–91 through 2013–14," Digest of Education Statistics 2015, September 2015, https://nces.ed.gov/programs/digest/d15/tables/dt15 _216.20.asp.

4. Education Commission of the States, "Open Enrollment 50-State Report: All Data Points," accessed February 1, 2018, http://ecs.force.com/mbdata/mbquest4e?rep=OE1705; Micah Ann Wixom, "Table 4.2: Numbers and Types of Open Enrollment Policies, by State: 2016," *Open Enrollment: Overview and 2016 Legislative Update*, Education Commission of the States, http:// www.ecs.org/ec-content/uploads/Open-Enrollment-Overview-and-2016-legislative-update.pdf.

5. "Table 13: Number of Public School Districts with More Than One School, and among Those Districts, Percentage That Offer Various School Choice Programs to Students within or outside the District, by State: 2001–12," Schools and Staffing Survey (SASS), National Center for Education Statistics, US Department of Education, http://nces.ed.gov/surveys/sass/tables /sass1112_2013311_d1s_013.asp. The Minnesota legislature established the first open enrollment policies in 1988, prior to its groundbreaking charter legislation, with expansion across the states during the 1990s.

6. No direct enrollment figures are available for students choosing schools under open enrollment policies.

7. In prepared remarks during the nomination hearings of Betsy DeVos, US Senator Lamar Alexander noted that "about 15 percent [of US students] attend a school other than their school of residence through open-enrollment programs." US Senate Committee on Health, Education, Labor and Pensions, "Alexander: Betsy DeVos Is on Our Children's Side," news release, January 17, 2017, http://www.help.senate.gov/chair/newsroom/press/alexander-betsy-devos-is-on-our -childrens-side.

8. Thomas D. Snyder, ed., *120 Years of American Education: A Statistical Portrait* (Washington, DC: National Center for Education Statistics, Office of Educational Research and Improvement, US Department of Education, 1993); and US Department of Education, National Center for Education Statistics, "Table 205.10—Private Elementary and Secondary School Enrollment and Private Enrollment as a Percentage of Total Enrollment in Public and Private Schools, by Region and Grade Level: Selected Years, Fall 1995 through Fall 2015, 2016," Digest of Education Statistics 2016, June 2017, https://nces.ed.gov/programs/digest/d16/tables/dt16_205.10.asp.

9. US Department of Education, National Center for Education Statistics, "Table 216.20."

10. Even the definition of charters is somewhat controversial. Here is the NCES definition: "A *public charter school* is a publicly funded school that is typically governed by a group or organization under a legislative contract (or charter) with the state, district, or other entity. The charter exempts the school from certain state or local rules and regulations. In return for flexibility and autonomy, the charter school must meet the accountability standards outlined in its charter. A school's charter is reviewed periodically by the entity that granted it and can be revoked if guidelines on curriculum and management are not followed or if the accountability standards are not met." National Center for Education Statistics, "Fast Facts: Charter Schools," accessed August 2, 2018, http://nces.ed.gov/fastfacts/display.asp?id=30.

11. US Department of Education, "School Choices for Parents," last modified January 14, 2009, http://www2.ed.gov/parents/schools/choice/definitions.html.

12. US Department of Education, National Center for Education Statistics, "Table 216.20." More recent magnet numbers appear proportionally consistent, if even higher relative to charters, representing enrollment at 2.52 million versus 2.19 million in charters. Morgan Polikoff and Tenice Hardaway, "Don't Forget Magnet Schools When Thinking about School Choice," *Evidence Speaks*, Brookings Institution, March 16, 2017, https://www.brookings.edu/research/dont-forget -magnet-schools-when-thinking-about-school-choice/.

13. J. Redford, D. Battle, and S. Bielick, *Homeschooling in the United States: 2012* (NCES 2016-096.REV) (Washington, DC: National Center for Education Statistics, Institute of Education Sciences, US Department of Education, April 2017), https://nces.ed.gov/pubs2016/2016096rev .pdf. Note that data collection methods shifted from telephone to paper and pencil for the 2012 data, causing some concerns regarding comparability with prior years; the NCES margin of error means that "the range of the estimate is from 1,543,000 to 2,003,000; alternatively, a national research association for the sector (NHERI) claims over 4% of US children in homeschooling, and puts the total figure at 2.3 million; Brian D. Ray, "Research Facts on Homeschooling: Homeschool Fast Facts," National Home Education Research Institute (NHERI), January 13, 2018, http:// www.nheri.org/research/research-facts-on-homeschooling.html.

14. Josh Cunningham, "School Vouchers," National Conference of State Legislatures, accessed July 12, 2018, http://www.ncsl.org/research/education/school-choice-vouchers.aspx; EdChoice, "Resource Hub – Fast Facts," accessed July 12, 2018, https://www.edchoice.org/resource-hub /fast-facts/#voucher-fast-facts; and Alexandra Usher and Nancy Kober, *Keeping Informed about School Vouchers: A Review of Major Developments and Research* (Washington, DC: Center on Education Policy, George Washington University, 2011).

15. EdChoice, "Resource Hub—Fast Facts," accessed 12 July 2018, https://www.edchoice.org /resource-hub/fast-facts/#taxcredit-scholarship-fast-facts; National Conference of State Legislatures, "Scholarship Tax Credits," accessed 12 July 2018, http://www.ncsl.org/research/education /school-choice-scholarship-tax-credits.aspx; Josh Cunningham, "Interactive Guide to School Choice Laws," June 15, 2017, National Conference of State Legislatures, http://www.ncsl.org /research/education/interactive-guide-to-school-choice.aspx#/.

16. EdChoice, "Resource Hub"; Josh Cunningham, "The Next Generation of School Vouchers: Education Savings Accounts," National Conference of State Legislatures, August 18, 2016, http://www.ncsl.org/research/education/the-next-generation-of-school-vouchers-education -savings-accounts.aspx; and Jimenez-Castellanos, W. J. Mathis, and K. G. Welner, *The State of Education Savings Account Programs in the United States* (Boulder, CO: National Education Policy Center, 2018), http://nepc.colorado.edu/publication/ESAs; Nevada's ESA program is not operating, pending litigation.

17. Elisabeth Leamy, "You Can Now Use a 529 to Pay for K–12 Tuition—So Should You?", On Parenting, *Washington Post*, February 28, 2018, https://www.washingtonpost.com/lifestyle /on-parenting/you-can-now-use-a-529-to-pay-for-k-12-tuition--so-should-you/2018/02/27 /885fb5a4-1aff-11e8-9de1-147dd2df3829_story.html?utm_term=.4b53d65690ca.

18. Nat Malkus, Richard V. Reeves, and Nathan Joo, *The Costs, Opportunities, and Limitations of the Expansion of 529 Education Savings Accounts*, Evidence Speaks Reports, vol. 2, no. 47, April 12, 2018 (Washington, DC: Brookings Institution), 1.; Figure 1 (below) sums estimates of vouchers, ESAs, and tax credit scholarships, but not all tax deductions/credits claimed for education.

19. Center for Public Education, "Charter Schools: Finding Out the Facts," March 2010, http://www.centerforpubliceducation.org/Main-Menu/Organizing-a-school/Charter-schools -Finding-out-the-facts-At-a-glance. Charter schools remain primarily an urban strategy; see, for example, Sara Mead, Ashley LiBetti Mitchel, and Andrew J. Rotherham, "The State of the Charter School Movement" (Washington, DC: Bellwether Education Partners, 2015); and National Charter School Resource Center: R. Lake, B. Dusseault, M. Bowen, A. Demeritt, and P. Hill, *The National Study of Charter Management Organization (CMO) Effectiveness: Report on Interim Findings* (Mathematica Policy Research and Center on Reinventing Public Education, 2010).

20. US Department of Education, National Center for Education Statistics, Digest of Education Statistics 2015 (NCES 2016-014), chap. 2; and US Department of Education, National Center for Education Statistics, "Fast Facts: Public School Choice Programs," accessed July 23, 2018, https://nces.ed.gov/fastfacts/display.asp?id=6.

21. US Senate Committee, "Alexander: DeVos Is on Our Children's Side."

22. "Table 105.30. Enrollment in Elementary, Secondary, and Degree-Granting Postsecondary Institutions, by Level and Control of Institution: Selected Years, 1869–70 through Fall 2026," US Department of Education, National Center for Education Statistics, Annual Report of the Commissioner of Education, 1870 to 1910; Biennial Survey of Education in the United States, 1919–20 through 1949–50; Statistics of Public Elementary and Secondary School Systems, 1959 through 1979; Statistics of Nonpublic Elementary and Secondary Schools, 1959 through 1980; 1985–86 Private School Survey; Common Core of Data (CCD), "State Nonfiscal Survey of Public Elementary and Secondary Education," 1985–86 through 2014–15; Private School Universe Survey (PSS), 1991–92 through 2013–14; National Elementary and Secondary Enrollment Projection Model, 1972 through 2026; Opening (Fall) Enrollment in Higher Education, 1959; Higher Education General Information Survey (HEGIS), "Fall Enrollment in Institutions of Higher Education" surveys, 1969, 1979, and 1985; Integrated Postsecondary Education Data System (IPEDS), "Fall Enrollment Survey" (IPEDS-EF:90-99); IPEDS Spring 2001 through Spring 2016, Fall Enrollment component; and Enrollment in Degree-Granting Institutions Projection Model, 2000 through 2026 (table prepared February 2017); Table 216.20. Number and enrollment of public elementary and secondary schools, by school level, type, and charter and magnet status: Selected years, 1990–91 through 2014–15. US Department of Education, National Center for Education Statistics, Common Core of Data (CCD), "Public Elementary/Secondary School Universe Survey," 1990–91 through 2014–15 (table prepared October 2016); Redford, Battle, and Bielick, *Homeschooling in the United States*; Ray, "Research Facts on Homeschooling"; http://dashboard.publiccharters.org /dashboard/schools/page/overview/year/2013; NHERI estimates 2.3 million homeschooled students, considerably above the earlier NCES estimates; undercounting in official statistics seems very likely; see Ray, "Research Facts on Homeschooling."

23. New NY Education Reform Commission, *Putting Students First: Final Action Plan* (Albany, NY, 2014), 17. The top districts in terms of charter school enrollment, in order, include New Orleans, Detroit, Washington DC, Flint (MI), Cleveland, Gary (IN), Kansas City (state not

specified, but we presume MO, since it has twenty years of history with charters), Hall County (GA), Victor Valley (CA), and Philadelphia. "Big, Not Easy," *Economist*, December 13, 2014.

24. US Department of Education, National Center for Education Statistics, "Table 216.30: Number and Percentage Distribution of Public Elementary and Secondary Students and Schools, by Traditional or Charter School Status and Selected Characteristics: Selected Years, 1999–2000 through 2014–15," Digest of Education Statistics 2016, October 2016, https://nces.ed.gov /programs/digest/d16/tables/dt16_216.30.asp.

25. S. Grady and S. Bielick, *Trends in the Use of School Choice: 1993 to 2007* (Washington, DC: National Center for Education Statistics, Institute of Education Sciences, US Department of Education, 2010), 19, table 4, and 22, table 6.

26. Carl F. Kaestle, "Clio at the Table: Historical Perspectives and Policymaking in the Field of Education," in *Clio at the Table: Using History to Inform and Improve Education Policy*, ed. Kenneth K. Wong and Robert Rothman, History of Schools and Schooling (New York: Peter Lang, 2009), 293.

27. David P. Baker, "Minds, Politics, and Gods in the Schooled Society: Consequences of the Education Revolution," *Comparative Education Review* 58, no. 1 (February 2014): 6.

28. The trend appears to continue; see Tom Chorneau, "States Adding Time to Compulsory Ed Requirement," *K–12 Daily*, November 29, 2017, https://www.cabinetreport.com/human -resources/states-adding-time-to-compulsory-ed-requirement.

29. National Center for Education Statistics, "Table 98: Number of Public School Districts and Public and Private Elementary and Secondary Schools: Selected years, 1869–70 through 2010–11," NCES, US Department of Education, Digest of Education Statistics 2012, November 2012, http://nces.ed.gov/programs/digest/d12/tables/dt12_098.asp.

30. National Center for Education Statistics, "Table 98."

31. On recent shifting boundaries of public and private realms, see Michael Johanek, "Private Citizenship and School Choice," in *The Choice Controversy*, ed. Peter W. Cookson Jr. (Newbury Park, CA: Corwin Press, 1992), 146–70.

32. Henry R. Levin, "An Economic Perspective on School Choice," in *Handbook of Research on School Choice*, ed. Mark Berends (New York: Taylor & Francis, 2009), 19.

33. William S. Koski and Rob Reich, "When Adequate Isn't: The Retreat from Equity in Educational Law and Policy and Why It Matters," *Emory Law Review* 56 (2007): 545–617.

34. John Stuart Mill, *On Liberty* (1859) Project Gutenberg, 201.

35. Whitney Bross, Douglas N. Harris, and Lihan Liu, *Extreme Measures: When and How School Closures and Charter Takeovers Benefit Students* (New Orleans: Education Research Alliance for New Orleans, 2016); see ibid., 1, for the estimate.

36. Valerie Strauss, "How Mike Pence Expanded Indiana's Controversial Voucher Program When He Was Governor," January 28, 2018, Answer Sheet (blog), *Washington Post*, https://www .washingtonpost.com/news/answer-sheet/wp/2018/01/28/how-mike-pence-expanded-indianas -controversial-voucher-program-when-he-was-governor/?utm_term=.b571f89849a3; the following textbook passage is quoted in the article: "Dinosaurs and humans were definitely on the earth at the same time and may have even lived side by side within the past few thousand years."

37. Audrey Watters, "The Business of Ed-Tech: December 2017 Funding Data," Hack Education, December 29, 2017, http://funding.hackeducation.com/2017/12/29/december; and Gordon Lafer, *The One Percent of Solution: How Corporations Are Remaking America One State at a Time* (Cornell University Press, 2017), loc. 3094–96 of 7642, Kindle.

38. Arianna Prothero, "Too Big to Fail? Why Large Cyber Charter Schools Rarely Get Shut Down," *Charters and Choice* (blog), *Education Week*, January 24, 2018, http://blogs.edweek.org

/edweek/charterschoice/2018/01/too_big_to_fail_why_massive_cyber_charter_schools_rarely_get_shut_down.html.

39. We should note that this book focuses on the choice of schooling offered to households, within the bounds of compulsory education laws, and on parental/guardian authority. Yet students have also clamored for more choice, including regarding the age up to which they are legally required to attend. At times that voice has been exercised via exiting the system, whether students were required to attend or not; and at times that voice was exercised through more organized, collective efforts.

Part One

1. Thomas Paine, *The Rights of Man* (1791–92; repr., New York: Penguin, 1984), 245; John Adams quoted in Eric Foner, introduction to *The Rights of Man*, by Paine, 7; John Stuart Mill, *On Liberty* (New York: Appleton-Century-Crofts, 1947), 107–10. Paragraph adapted from Michael Johanek, "Private Citizenship and School Choice," in *The Choice Controversy*, ed. Peter W. Cookson Jr. (Newbury Park, CA: Corwin Press, 1992), 149. For Adam Smith's ideas on distributing expenses and decision-making, see E. G. West, "Tom Paine's Voucher Scheme for Public Education," *Southern Economic Journal* 33, no. 3 (January 1967): 382.

2. See, for example, Paul T. Hill, *Strife and Progress: Portfolio Strategies for Managing Urban Schools* (Washington, DC: Brookings Institution Press, 2013).

3. George S. Counts, *The American Road to Culture: A Social Interpretation of Education in the United States* (New York: John Day, 1930), 3.

4. Counts, 4.

5. Counts, 5.

6. Counts, 5. "These practical responses of society, rooted in the folkways and mores of the population, possess a validity and a vitality which no purely theoretic pronouncements . . . can hope to attain . . . they . . . reflect the genius of a given people, the history of a particular civilization, and the conditions of life in a certain natural setting. In a word, they constitute the living theory of education of a country, the theory which has been made flesh and endowed with the breath of life" (ibid.).

7. Theodore R. Sizer, preface to Nancy Beadie and Kim Tolley, *Chartered Schools: Two Hundred Years of Independent Academies in the United States, 1727–1925*, Studies in the History of Education (New York: RoutledgeFalmer, 2002), xi.

8. Bernard Bailyn, *Education in the Forming of American Society: Needs and Opportunities for Study* (Chapel Hill: University of North Carolina Press, published for the Omohundro Institute of Early American History and Culture, Williamsburg, Virginia), loc. 251–52 of 2569, Kindle.

9. Thomas Nashe, *Pierce* Penilesse, 1592, from John Dover Wilson,. *Life in Shakespeare's England: A Book of Elizabethan Prose*, 2nd ed., Cambridge Anthologies (Cambridge: University Press, 1913), 142.

10. Bailyn, *Education in the Forming of American Society*, loc. 343. Bailyn's introductory historiographical essay focuses on developments within the settler communities in the colonies and later United States.

11. Bailyn, *Education in the Forming of American Society*, loc. 274–442. Later work qualified Bailyn's thesis regarding the stability of families, especially for northeastern colonies; see Maris A. Vinovskis, "Explorations in Early American Education," *History of Education Quarterly* 37, no. 2 (1997): 111.

12. Bailyn, *Education in the Forming of American Society*, loc. 401.

13. Bailyn, loc. 378–80. The quote, part of Ulysses's famous speech in *Troilus and Cressida* extolling the ordered, hierarchical, patriarchal world in which all had their place, finishes: "Oh, when degree is shak'd, / Which is the ladder to all high designs, / The enterprise is sick" (1.3.104–6).

14. Lawrence A. Cremin, *American Education: The Colonial Experience, 1607–1783*, 1st ed. (New York: Harper & Row, 1970), 519.

15. Old Deluder Satan Law of 1647, excerpted from *The Laws and Liberties of Massachusetts*, 1648 edition, in the Henry E. Huntington Library, with an introduction by Max Farrand. repr. Harvard University Press, 1929, available at Mass.gov, accessed July 13, 2018, https://www.mass .gov/files/documents/2016/08/ob/deludersatan.pdf.

16. Cremin, *American Education: The Colonial Experience*; see also Joel Perlmann, Silvana R. Siddali, and Keith Whitescarver, "Literacy, Schooling, and Teaching among New England Women, 1730–1820," *History of Education Quarterly* 37, no. 2 (1997).

17. The quote is from the 1642 Massachusetts school law, cited in Marcus W. Jernegan, "Compulsory Education in the American Colonies," *School Review*, January–December 1918, 740–41fn1.

18. For the history of testing in US schools, in part as a way of representing standards, see William J. Reese, *Testing Wars in the Public Schools: A Forgotten History* (Cambridge, MA: Harvard University Press, 2013).

19. Bailyn, *Education in the Forming of American Society*, loc. 455.

20. Author Johanek thanks colleague John Puckett for this example. We at Penn have obviously benefited from Franklin's decision to flee to Philadelphia.

21. From Franklin's autobiography, cited at National Humanities Center, "Benjamin Franklin's Junto Club & Lending Library of Philadelphia," accessed March 8, 2016, http:// nationalhumanitiescenter.org/pds/becomingamer/ideas/text4/juntolibrary.pdf.

22. Bailyn, *Education in the Forming of American Society*, loc. 526.

23. Bailyn, loc. 564.

24. Relatedly, Sidney Mead explained the rise of religious choice in the United States as the result of the inability of religious groups to enforce compliance in the colonies. See Jerald C. Brauer, Sidney Earl Mead, and Robert N. Bellah, *Religion and the American Revolution* (Philadelphia: Fortress Press, 1976).

25. Bailyn, *Education in the Forming of American Society*, 41.

26. Bailyn, 48.

27. Bailyn, 49.

28. Carl F. Kaestle, "Common Schools before the Common School Revival: New York Schooling in the 1790s," *History of Education Quarterly* 12 (1972): 465.

29. Kenneth A. Lockridge, *Literacy in Colonial New England: An Enquiry into the Social Context of Literacy in the Early Modern West*, 1st ed. (New York: Norton, 1974); and Perlmann, Siddali, and Whitescarver, "Literacy, Schooling, and Teaching among New England Women," 117–39.

30. The United States population did not drop below 50% rural until the 1920 census. In 1790, only 5% of the population lived in areas of 2,500 or more people. At the advent of the Civil War, the United States was still 80% rural. See US Bureau of the Census, "Series A 57-72. Population in Urban and Rural Territory, by Size of Place: 1790 to 1970," *Bicentennial Edition: Historical Statistics of the United States, Colonial Times to 1970*, (US Department of Commerce, 1975), part 1, chapter A, 11, https://www2.census.gov/library/publications/1975/compendia/hist_stats_colonial -1970/hist_stats_colonial-1970p1-chA.pdf.

31. US Bureau of the Census, "Series A 57-72"; Centers for Disease Control, "Achievements

in Public Health, 1900-1999: Family Planning," *Morbidity and Mortality Weekly Report* 48, no. 47: 1073–80, http://www.cdc.gov/mmwr/preview/mmwrhtml/mm4847a1.htm.

32. See Carl F. Kaestle, *Pillars of the Republic: Common Schools and American Society, 1780– 1860*, ed. Eric Foner, American Century Series (New York: Hill and Wang, 1983); Kaestle, *The Evolution of an Urban School System: New York City, 1750–1850* (Cambridge, MA: Harvard University Press, 1973); Kaestle, "Common Schools before the Common School Revival: New York Schooling in the 1790s," *History of Education Quarterly* 12 (1972): 465–500; Cremin, *American Education: The Colonial Experience*; Claudia Goldin and Lawrence F. Katz, "The "Virtues" of the Past: Education in the First Hundred Years of the New Republic," in *NBER Working Paper Series, Working Paper 9958* (Cambridge, MA: National Bureau of Economic Research, 2003), 1–56, http://www.nber.org/papers/w9958; and Maris A. Vinovskis, "Explorations in Early American Education," *History of Education Quarterly* 37, no. 2 (1997): 111–16.

33. See Perlmann, Siddali, and Whitescarver, "Literacy, Schooling, and Teaching among New England Women," 124; Cremin, *American Education: The Colonial Experience*, 186–87; Kaestle,; Beadie and Tolley, *Chartered Schools*; and James Axtell, *The School upon a Hill: Education and Society in Colonial New England* (New York: Norton, 1976).

34. We use the terminology set out by Kim Tolley, "Mapping the Landscape of Higher Schooling, 1727–1850," in *Chartered Schools: Two Hundred Years of Independent Academies in the United States, 1727-1925*, ed. Nancy Beadie and Kim Tolley, Studies in the History of Education (New York: RoutledgeFalmer, 2002), 19–43.

35. Nancy Beadie, "Toward a History of Education Markets in the United States," *Social Science History* 32, no. 1 (2008): 49.

36. Jon Teaford, "The Transformation of Massachusetts Education, 1670–1780," *History of Education Quarterly* 10 (1970): 301, quoted in Beadie, "Toward a History of Education Markets," 50.

37. Theodore R. Sizer, preface to Beadie and Tolley, *Chartered Schools*, xii. The term *academy* was used by a good range of institutions, not all of which match the definition used in this discussion, which follows the definitions for academy, venture school, dame school, church school, mechanics institutes, Latin grammar schools, town schools, and so on, as set out in Tolley, "Mapping the Landscape of Higher Schooling," in Beadie and Tolley, *Chartered Schools*, 19–22.

38. Kim Tolley, "Mapping the Landscape of Higher Schooling," in Beadie and Tolley, *Chartered Schools*, 21.

39. Kim Tolley and Nancy Beadie, "A School for Every Purpose: An Introduction to the History of Academies in the United States," in Beadie and Tolley, *Chartered Schools*, 16fn2.

40. See, for example, "Symposium: Reappraisals of the Academy Movement," in *History of Education Quarterly* 41, no. 2 (Summer 2001): 216–70.

41. Beadie and Tolley, *Chartered Schools*, 3. Later in the text, "more like they do today" refers to the longer required years of study, a graded and sequenced curriculum, provision by publicly operated institutions, professionalized educators, and so on.

42. Edward Branley, "NOLA History: The Old Ursuline Convent in the French Quarter," Go NOLA, March 30, 2011, http://gonola.com/2011/03/30/nola-history-the-old-ursuline-convent-in -the-french-quarter.html; and Mary D. McConaghy, Michael Silberman, and Irina Kalashnikova, "Introduction: From Franklin's Vision to Academy to University of Pennsylvania," University of Pennsylvania Archives & Record Center, 2004, http://www.archives.upenn.edu/histy/features /1700s/penn1700s.html. Primary documents and other materials regarding Franklin Academy can also be found at the Penn Archives & Record Center link.

43. United States Census Bureau, "Table 2: Population, Housing Units, Area Measurements,

and Density: 1790 to 1990," *1990 Census of Population and Housing* (CPH-2), accessed July 23, 2018, http://www.census.gov/population/www/censusdata/files/table-2.pdf.

44. J. M. Opal, "Exciting Emulation: Academies and the Transformation of the Rural North, 1780s–1820s," *Journal of American History* 91, no. 2 (2004): 448.

45. Henry Barnard, "Table III: Educational Statistics of the United States in 1850," *American Journal of Education* 1 (1850): 368; also quoted in Beadie and Tolley, *Chartered Schools*. In 1850, per Barnard, there were 6,100 chartered schools (incorporated academies), and in 2010/11, NCES counted 5,274 charters nationally (ibid.). Sizer considered Barnard's estimate as "probably conservative." Theodore R. Sizer, *The Age of the Academies*, Classics in Education (New York: Bureau of Publications, Teachers College, Columbia University, 1964), 1. Regarding issues with statistics of nineteenth-century schooling, see Claudia Dale Goldin and Lawrence F. Katz, *The Race between Education and Technology* (Cambridge, MA: Belknap Press of Harvard University Press, 2008), chap. 4.

46. J. M. Opal, "Exciting Emulation: Academies and the Transformation of the Rural North, 1780s–1820s." *Journal of American History* 91, no. 2 (2004): 448.

47. The quote is from Theodore R. Sizer, "The Academies: An Interpretation," in *Age of the Academies*, 40; and the statistic is from Kathyrn Kerns, "Antebellum Higher Education for Women in Western New York State," (PhD diss., University of Pennsylvania, 1993), 155–92; both quoted in Nancy Beadie, "Academy Students in the Mid-Nineteenth Century: Social Geography, Demography, and the Culture of Academy Attendance," *History of Education Quarterly* 41 no. 2 (2001): 251–52.

48. Opal, "Exciting Emulation, 451; Beadie, "Academy Students in the Mid-Nineteenth Century," 255–56.

49. Beadie, "Academy Students in the Mid-Nineteenth Century," 253.

50. Beadie, 251–62.

51. Sizer, *Age of the Academies*, 38.

52. Beadie and Tolley, *Chartered Schools* 30–31.

53. See C. F. Kaestle, *Joseph Lancaster and the Monitorial School Movement: A Documentary History* (New York: Teachers College Press, 1973).

54. Opal, "Exciting Emulation," 456.

55. Sizer, *Age of the Academies*, 1.

56. For the American as "hustler," see Walter A. McDougall, *Throes of Democracy: The American Civil War Era, 1829–1877*, 1st ed. (New York: Harper, 2008), xvi.

57. Tolley and Beadie, "A School for Every Purpose," 6.

58. Hammond, "New England Academies and Classical Schools," excerpted in Sizer, *Age of the Academies*, 136. "If there can be found on earth . . . a republic where there is a perfect equality of rights and privileges, and a perfect reciprocity of sympathy and social fellowship, independent absolutely of the distinctions of the outside world, that realization is a community of students in an American Academy or College" (ibid.).

59. From Alexis de Tocqueville, *Democracy in America*, (London: Saunders and Otley, 1835), quoted in Sizer, *Age of the Academies*, 15.

60. Sizer, *Age of the Academies*, 15. "The academy was the American's compromise between practical education and the education traditionally held valuable" (ibid., 19).

61. Opal, "Exciting Emulation," 445–70.

62. *Public* here being used in the sense of government-sponsored institutions, including the emerging common schools.

63. Edward Hitchcock, *The American Academic System Defended: An Address Delivered at*

the Dedication of the New Hall of Williston Seminary, in Easthampton, January 28, 1845 (Amherst: J. S. & C. Adams, Printers, 1845), quoted in Sizer, *Age of the Academies*, 123.

64. Alcott's "conversations" approach grew out of a heady mix of transcendentalist Christian thinking of the era; one of Temple School's teachers, Elizabeth Peabody, published *A Record of a School* in 1835 (with later editions titled *A Record of Mr. Alcott's School*) and went on to become a pioneer for kindergarten in the United States. It seems her warnings to Alcott urging him not to publish his book recording conversations with the school's children were not heeded, unfortunately; controversy arising from that, as well as parents' reaction to the admittance of a mulatto to the school, led to its closure after six years of operation. See Amos Bronson Alcott, *Conversations with Children on the Gospels*, 2 vols. (Boston: J. Munroe, 1836); and Elizabeth Palmer Peabody, *Record of a School: Exemplifying the General Principles of Spiritual Culture* (Boston: James Munroe and Company, 1835.)

65. Mann quoted in William J. Reese, "Changing Conceptions of 'Public' and 'Private' in American Educational History," chap. 5 in *History, Education, and the Schools*, 1st ed. (New York: Palgrave Macmillan, 2007), 101.

66. Reese, "Changing Conceptions of 'Public' and 'Private'"; for related and subsequent context, see Tracy L. Steffes, *School, Society, and State: A New Education to Govern Modern America, 1890–1940* (Chicago: University of Chicago Press, 2012).

67. Kaestle, *Pillars of the Republic*, 221.

68. David B. Tyack, *The One Best System: A History of American Urban Education* (Cambridge, MA: Harvard University Press, 1974).

69. See Nancy Beadie and Kim Tolley, "Legacies of the Academy," in Beadie and Tolley, *Chartered Schools*, 331–51.

70. Kaestle, *Pillars of the Republic*, 221.

71. Michael S. Katz, *A History of Compulsory Education Laws*, Fastback Series (Bloomington, IN: Phi Delta Kappa Educational Foundation, 1976), 15.

72. Tracy L. Steffes, *School, Society, and State*, 151–52.

73. The rate was relatively flat if fluctuating for white youth, at about 50%; black school participation rose dramatically from the Civil War to 1880, more than tripling after the war to reach 34% in 1880; it then remained flat until the early twentieth century. Snyder, *120 Years of American Education*, 6.

74. M. S. Katz, *Compulsory Education Laws*, 19.

75. Edson quoted in M. S. Katz, 23.

76. Ellwood Cubberley, *Changing Concepts of Education* (Boston: Houghton Mifflin: 1939), 63, quoted in Ethan L. Hutt, "Formalism over Function: Compulsion, Courts, and the Rise of Educational Formalism in America, 1870–1930," *Teachers College Record* 114, no. 1 (2012): 3.

77. Steffes, *School, Society, and State*, 121.

78. On state/family trade-offs and tensions, see Ethan L. Hutt, "Formalism over Function"; Stephen Provasnik, "Judicial Activism and the Origins of Parental Choice: The Court's Role in the Institutionalization of Compulsory Education in the United States, 1891–1925," *History of Education Quarterly* 46, no. 3 (2006): 311–47; and Claudia Goldin and Lawrence Katz, "Mass Secondary Schooling and the State: The Role of State Compulsion in the High School Movement," in *NBER Working Paper Series* (Cambridge, MA: National Bureau of Economic Research, 2003).

79. Many educators appear to have joined this resistance, contrary to prior characterizations in the literature. See Provasnik, "Judicial Activism and Parental Choice."

80. Jack Dougherty, "A Rite of Adolescence? Review of Stephen Lassonde, *Learning to Forget: Schooling and Family Life in New Haven's Working Class, 1870–1940* [. . .]," *Reviews in American History* 34, no. 2 (2006): 201.

81. Dougherty, 201. On Leonard Covello, see Michael C. Johanek and John L. Puckett, *Leonard Covello and the Making of Benjamin Franklin High School: Education as if Citizenship Mattered* (Philadelphia, PA: Temple University Press, 2007); for immigrant and family experiences of schooling, see Stephen Lassonde, *Learning to Forget: Schooling and Family Life in New Haven's Working Class, 1870–1940* (New Haven, CT: Yale University Press, 2005); and William W. Cutler, *Parents and Schools: The 150-Year Struggle for Control in American Education* (Chicago: University of Chicago Press, 2000).

82. Cutler, *Parents and Schools*.

83. The practice seems to cross national boundaries as well; for the UK, see Richard Adams, "One in Four Families Move House to Secure School Place—Survey," *Guardian*, September 1, 2015, http://www.theguardian.com/education/2015/sep/02/one-in-four-families-move-house-to -secure-school-place-survey.

84. Goldin and Katz, "Mass Secondary Schooling and the State," 28.

85. Recent scholarship revisits prior understandings of compulsory schooling laws; for example, see Provasnik, "Judicial Activism and Parental Choice."

86. Teacher quoted in James Anderson, *The Education of Blacks in the South, 1860–1935* (1988), 5, cited in James Forman Jr., "The Secret History of School Choice: How Progressives Got There First," *Georgetown Law Journal* 93, no. 4 (2005) 294; illiteracy rate, ibid., 1295. For other work on this period, see Christopher M. Span, *From Cotton Field to Schoolhouse: African American Education in Mississippi, 1862–1875*, 1st ed. (Chapel Hill: University of North Carolina Press, 2009); Span, "Post-Slavery? Post-Segregation? Post-Racial? A History of the Impact of Slavery, Segregation, and Racism on the Education of African Americans," *National Society for the Study of Education* 114, no. 2 (2015): 53–74; Hilary Green, *Educational Reconstruction: African American Schools in the Urban South, 1865–1890*. Reconstructing America, 1st ed. (New York: Fordham University Press, 2016); and Johann N. Neem, *Democracy's Schools: The Rise of Public Education in America*, How Things Worked (Baltimore, Maryland: John Hopkins University Press, 2017), chap. 5. Neem explores the ways the "school question" was refracted across North and South, Catholics and African Americans, particularly after the Civil War: "While southern African Americans and northern philanthropists were promoting public education in the South, northerners were wondering whether the schools could bring together a diverse nation" (ibid., 169).

87. The Third Plenary Council of 1884 ratcheted up the emphasis on building a parallel school system, a theme in prior councils dating back to the first and second councils in 1852 and 1866, respectively. Francis P. Cassidy, "Catholic Education in the Third Plenary Council of Baltimore," part 1, *Catholic Historical Review* 34, no. 3 (1948): 257–305; and Jay P. Dolan, *The American Catholic Experience: A History from Colonial Times to the Present* (Notre Dame, IN: University of Notre Dame Press, 1992).

88. Another dual system arose in the South prior to but especially following the Civil War, a set of schools run by freed African Americans. James Forman notes: "In state after state, in the absence of a formal education system, blacks began to build schools and hire teachers. Historian Herbert Gutman found that in the fall of 1866, at least half of the schools in Arkansas, Florida, Georgia, Kentucky, Louisiana, Maryland, and Texas were sustained by blacks. In Alabama, the Carolinas, Tennessee, and Virginia, blacks supported twenty-five to forty-nine percent of the schools. These efforts initially surprised Freedman's Bureau agents who surveyed the region shortly after the Civil War expecting to find no functioning schools for blacks." Forman, "The Secret History of School Choice," 1293.

89. Philip Gleason, William D. Borders, Daniel E. Pilarczyk, and William E. McManus, "Baltimore III and Education," *U.S. Catholic Historian* 4, no. 3/4, Historians & Bishops in Dialogue: A Centenary Celebration of the Third Plenary Council of Baltimore 1884–1984 (1985): 277.

90. Robert D. Cross, "Origins of the Catholic Parochial Schools in America," *American Benedictine Review* 16 (1965): 197; F. Michael Perko references Cross's work in *Enlightening the Next Generation: Catholics and Their Schools, 1830–1980* (New York: Garland, 1988).

91. *The Memorial Volume: A History of the Third Plenary Council of Baltimore, November 9– December 7, 1884* (Baltimore, 1885), 53, quoted in Gleason et al., "Baltimore III and Education," 277fn9.

92. Bernard J. Meiring, *Educational Aspects of the Legislation of the Councils of Baltimore, 1829–1884* (University of California, Berkeley, 1963), quoted in Gleason et al., "Baltimore III and Education," 277.

93. Meiring, *Educational Aspects*, quoted in Philip Gleason, William D. Borders, Daniel E. Pilarczyk, and William E. McManus, "Baltimore III and Education," p.277.

94. National Education Association, *Journal of Proceedings and Addresses . . . 1890* (Topeka, 1890), 181; quoted in Gleason, et al., "Baltimore III and Education," 278fn11. St. Paul's Archbishop Ireland, while seeing the parish school as a last resort, lamented to the National Education Association's annual meeting in Topeka "the chilling and devastating blast of unbelief . . . the swelling tide of irreligion . . . the materialism which sees not beyond the universe a living, personal God, or the agnosticism which reduces him to an indescribable perhaps" (ibid.).

95. Weisz quoted in Timothy Walch, "The Past before Us: Historical Models for Future Parish Schools," in *Catholic Schools in the Public Interest: Past, Present and Future Directions*, ed. Patricia A. Bauch, OP (Charlotte, NC: Information Age Publishing, 2014), 9; and Perko, *Enlightening the Next Generation*, v.

96. Lawrence A. Cremin, *American Education: The Metropolitan Experience, 1876–1980*, 1st ed. (New York: Harper & Row, 1988), 127.

97. Benjamin Justice, "The Blaine Game: Are Public Schools Inherently Anti-Catholic?," *Teachers College Record* 109, no. 9 (2007): 2185.

98. The typology draws from, among other sources, Walch, "The Past before Us," 3–19.

99. Ann Marie Ryan, "Keeping 'Every Catholic Child in a Catholic School' during the Great Depression, 1933–1939," *Catholic Education: A Journal of Inquiry and Practice* 11, no. 2 (December 2007):159. This became the motto of the Catholic hierarchy after the Third Plenary Council (ibid.).

100. "The best known action taken by the Council in 1884 was to shift from the language of exhortation in respect to parochial schools to that of command." Gleason et al., "Baltimore III and Education," 273. The council arguably reflected an increased assertion by the Church of its moral authority in a world viewed hostile to religious belief and hierarchy; the council also instigated the development of the Baltimore Catechism, long a core element within US Catholic education.

101. James Gibbons, "Pastoral Letter of 1884 (Third Plenary Council of Baltimore)," from *Memorial Volume: A History of the Third Plenary Council of Baltimore* (Baltimore, 1885), reproduced at CatholicCulture.org, accessed July 24, 2018, https://www.catholicculture.org/culture /library/view.cfm?recnum=518#christianed.

102. Gibbons, "Pastoral Letter of 1884."

103. Gibbons, "Pastoral Letter of 1884."

104. F. Michael Perko, SJ, noted, as late as 1988, that "it is a misnomer to call Catholic schooling a system. . . . More accurately, Catholic schooling is best viewed as a network or quasi-system, tied together by some common coordinative structures and a similar mission, but strongly shaped by the needs and desires of the local community." Perko, *Enlightening the Next Generation*, vi.

105. Cremin, *American Education: The Metropolitan Experience*, 127.

106. Cremin, 127.

107. Cremin, 127. French Catholics arrived in the colonial period, as stated above, with German and Irish immigration growing in the mid-nineteenth century, followed by Catholic immigration from southern and eastern Europe in the late nineteenth/early twentieth centuries. By 1920, nearly twenty million Catholics resided in the United States. There was wide variation in the social network of parish communities across different ethnic groups, of course, and in the differing contexts of rural, small town, and urban parish life. See Dolan, *The American Catholic Parish*; Perko, *Enlightening the Next Generation*; and Cross, "Origins of the Catholic Parochial Schools in America," 194–209.

108. In cities where linguistic diversity was better accommodated in public systems, parish schools found inroads more limited. For how this supported "patriotic pluralism," see Jeffrey E. Mirel, *Patriotic Pluralism: Americanization Education and European Immigrants* (Cambridge, MA: Harvard University Press, 2010).

109. Diane Ravitch, *The Great School Wars: A History of the New York City Public Schools* (Baltimore: Johns Hopkins University Press, 2000), 141.

110. Ravitch, 141.

111. Ravitch sees parallels between activist Preston Wilcox's stance in the community-control controversy of the mid-1960s and Bishop John Hughes's battle with the Public School Society for public funding in the mid-nineteenth century; Wilcox proposed that "the interests and values of blacks were so divergent from those of the Board of Education that only the local community could administer the schooling of its children"; that is, the school should be run by the community with public dollars. "Hughes had had the same objections to the Public School Society and had sought the same remedy. . . . Hughes wanted the schools to reinforce Catholicism; Wilcox wanted IS201 to affirm the strengths of black culture. The outlook of each was based on the premise that his group had to free itself from the assimilationism of the common school concept and to control publicly funded schools of its own, for its own purposes." Diane Ravitch, *The Great School Wars: A History of the New York City Public Schools* (Baltimore: Johns Hopkins University Press, 2000), 296–97.

112. Considering these private systems as a part of US mass education provides a useful lens for the period; see David P. Baker, "Schooling All the Masses: Reconsidering the Origins of American Schooling in the Postbellum Era," *Sociology of Education* 72, no. 4 (1999): 197–215.

113. Catholic school enrollment would not peak, however, until the mid-1960s, by then more than doubling again from its 1930 enrollment. Bruce S. Cooper and Steven D'Agustino, "Catholic School Survival and the Common Good," in Bauch, *Catholic Schools in the Public Interest*, 254.

114. Arguably, professionalism in Catholic education lagged in time relative to the professionalization efforts in public schools, especially in larger urban systems; countering secularism while also recognizing the knowledge that its institutions produced caused considerable discomfort. Tensions between the sacred and secular could be seen in attitudes toward the preparation of Catholic educators, and yet the 1884 council clearly saw an urgent need to improve the education of the clergy and laity teaching in parish schools. One historian views the formation of the Department of Education at Catholic University at the turn of the twentieth century as both "radical and prophetic." As late as 1955, Philadelphia's Cardinal Archbishop O'Hara, reflecting continued skepticism toward any secular science of education, remarked: "The secularist, who denies the existence of the soul, writes a thousand books to explain what makes Johnny tick. The Catholic teacher who follows up the secularist, up a dozen blind alleys, wastes precious time and risks failure. The good nun who spends as much time praying for Johnny as teaching him, takes Johnny as he is, soul and all, and never has to worry about his conditioned reflexes." John

F. Murphy, "Professional Preparation of Catholic Teachers in the Nineteen Hundreds," *Notre Dame Journal of Education* 7 (1976): 126, cited in Perko, *Enlightening the Next Generation*, 246.

115. While other private schools existed, both independent and affiliated with other religious institutions, the predominance of the Catholic schools numerically and in the minds of public educators at the time warrants particular attention.

116. Baker, "Schooling All the Masses," 199–200, 204. It is worth noting that Catholic schools never enrolled more than a fraction of the total K–12 student population, as the private sector overall hovered around 10% for this period. National Center for Education Statistics, "Table 3: Enrollment in Educational Institutions, by Level and Control of Institution: Selected Years, 1869–70 through Fall 2021," NCES, US Department of Education, Institute of Education Sciences, January 2013, with author calculations. Catholic school enrollment peaked in the early 1960s, at "more than 5.2 million students in almost thirteen thousand schools across the nation." National Catholic Education Association, *United States Catholic Elementary and Secondary Schools 2014–2015: The Annual Statistical Report on Schools, Enrollment, and Staffing*, accessed June 9, 2015, https://www.ncea.org/data-information/catholic-school-data.

117. US Bureau of Education, *Report of the Commissioner of Education for the Year 1886–87* (Washington, DC: Government Printing Office, 1888), 90, 65, cited in Robert N. Gross, *Public vs. Private: The Early History of School Choice in America* (New York: Oxford University Press, 2018), 2.

118. Joshua Young, "Moral Education," *Lend a Hand* 5, no. 5 (May 1890): 314, quoted in Robert N. Gross, "A Marketplace of Schooling: Education and the American Regulatory State, 1870–1930," PhD diss., University of Wisconsin–Madison, 2013, 3.

119. Gross, "A Marketplace of Schooling," 72. See also Gross, *Public vs. Private*.

120. Gross, "A Marketplace of Schooling," 70–71.

121. Philip Gleason, "American Catholic Higher Education: A Historical Perspective," *The Shape of Catholic Higher Education*, ed. Robert Hassenger (Chicago: University of Chicago, 1967), 27, quoted in Perko, *Enlightening the Next Generation*, 194. Different ethnic groups within the Catholic community were at generally different stages, of course, with the Irish and Germans predominantly at second- and third-generation phases by 1900, while Poles, Slavs, Italians, Czechs, for example, were predominantly in their first and second generations.

122. The phrase "peaceable adjustments" is from nineteenth-century Bishop Thomas Jefferson Jenkins, quoted in Benjamin Justice, *The War That Wasn't: Religious Conflict and Compromise in the Common Schools of New York State, 1865–1900* (Albany: State University of New York Press, 2005), loc. 74–76 of 3881, Kindle.

123. Justice, loc. 3170.

124. *Encyclopedia of Educational Reform and Dissent*, ed. Thomas C. Hunt, James C. Carper, Thomas J. Lasley, II and C. Daniel Raisch (Thousand Oaks, CA: SAGE Publications, 2010), s.v. "Faribault-Stillwater Plan," by Timothy Walch, 372–73; and *Encyclopedia of Educational Reform and Dissent*, s.v. "Lowell Plan," by Timothy Walch, 531–32.

125. Cremin, *American Education: The Metropolitan Experience*, 130–31; *Encyclopedia of Educational Reform and Dissent*, s.v. "Faribault-Stillwater Plan"; and Justice, *The War That Wasn't*, loc. 224.

126. Edward M. Connors, *Church-State Relationships in Education in the State of New York* (Washington, DC: Catholic University of America Press, 1951), 112.

127. The board and the parish could terminate the agreement at the end of any school year, with thirty days' notice.

128. Justice, *The War That Wasn't*, loc. 2741–42. German Catholics maintained their Nativity's parish school, however, presumably to maintain linguistic and cultural identity there.

129. Justice, loc. 3002.

130. *Encyclopedia of Educational Reform and Dissent*, s.v. "Poughkeepsie Plan," by Timothy Walch, 719.

131. "Religious Garb in Poughkeepsie," *School Journal*, January 29, 1898, 128. Skinner ruled against the use of religious garb in another case, in Corning, in April 1898.

132. "Religion in the Schools: State Supt. Skinner Finds the 'Poughkeepsie Plan' Unlawful," *New York Times*, December 24, 1898, 12.

133. "State Supt. Skinner Finds the 'Poughkeepsie Plan' Unlawful." On the Poughkeepsie Plan, see also *Encyclopedia of Educational Reform and Dissent*, s.v. "Poughkeepsie Plan," 718–19; and Justice, *The War That Wasn't*, loc. 2655–83.

134. Edmund Platt, *The Eagle's History of Poughkeepsie from Earliest Settlements, 1683 to 1905* (Poughkeepsie, NY: Platt & Platt, 1905), 253.

135. It would appear, though, that much remains to be learned about local accommodations even within growing state and professional supervision of public schooling in this era.

136. Walch, "The Past before Us," 13; see also Jeffrey E. Mirel, *Patriotic Pluralism: Americanization Education and European Immigrants* (Cambridge, MA: Harvard University Press, 2010), 113–18.

137. Mirel, *Patriotic Pluralism*.

138. Cross, "Origins of the Catholic Parochial Schools in America," 203.

139. Cross, 204, quoted in Perko, *Enlightening the Next Generation*, 327.

140. Cross, 202, quoted in Perko, 325.

141. Mirel, *Patriotic Pluralism*, 114. The newspaper, still in operation, claims to be the oldest continuously published Polish-language newspaper.

142. Cross, "Origins of the Catholic Parochial Schools," 203, quoted in Perko, *Enlightening the Next Generation*, 326.

143. Quoted in Mirel, *Patriotic Pluralism*, 114.

144. Many Catholic pastors themselves expressed ambivalence at the task of running a parish school; knowing the poverty of many of their parishioners, many longed for any arrangement that could relieve their community of the financial burden, and allow more singular focus on the challenges of the spirit and of the parish's social welfare concerns.

145. Gross, "A Marketplace of Schooling," 69.

146. Gross, 187.

147. Robert N. Gross, "Public Regulation and the Origins of Modern School-Choice Policies in the Progressive Era," *Journal of Policy History* 26, no. 4 (2014): 526.

148. Walch, "The Past before Us," 11.

149. Reverend Patrick J. McCormick, "Standards in Education," *Catholic Educational Association Bulletin* 14 (1917): 81–82, cited in Gross, *Public vs. Private*, 101.

150. Gross, "Public Regulation and Modern School-Choice Policies," 525, 524; and Ann Marie Ryan, "Negotiating Assimilation: Chicago Catholic High Schools' Pursuit of Accreditation in the Early Twentieth Century." *History of Education Quarterly* 46, no. 3 (2006): 348–81. Fr. McCormick's discourse, it should be noted, starts with reference to those in Ancient Persia and Sparta, tracing standards from there to 1917. Patrick J. McCormick, "Standards in Education," *Catholic Educational Association Bulletin* 14 (1917): 70–83.

151. Howard Weisz, "Irish-American Attitudes and the Americanization of the English-Language Parochial School," *New York History* 53 (1972): 175, cited in Perko, *Enlightening the Next Generation*, 162–81; partially quoted in Walch, "The Past before Us," 11. Weisz notes the tension this caused parish schools, though: "If parochial schools were not demonstrably American, then they could not survive pressure from their enemies, and if there were not different, then they

had no reason to exist." Weisz, 158. Certainly some Catholics saw in the efforts to mimic public schools a threat to their distinctive value, pushing back on the convergence of models. Editor Maurice Egan complained of the proliferation of courses in American Catholic schools; "it savors too much of the pretentious system of brain stuffing and stifling adopted in the public schools." Weisz, 168, quoted in Walch, 9.

152. Quoted in Gross, "Public Regulation and Modern School-Choice Policies," 513.

153. Thernstrom coined the phrase "permanent transients" in reference to nineteenth-century Irish residents of Newburyport, Massachusetts. Stephan Thernstrom, *Poverty and Progress: Social Mobility in a Nineteenth Century City* (Cambridge, MA: Joint Center for Urban Studies of the Massachusetts Institute of Technology and Harvard University/Harvard University Press, 1964).

154. Robert N. Gross, "A Marketplace of Schooling," 170.

155. We acknowledge the very useful work of Robert Gross in arguing the role of regulation in creating/stimulating the market for a blended public/private schooling market; see Gross, "A Marketplace of Schooling"; and Gross, "Public Regulation and Modern School-Choice Policies." He notes also the general adoption of diocesan systems of the measurement/efficiency efforts under way in public systems: "As parochial schools continued to grow, becoming ever more centralized and bureaucratic, Catholics' demand for educational measurement kept pace with public school reformers."' Gross, "A Marketplace of Schooling," 185.

156. J Kenneth T. Jackson, *Crabgrass Frontier: The Suburbanization of the United States* (New York: Oxford University Press, 1985), loc. 4726–27 of 9107, Kindle. Two recent works put the total for the decades just after World War II at between thirteen million and thirty-five million new units constructed; see Martin Filler, "Living Happily Ever After," *New York Review of Books*, April 12, 2016, https://www.nybooks.com/articles/2016/04/21/houses-living-happily-ever-after/.

157. Kenneth Fox, *Metropolitan America: Urban Life and Urban Policy in the United States, 1940–1980* (Jackson: University Press of Mississippi, 1986); Dolores Hayden, *Building Suburbia: Green Fields and Urban Growth, 1820–2000*, 1st ed. (New York: Pantheon Books, 2003); Jon C. Teaford, *City and Suburb: The Political Fragmentation of Metropolitan America, 1850–1970*, Johns Hopkins Studies in Urban Affairs (Baltimore: Johns Hopkins University Press, 1979); and Teaford, *The Metropolitan Revolution: The Rise of Post-Urban America*, (New York: Columbia University Press, 2006).

158. Lewis Mumford, *The City in History* (New York: Harcourt, 1961), 486. Four decades earlier, Mumford lamented the "repulsion" from cities into suburbs: "Having failed to create a common life in our modern cities, we have builded Suburbia, which is a common refuge from life, and the remedy is an aggravation of the disease!" Mumford, "The Wilderness of Suburbia," *New Republic*, September 7, 1921, 45.

159. Jackson, *Crabgrass Frontier*, loc. 7638–39.

160. Jackson, loc. 4857.

161. John Bodnar, "Unruly Adults: Social Change and Mass Culture in the 1950s," *OAH Magazine of History* 26, no. 4 (2012): 23.

162. Bodnar, "Unruly Adults: Social Change and Mass Culture in the 1950s," *OAH Magazine of History* 26, no. 4 (2012): 23. See also Penny Von Eschen, "Rethinking Politics and Culture in a Dynamic Decade," *OAH Magazine of History* 26, no. 4 (2012): 9–12. In Tennessee Williams's *Streetcar Named Desire*, a decorated war hero rapes his wife, challenging the "inherent virtue of Americans and their ability to govern their darkest impulses"; Bodnar, "Unruly Adults," 22.

163. David Greenberg, "The Pledge of Allegiance: Why We're Not One Nation 'Under God,'" *Slate*, June 28, 2002, http://www.slate.com/articles/news_and_politics/history_lesson/2002/06

/the_pledge_of_allegiance.html; and Jeffrey Owen Jones, "The Man Who Wrote the Pledge of Allegiance," *Smithsonian Magazine*, November 2003, https://www.smithsonianmag.com/history/the-man-who-wrote-the-pledge-of-allegiance-93907224/.

164. Benjamin Fine, "Progressive Unit in Teaching to Die," *New York Times*, June 21, 1955, 33. K–12 enrollments roughly double from 1945 to 1968, from nearly twenty-five million to more than fifty million students, per "Table 9: Enrollment in Regular Public and Private Elementary and Secondary Schools, by Grade Level: 1869–70 to Fall 1992," in Snyder, *120 Years of American Education*, 36–37). For further background on the PEA, see Patricia Albjerg Graham, *Progressive Education from Arcady to Academe: A History of the Progressive Education Association, 1919–1955*, Teachers College Studies in Education (New York: Teachers College Press, 1967); and "Educational Group Moves to Dissolve," *New York Times*, June 26, 1955, 54.

165. With numerous caveats in mind, "school reform" stands here for dominant directions, especially at the level of discourse, in policies regarding school improvement.

166. Arthur Eugene Bestor, Clarence J. Karier, and Foster McMurray, *Educational Wastelands: The Retreat from Learning in Our Public Schools*, 2nd ed. (Urbana: University of Illinois Press, 1985); quoted in Theodore R. Sizer and Molly Schen, "Arthur Bestor's *Educational Wastelands*," *History of Education Quarterly* 27, no. 2 (Summer 1987): 259.

167. Milton Friedman, "The Role of Government in Education," in Robert A. Solo, *Economics and the Public Interest [Essays Written in Honor of Eugene Ewald Agger]* (New Brunswick, NJ: Rutgers University Press, 1955), 123–44.

168. Friedman quoted in Solo, 144.

169. See, for example, Chris Taylor, Julie McLeod, Tim Butler, and Carol Vincent, "Review Symposium: Education Policy, Space and the City: Markets and the (in)Visibility of Race," *British Journal of Sociology* 32, no. 5 (2011): 805–20; and Annette Lareau and Kimberly Goyette, eds., *Choosing Homes, Choosing Schools* (New York: Russell Sage Foundation, 2014). For another example, during the half century after World War II, while the percent of the population living in rural areas plummeted, the percent in central cities remained relatively stable. However, the proportion in suburbs grew dramatically. Having doubled between 1900 and 1950, the share of suburban dwellers doubled again between 1950 and 2000. Essayist William Schneider declared, "The third century of American history is shaping up as the suburban century." William Schneider, "The Suburban Century Begins," *Atlantic Monthly*, July 1992, 33.

170. PBS, "Population," *The First Measured Century*, accessed March 9, 2015, http://www.pbs.org/fmc/book/1population6.htm. There are some unclear stats here; for example, John L. Rury and Argun Saatcioglu, in "Suburban Advantage: Opportunity Hoarding and Secondary Attainment in the Postwar Metropolitan North," *American Journal of Education* 117, no. 3 (2011): 307-42, claim that one-third of 17-year-olds in suburbs in 1940, rising to 60% in 1980; but the US Department of Education puts the K–12 percentage at 34 percent, breaking out urban, suburban, town, and rural.

171. See Kevin M. Kruse and Thomas J. Sugrue, eds., *The New Suburban History*, Historical Studies of Urban America (Chicago: University of Chicago Press, 2006).

172. Argun Saatcioglu and John L. Rury, "Education and the Changing Metropolitan Organization of Inequality: A Multilevel Analysis of Secondary Attainment in the United States, 1940–1980," *Historical Methods* 45, no. 1 (2012): 21–40.

173. Isabel Wilkerson, *The Warmth of Other Suns: The Epic Story of America's Great Migration* (New York: Vintage Books, 2011), loc. 271–73 of 11057, Kindle.

174. Wilkerson, loc. 274.

175. Wilkerson, loc. 274–76.

176. Rury and Saatcioglu, "Suburban Advantage," 307–42.

177. Lareau and Goyette, *Choosing Homes, Choosing Schools*; Richard R. W. Brooks and Carol M. Rose, *Saving the Neighborhood: Racially Restrictive Covenants, Law, and Social Norms* (Cambridge, MA: Harvard University Press, 2013).

178. Quoted in Jackson, *Crabgrass Frontier*, loc. 4792–93.

179. David Ment, "Patterns of Public School Segregation, 1900–1940: A Comparative Study of New York City, New Rochelle, and New Haven," in *Schools in Cities: Consensus and Conflict in American Educational History*, ed. Ronald K. Goodenow and Diane Ravitch (New York: Holmes & Meier, 1983), 72.

180. According to the Chicago Real Estate Board in 1950, mixing neighbors could violate their written code of ethics: "A realtor should never be instrumental in introducing into a neighborhood . . . members of any race or nationality or any individual whose presence would be clearly detrimental to property values in that neighborhood." James Alan McPherson, "'In My Father's House There Are Many Mansions—and I'm Going to Get Me Some of Them, Too,'" *Atlantic Monthly*, April 1972, 52–53. In 1950, the words "race" and "nationality" were dropped from this statement in the code.

181. McPherson, 51. These contract sales likely constituted the vast majority of sales to black families, as the black population of northern cities like Chicago spiked, jumping from 278,000 in 1940 to 813,000 in 1960. The opportunity for contract sellers owing to blacks' restricted access to credit and housing markets was noted at the time. Beryl Satter, *Family Properties: Race, Real Estate, and the Exploitation of Black Urban America* (New York: Henry Holt, 2010), 5.

182. Satter, *Family Properties*, 5.

183. Satter, 5. Her (Satter's) father's research "estimated that 85 percent of the properties purchased by blacks were sold on contract" (4).

184. Satter, 5.

185. Among many sources, see Thomas J. Sugrue, *The Origins of the Urban Crisis: Race and Inequality in Postwar Detroit: With a New Preface by the Author* (Princeton, NJ: Princeton University Press, 2005).

186. Along Satter's general line of argument, see Davison M. Douglas, *Jim Crow Moves North: The Battle over Northern School Segregation, 1865–1954.* (Cambridge: Cambridge University Press, 2005); Richard Kluger, *Simple Justice: The History of Brown v. Board of Education and Black America's Struggle for Equality* (New York: Vintage Books, 1977); and James T. Patterson, *Brown v. Board of Education: A Civil Rights Milestone and Its Troubled Legacy,* (Oxford: Oxford University Press, 2001)

187. Ansley T. Erickson, "The Rhetoric of Choice: Segregation, Desegregation, and Charter Schools," *Dissent*, Fall 2011, 42.

188. Erickson, 42-43; Erickson in Michael B. Katz and Mike Rose, *Public Education under Siege* (Philadelphia: University of Pennsylvania Press, 2013); Karen Benjamin, "Suburbanizing Jim Crow: The Impact of School Policy on Residential Segregation in Raleigh," *Journal of Urban History* 38, no. 2 (2012): 225; and Andrew R. Highsmith and Ansley T. Erickson, "Segregation as Splitting, Segregation as Joining: Schools, Housing, and the Many Modes of Jim Crow," *American Journal of Education* 121, no. 4 (2015): 563–95. On Flint, see Erickson, *Making the Unequal Metropolis: School Desegregation and Its Limits*, Historical Studies of Urban America (Chicago: University of Chicago Press, 2016).

189. Charles T. Clotfelter, *After* Brown: *The Rise and Retreat of School Desegregation* (Princeton, NJ: Princeton University Press, 2011), loc. 178, Kindle.

190. Patterson, *Brown v. Board of Education*, xvii. Spending in black southern schools had been rising, "reflecting belated efforts by white officials to deflect mounting legal challenges to

segregation"; in 1940, spending in black southern schools was at only 45% of per pupil spending in white southern schools (ibid., xvi–xvii).

191. Patterson, 25.

192. Highsmith and Erickson, "Segregation as Splitting, Segregation as Joining."

193. Patterson, *Brown v. Board of Education*, 5. In Chicago, "some 90 percent of . . . black teachers . . . were placed in schools that were 95 percent or more black. Kluger, *Simple Justice*, 461, quoted in Patterson, *Brown v. Board of Education*, 5.

194. Highsmith and Erickson, "Segregation as Splitting, Segregation as Joining," 585.

195. Brown v Board of Education of Topeka, 347 U.S. 483 (1954).

196. Clive Webb, ed., *Massive Resistance: Southern Opposition to the Second Reconstruction* (New York: Oxford University Press, 2005), loc. 297 of 3663, Kindle.

197. Clotfelter, *After Brown*, 22, On southern reactions, see Gareth D. Pahowka, "Voices of Moderation: Southern Whites Respond to *Brown v. Board of Education*," *Gettysburg Historical Journal* 5, no. 1 (2006): 44–66; James E. Ryan, *Five Miles Away, a World Apart: One City, Two Schools, and the Story of Educational Opportunity in Modern America* (Oxford: Oxford University Press, 2010), 35–36; and Street Law and the Supreme Court Historical Society, "Immediate Reaction to the Decision: Comparing Regional Media Coverage," *Landmark Cases of the U.S. Supreme Court*, accessed July 24, 2018, http://landmarkcases.org/en/Page/507/Immediate _Reaction_to_the_Decision_Comparing_Regional_Media_Coverage. Clotfelter appears to characterize the southern reaction more stridently than other commentators, or at least not to distinguish as deliberately the Deep South versus other areas.

198. In Alabama, black per capita spending went from 33% to 80% of white spending; in Mississippi, it reached just 30%, though up from 17% in 1940. Clotfelter, *After* Brown, table 1.1.

199. Jim Carl, *Freedom of Choice: Vouchers in American Education*, Praeger Series on American Political Culture (Santa Barbara, CA: Praeger, 2011), 3, chap. 2.

200. Carl, 3.

201. Carl, 48–49.

202. Quoted in Patterson, *Brown v. Board of Education*, 101.

203. Of eleven southern states, only Virginia created a state-level Pupil Placement Board. James Ryan notes in his very useful history that Virginia's Pupil Placement Board discarded the "deeply rooted tradition" of "local control over public schools." "Local control was a fine tradition, it appeared, as long as localities exercised that control to resist rather than promote integration." Ryan, *Five Miles Away*, 41.

204. Criteria included "available room and teaching capacity, available transportation, adequacy of a student's scholastic aptitude and preparation, psychological qualifications of the pupil for the type of teaching and associations involved, effect of the admission of the pupil on the academic progress of others, possibility of breaches of peace or ill will or economic retaliation with the community, home environment of the pupil, morals, conduct, health and personal conduct of the pupil." Reed Sarratt, *The Ordeal of Desegregation: The First Decade* (New York: Harper & Row, 1966), 32.

205. Ryan, *Five Miles Away*, 48–51.

206. Sarratt, *The Ordeal of Desegregation*, 222–30.

207. Ryan, *Five Miles Away*, 47–51.

208. Patterson, *Brown v. Board of Education*, chap. 5.

209. Federal Judicial Center, "Bush v. Orleans Parish School Board and the Desegregation of New Orleans Schools, Historical Documents," accessed July 26, 2018, http://199.107.17.13/history /home.nsf/page/tu_bush_doc_6.html; the document's source is US Congress, *Congressional Record*, 84th Cong., 2d sess., 1956, 102, pt. 4: 4515–16.

210. Robert F. Kennedy, remarks at the Kentucky Centennial Celebration of the Emancipation Proclamation, March 18, 1963; see also Kristen Green, *Something Must Be Done about Prince Edward County: A Family, a Virginia Town, a Civil Rights Battle* (New York: Harper, 2015).

211. Among many sources on Little Rock, see Patterson, *Brown v. Board of Education*, 109–112; and Sondra Hercher Gordy, *Finding the Lost Year: What Happened When Little Rock Closed Its Public Schools* (Fayetteville: University of Arkansas Press, 2009).

212. As James Ryan argues, the real winners were the southern, metropolitan area white parents, who brought no overbearing or particular ideology to the table. They sought simply to protect their interests, and their ability to choose schooling chief among them. Neither massive resistance nor massive desegregation advanced those interests. Desegregation was less threatening to their interests than shuttering schools, so they chose the former over the latter. Massive integration was more threatening than token integration, so they chose the latter over the former. They won both times, in legislative arenas and in the courts. Ryan, *Five Miles Away,* 61.

213. Ryan, 42–51.

214. Patterson, *Brown v. Board of Education*, 113. Even within the more moderate border states, 45% of black students still attended all-black schools in 1964. In Los Angeles in 1963, nearly no whites attended Jordan High in Watts, and nearly no blacks attended South Gate High—a mile away. Patterson, *Brown v. Board of Education*, 113. While interracial exposure in schools has risen, "in the late 1960s, 76.6 percent of black children attended majority black schools. In 2010, 74.1 percent of black children attended majority nonwhite schools." A. Austin, *The Unfinished March: An Overview* (Washington, DC: Economic Policy Institute, 2013), 3.

215. In terms of racial integration, James Ryan aptly claims that "desegregation was like an unreliable car: it took forever to warm up, ran well for a brief period, and then sputtered and eventually died." Ryan, *Five Miles Away*, 59.

216. Patterson, *Brown v. Board of Education*, 162–63.

217. Gary Orfield, "The 1964 Civil Rights Act and American Education," in *Legacies of the 1964 Civil Rights Act*, ed. Bernard Grofman, Race, Ethnicity, and Politics (Charlottesville: University Press of Virginia, 2000), 89–128.

218. The plaintiffs in *Green*—rural black students bused across the county to maintain segregated schools—had been given the option under a recently adopted "freedom of choice" plan to attend any school in the district. Though residential patterns were not highly segregated, no whites chose to attend all-black Watkins on the west side of rural New Kent County, Virginia, and few blacks chose to attend largely white New Kent on the east side. The court found that taking down the legal fence of segregation was insufficient, and that *Brown II* required the school board to "come forward with a plan that promises realistically to work, and promises realistically to work *now*." Green v. County School Board of New Kent County, 391 U.S. 430 (1968), accessed July 27, 2018, https://supreme.justia.com/cases/federal/us/391/430/#tab-opinion-1947387. In recognition of the *Green* decision, Georgia Governor Lester Maddox ordered all state flags be flown at half-staff. In a span of four years, all three branches of the federal government had stepped in actively to support school integration efforts—a convergence that would last only seven months, however. Once Nixon assumed office in January 1969, the executive branch backed off its support for school integration, HEW ended its fund cutoff power, the Justice Department shifted to arguing for less desegregation, and Nixon's appointments over time to the Supreme Court assured a limit to court activism. Nonetheless, from the mid-1960s, federal courts asserted their authority in pursuit of less glacial integration approaches. Three years later, in a pivotal case, the *Swann* decision initiated the first court-ordered desegregation busing in Charlotte-Mecklenburg, North Carolina. Court-mandated desegregation busing spread quickly across the South after

the decision, and its opposition figured prominently in Nixon's 1972 reelection. The Supreme Court's *Keyes* decision the following year extended the *Swann* decision, mandating integration in northern cities as well, including via busing. For a cogent presentation of the 1964–73 legal and policy history, see Ryan, *Five Miles Away*, chap. 1–2.

219. Worthy of greater study, a handful of cities have supported urban students commuting from urban centers to suburban districts—for example, Boston/Springfield, Milwaukee, and St. Louis; see James E. Ryan and Michael Heise, "The Political Economy of School Choice," *Yale Law Journal* 111 (April 26, 2002), fn.130, referencing Susan E. Eaton, *The Other Boston Busing Story: What's Won and Lost across the Boundary Line* (New Haven, CT: Yale University Press, 2001); Richard D. Kahlenberg, *All Together Now: Creating Middle-Class Schools Through Public School Choice*, Brookings Institution Press, 2001; Joseph P. Viteritti, Choosing Equality, Brookings Institution Press, 1999; and Amy Stuart Wells and Robert L. Crain, *Stepping Over the Color Line: African-American Students in White Suburban Schools* (New Haven, CT: Yale University Press, 1997). More recent efforts by districts pursuing socioeconomic integration, including via "controlled choice" variations and magnets, are profiled in Richard D. Kahlenberg, "School Integration in Practice: Lessons from Nine Districts," Century Foundation, October 14, 2016, https://tcf.org/content/report/school-integration-practice-lessons-nine-districts/.

220. The fact that "busing" became shorthand for an approach to desegregation—though busing itself had existed and grown for decades, often in support of segregated schooling—receives valuable historical treatment in Matthew F. Delmont, *Why Busing Failed: Conservative Politics, TV News, and the Backlash to Integration*, American Crossroads (Oakland: University of California Press, 2016).

221. Jack Schneider, "Escape from Los Angeles: White Flight from Los Angeles and Its Schools, 1960–1980," *Journal of Urban History* 34, no. 6 (2008): 995–1012. The 1965 Watts riots engulfed the city, echoing other urban unrest across the country.

222. From Los Angeles, the exodus of white families with children came first, before any flattening or decline in the overall white population in the city. Schneider, "Escape from Los Angeles," 995–1012. Denver exploded even before the 1973 *Keyes* decision came down ordering integration; some twenty-three school buses were bombed, as was the judge's home. A local journalist observed at an anniversary event: "In 1968, there were 68,000 white families in Denver schools. In 1995, another ruling ended court-ordered busing. And by then, there were just 18,000 white families in the district. And now in Denver's schools, minorities are mostly congregated in the worst schools." Jenny Brundin, "40 Years since Keyes," Colorado Public Radio, February 4, 2013, http://www.cpr.org/news/story/40-years-keyes. Private school enrollment between 1970 and 1980 rises significantly in percentage terms in the South, and slightly in the West, though not in other regions; the Northeast and Midwest saw a decline in the percentage in private schools from 1960 forward as rates in each region begin to converge. Highest rates still apply to northeast, midwest, and border states. See table 4.1 in Clotfelter, *After* Brown, 104.

223. Ryan, *Five Miles Away*, 106.

224. US Commission on Civil Rights, *School Desegregation in Tacoma, Washington: A Staff Report of the US Commission on Civil Rights* (Washington, DC: US Commission on Civil Rights, 1979). While Tacoma's is often referred to as the first magnet school in the United States, there certainly appear to have been a good number of magnet programs years earlier (e.g., SPARC aerospace academy in 1962 or, in 1967, the Parkway "school without walls" program, both in Philadelphia).

225. A later study would characterize magnet schools by four criteria: "1. A distinctive school curriculum based on a special theme or method of instruction 2. A unique district role and pur-

pose for voluntary desegregation 3. Voluntary choice of the school by student and parent 4. Open access to school enrollment beyond a regular attendance zone." *Final Report of a National Study for US Department of Education Office of Planning, Budget and Evaluation Contract*, no. 300-81-0420. Today, the Department of Education defines a magnet school as "a public elementary school, public secondary school, public elementary education center, or public secondary education center that offers a special curriculum capable of attracting substantial numbers of students of different racial backgrounds." US Department of Education, "Magnet Schools Assistance: Program Description," accessed July 1, 2015, http://www2.ed.gov/programs/magnet/index.html. US Senator Moynihan called Boston Latin, founded in 1635, "the first form of 'Magnet school,'" (as do others—e.g., Nolan Estes, below) and noted other "renowned" magnets (here, selective admissions high schools, apparently) including Lowell (San Francisco), Central (Philadelphia), Late Tech (Chicago), and several in New York City. "Testimony of Daniel Patrick Moynihan on S. 38, the Magnet School Expansion Act of 1987 before the Subcommittee on Education," *Committee on Labor and Human Resources* (Washington, DC: United States Senate, 1987). Others include in the magnet concept early specialized theme schools that were largely technical, dating to the early twentieth century: "Programs tended to be geared to the student who would end his education with a high school graduation; and skill acquisition, mainly in the trades, was the goal of students who elected to attend such programs." Nolan Estes, Daniel U. Levine, and Donald R. Waldrip, eds., *Magnet Schools: Recent Developments and Perspectives* (Austin, TX: Morgan Printing and Publishing., 1990), vii–viii.

226. Irwin Krigsman and Leo Winchell, *Exemplary Magnet Program: Title III, ESEA: Final Report, 1969–72, Tacoma School District* (Olympia, WA: Washington Office of the State Superintendent of Public Instruction, 1972), 3–4.

227. US Commission on Civil Rights, *School Desegregation in Tacoma*, 8.

228. US Commission on Civil Rights, *School Desegregation in Tacoma*, 8–10. McCarver was a junior high school prior to its conversion to a magnet elementary school.

229. A citizens' committee, established by the school board, proposed an expansion to completely open district enrollment for fall 1976; it was rejected by the school board in the summer of 1967, claiming too little time for implementation by the start of the school year. US Commission on Civil Rights, *School Desegregation in Tacoma*.

230. Irwin Krigsman and Leo Winchell, *Exemplary Magnet Program: Title III, ESEA: Final Report, 1969–72, Tacoma School District* (Olympia, WA: Washington Office of the State Superintendent of Public Instruction, 1972), 1.

231. US Commission on Civil Rights, *School Desegregation in Tacoma*, 10.

232. Alex Sergienko, "In the Beginning: How a Small City in the Pacific Northwest Invented Magnet Schools," *Education Next*, Spring 2005, 47. As to the specific notion of a magnet school, Sergienko claimed, "We stumbled on an article about someone in Pittsburgh advocating the establishment of a school that would do something so well that students would want to enroll. They called it a 'magnet school.'" Sergienko later became superintendent of Tacoma Public Schools (1974–79), a post from which he was removed a year before his contract ended; two teacher strikes occurred during his tenure. He then served as superintendent of Peters Township near Pittsburgh, leaving there "without explanation" after four years. In 1970, Tacoma became the first school district to desegregate without a court order. The district later received the NAACP's Lamplighter Award. Sergienko had succeeded Dr. Angelo Giaudrone, serving from 1965 to 1974; Giaudrone was superintendent when the first magnet was formed. Giaudrone was also critical in establishing Tacoma Community College in 1965, then under the district's administration; an arts building was named after him in 1968. He had served in Ellensburg, Washington, previously as

superintendent, and served for seventeen years in Tacoma. Giaudrone Middle School was named in his honor. "Angelo Giaudrone Discusses Retirement," *Ellensburg Daily Record*, August 21, 1973, https://news.google.com/newspapers?id=PHVUAAAAIBAJ&sjid=Ao8DAAAAIBAJ&pg=6942%2C2564734.

233. Sergienko, "In the Beginning," 47; and US Commission on Civil Rights, *School Desegregation in Tacoma*.

234. Krigsman and Winchell, *Exemplary Magnet Program*. According to a staff report of the US Civil Rights Commission: "The success of the concept was apparent after the 2-year operation of McCarver's exemplary magnet program because many black students opted for schools in outlying areas while more and more white students chose McCarver. Black enrollment at McCarver declined from more than 86 percent in 1967 to just over 53 percent by October 1969." US Commission on Civil Rights, *School Desegregation in Tacoma*, 17.

235. On Chicago's early history with magnets, see Nicholas Kryczka, "From Racial Liberalism to Neoliberalism: Class, Choice, and Magnet Schools in Post-Civil Rights Chicago," presented at the American Educational Research Association, New York City, April 16, 2018.

236. Rolf K. Blank, Robert A. Dentler, D. Catherine Baltzell, Kent Chabotar, *Survey of Magnet Schools: Analyzing a Model for Quality Integrated Education* (Washington, DC: Abt Associates for the Office of Planning, Budget, and Evaluation, Department of Education, 1983), 13–15.

237. Lauri Steel and Roger Levine, *Educational Innovations in Multiracial Contexts: The Growth of Magnet Schools in American Education* (Palo Alto, CA: American Institutes for Research in the Behavioral Sciences for the Office of the Under Secretary, US Department of Education, 1994), 106.

238. Blank et al., *Survey of Magnet Schools*, 221.

239. Martha Minow, "Confronting the Seduction of Choice: Law, Education, and American Pluralism," *Yale Law Journal* 120 (2011): 823–26. See also the discussion in Sigal R. Ben-Porath, *Tough Choices: Structured Paternalism and the Landscape of Choice*, Princeton, NJ: Princeton University Press, 2010.

240. US Senate Committee on Labor and Human Resources, "Testimony of Daniel Patrick Moynihan on S. 38, the Magnet School Expansion Act of 1987 before the Subcommittee on Education," (Washington, DC: United States Senate, 1987), 8; and Green v. County School Board of New Kent County, 391 U.S. 430 (1968).

241. US Senate Committee on Labor and Human Resources "Testimony of Daniel Patrick Moynihan," 8.

242. US Senate Committee on Labor and Human Resources, "Testimony of Daniel Patrick Moynihan," 9. Nixon proposed federal aid to address the "emergency" of desegregation efforts; the Emergency School Aid Act was passed in 1972; funding was folded into block grants in 1981; magnets have received support under the Magnet Schools Assistance Program (MSAP) since 1985, with largely flat and recently declining support.

243. Grace Chen quoted in Minow, "Confronting the Seduction of Choice," 826.

244. Scott Gelber, "'The Crux and the Magic': The Political History of Boston Magnet Schools, 1968–1989," *Equity & Excellence in Education* 41, no. 4 (2008): 456.

245. Gelber, "'The Crux and the Magic,'" 456. Regular city schools could deviate as much as 25% from the overall profile. The overall mix was shifting rapidly; white K–12 enrollment dropped 17% between 1974 and 1976 (ibid.).

246. Gelber, "'The Crux and the Magic,'" 456. Gelber's study examines the "conflicting parental perceptions in Boston" and "the manner in which perceptions of magnet programs were affected by the evolution of parental attitudes over the course of several decades" (ibid., 454). He

notes the clear tension: if the magnets are seen as elite, they symbolize the inequity that busing meant to counter; if they do not appear superior, they could not promote voluntary integration. Per Gelber and other accounts, the limited magnet approach failed to mollify the virulent anti-busing sentiment and activity in Boston, starting with ROAR's disruption of district nine's Citywide Coordinating Council's first community hearing. At the height of their prominence, Boston magnets enrolled a third of all city students. Other magnets arose from court orders in Los Angeles, Houston, Louisville, Dallas, Milwaukee, and San Diego; and from threatened court orders in Cincinnati, Bridgeport (CT), Seattle, and Chicago. Montclair (NJ), St. Paul, and Cambridge (MA) developed voluntary magnets, the latter within a wider "controlled choice" scheme meant to avoid the fate of neighboring Boston. Charles B. McMillan, *Magnet Schools: An Approach to Voluntary Desegregation*, Fastback vol. 141 (Bloomington, IN: Phi Delta Kappa Educational Foundation, 1980).

247. Claire Smrekar and Ellen B. Goldring, *School Choice in Urban America: Magnet Schools and the Pursuit of Equity*, Critical Issues in Educational Leadership Series, New York: Teachers College Press, 1999: 7; for further background on magnets, see Rolf K. Blank, Roger E. Levine, and Lauri Steel, "After 15 Years: Magnet Schools in Urban Education," in *Who Chooses? Who Loses?*, ed. Bruce Fuller and Richard F. Elmore with Gary Orfield (New York: Teachers College Press, 1996); Corrine M. Yu and William L. Taylor, *Difficult Choices: Do Magnet Schools Serve Children in Need?*, Citizens Commission on Civil Rights, Washington, DC: Citizens Commission on Civil Rights, Washington, DC.; Vanderbilt Univ., Nashville.; Inst. for Public Policy Studies; Spencer Foundation, Chicago; Pew Charitable Trusts, Philadelphia, 1997.

248. Christine H. Rossell and David J. Armor. "The Effectiveness of School Desegregation Plans, 1968-1991," *American Politics Research* 24, no. 3 (1996): 267-302.

249. Minow, "Confronting the Seduction of Choice," 827.

250. Erica Frankenberg and Genevieve Siegel-Hawley. *Rethinking Magnet Schools in a Changing Landscape: A Report to Magnet Schools of America* (Civil Rights Project: University of California at Los Angeles, 2008), 12.

251. Erica Frankenberg and Genevieve Siegel-Hawley, "Choosing Diversity: School Choice and Racial Integration in the Age of Obama," *Stanford Journal of Civil Rights and Civil Liberties* 6 (2010): 244; Sarah Reckhow and Jeffrey W. Snyder, "The Expanding Role of Philanthropy in Education Politics," *Educational Researcher* 43, no. 4 (2014): 186-95; and Reckhow, *Follow the Money: How Foundation Dollars Change Public School Politics*, Oxford Studies in Postwar American Political Development (Oxford: Oxford University Press, 2013).

252. John E. Coons, William H. Clune, and Stephen D. Sugarman, "Educational Opportunity: A Workable Constitutional Test for State Financial Structures." *California Law Review* 57, no. 2 (1969): 307.

253. Coons, Clune, and Sugarman, "Educational Opportunity," 332, 319. For further development of their thought, see John E. Coons, William H. Clune, and Stephen D. Sugarman, *Private Wealth and Public Education* (Cambridge, MA: Belknap Press of Harvard University Press, 1970); and Sugarman, "Jack Coons: School Choice Champion," *Journal of School Choice*, 4 (2010): 191-94.

254. James E. Ryan and Michael Heise, "The Political Economy of School Choice," *Yale Law Journal* 111 (April 26, 2002): 2062.

255. Charles Cobb, "Prospectus for a Summer Freedom School Program in Mississippi," Student Nonviolent Coordinating Committee, December 1963, available at Education and Democracy, http://www.educationanddemocracy.org/FSCfiles/B_05_ProspForFSchools.htm. For a history of Freedom Schools, see Daniel Perlstein, "Teaching Freedom: SNCC and the Creation

of the Mississippi Freedom Schools," *History of Education Quarterly* 30, no. 3 (Fall 1990): 297; Doug McAdam, *Freedom Summer* (New York: Oxford University Press, 1988); Staughton Lynd, "The Freedom Schools, An Informal History," *Solidarity*, January/February 2004, https://www .solidarity-us.org/node/477; "Burgland High School Walkout," McComb Legacies, accessed February 27, 2017, http://mccomblegacies.org/burglund-high-school-walkout/; and Jon N. Hale, *The Freedom Schools: Student Activists in the Mississippi Civil Rights Movement* (New York: Columbia University Press, 2016).

256. "Structurally, the Mississippi Summer Project is organized and run by COFO, the Council of Federated Organizations, a coalition of SNCC, CORE, NAACP, and SCLC, with SNCC's Bob Moses as Director and CORE's Dave Dennis as second in command." Civil Rights Movement Veterans, "Organizational Structure of Freedom Summer, 1964," accessed February 27, 2017, http://www.crmvet.org/tim/fs64orgs.htm.

257. Cobb, "Prospectus for a Summer Freedom School Program."

258. Quoted in Hale, *The Freedom Schools*, 172–73. For one back story to recent desegregation litigation and African American frustration with desegregation's impacts on their schools, see Sarah Garland, *Divided We Fail: The Story of an African American Community That Ended the Era of School Desegregation* (Boston: Beacon Press, 2013).

259. Howard Zinn, "Schools in Context: The Mississippi Idea," *Nation* 199, no. 16 (1964): 374–75.

260. Quote from Zinn, 375. Zinn continued: "Would it be possible to declare boldly that the aim of the schools is to find solutions for poverty, for injustice, for race and national hatred, and to turn all educational efforts into a national striving for those solutions?"; for further context, see also Charles Cobb, "SNCC: The Importance of Its Work, the Value of Its Legacy," SNCC Legacy Project, accessed July 25, 2018, http://www.sncclegacyproject.org/about/legacy; James Forman Jr., "The Secret History of School Choice: How Progressives Got There First." *Georgetown Law Journal* 93, no. 4 (2005): 1295–30; Leslie K. Etienne, "A Historical Narrative of the Student Nonviolent Coordinating Committee's Freedom Schools and their Legacy for Contemporary Youth Leadership Development Programming" (PhD diss., Antioch University, 2012), http:// aura.antioch.edu/etds/6. Some claimed too many free schools catered to those able and willing to escape engagement with the day's social challenges; see, for example, Kozol, *Free Schools*.

261. Lizabeth Cohen, *A Consumers' Republic: The Politics of Mass Consumption in Postwar America*, 1st ed. (New York: Knopf/Random House, 2003); and Victor Alexis Pestoff, Taco Brandsen, and Bram Verschuere, *New Public Governance, the Third Sector and Co-Production*, Routledge Critical Studies in Public Management (New York: Routledge, 2012).

262. See, for example, Gary Orfield and John T. Yun, "Resegregation in American Schools" (Cambridge, MA: The Civil Rights Project, Harvard University, 1999); Genevieve Siegel-Hawley and Erica Frankenberg, "Magnet School Student Outcomes: What the Research Says," in *Research Briefs* (The National Coalition on School Diversity, 2011); Erica Frankenberg and Genevieve Siegel-Hawley, "The Forgotten Choice? Rethinking Magnet Schools in a Changing Landscape" (Civil Rights Project, University of California Los Angeles, 2008); Frankenberg and Siegel-Hawley, "Choosing Diversity"; and Claire Smrekar and Robert L. Crowson, "Localism Rediscovered: Toward New Political Understandings in School District Governance," *Peabody Journal of Education* 90, no. 1 (2015): 1–8.

263. Recent "community school" efforts being largely distinct from earlier community control movements; on community-centered education's history, see Michael C. Johanek and John L. Puckett, *Leonard Covello and the Making of Benjamin Franklin High School: Education as If Citizenship Mattered* (Philadelphia: Temple University Press, 2007). Current efforts emphasize

service to full range of children's and families' needs, an efficiency of service delivery, and a more holistic approach to schooling.

264. The deliberate and sustained development of an alternative public-private infrastructure does distinguish the recent movement of charters.

265. See A. S. Neill, *Summerhill: A Radical Approach to Child Rearing* (New York: Hart, 1960); and Paul Goodman, *Growing Up Absurd: Problems of Youth in the Organized Society* (New York: Vintage Books, 1960). Jonathan Kozol famously critiqued the apolitical free schools in his *Free Schools* (Boston: Houghton Mifflin, 1972).

266. Ron Miller, *Free Schools, Free People: Education and Democracy after the 1960s* (Albany: State University of New York Press, 2002), 121-22.

267. Estimates drawn particularly from Miller, *Free Schools, Free People*, 121-22, and Tate Hausman, "A History of the Free School Movement" (senior honors thesis, Brown University, 1998), 26-28; for further background on the free schools, see Richard Neumann, *Sixties Legacy: A History of the Public Alternative Schools Movement, 1967-2001*, History of Schools and Schooling (New York: P. Lang, 2003); B. Cooper, "The Dissenting Tradition in American Education by James C. Carper and Thomas C. Hunt, New York: Peter Lang, 2007. *American Journal of Education* 114, no. 3 (2008); Lawrence A. Cremin, "The Free School Movement: A Perspective," in *Alternative Schools: Ideologies, Realities, Guidelines*, ed. Terrence E. Deal and Robert R. Nolan (Chicago: Nelson-Hall, 1978), 203-10.

268. For historian Peter Clecak, the era questioned authority broadly: "In the 1960s, authority went on the defensive in nearly every region of American civilization. . . . Gay men and lesbians rejected the authority of straight culture. Women denied the authority of men. Children abandoned parental authority. Blacks and other minorities rejected the authority of whites. . . . Radicals spurned the authority of bourgeois ideas and institutions." Clecak, *America's Quest for the Ideal Self: Dissent and Fulfillment in the 60s and 70s* (New York: Oxford University Press, 1983), 19, quoted in Hausman, "A History of the Free School Movement," 14.

269. Neill, *Summerhill*, 2.

270. Neill, *Summerhill*, 57-58.

271. John Caldwell Holt, *Freedom and Beyond*, Innovators in Education (Portsmouth, NH: Boynton/Cook Publishers, 1995), 223, quoted in Ron Miller, *Free Schools, Free People: Education and Democracy after the 1960s* (Albany: State University of New York Press, 2002), 100. Across a diverse and fragile mix of small free schools, some common elements surfaced in a contemporary study: a willful rejection of the conventional school system; a sharing of the consummate belief that freedom in education can be put into practice; and an active affirmation of self-determination instead of a passive reliance on the public system. Bruce S. Cooper, *Free and Freedom Schools: A National Survey of Alternative Programs* (Washington, DC: President's Commission on School Finance, 1971), 2.

272. In 1971, the Summerhill Society claimed a membership high of eight hundred; Miller, *Free Schools*, 123; general sources used include Hausman, "A History of the Free School Movement"; Miller, *Free Schools*; Graubard, Allen. *Free the Children; Radical Reform and the Free School Movement*. 1st ed. New York: Pantheon Books, 1972; Neumann, *Sixties Legacy*; Malcom Levin, "Understanding the Alternative Schools Movement," *Curriculum Inquiry* 9, no. 4 (1979): 337-49; Herbert R. Kohl, "Closing Time for Open Ed?," *New York Review of Books*, December 13, 1973; and Judith Kafka, "Free Schools, Free People: Education and Democracy after the 1960s/Sixties Legacy: A History of the Public Alternative Schools Movement, 1967-2000," *History of Education Quarterly* 45, no. 1 (2005): 134.

273. For professor Ira Shor, the era promised "great historical change," and yet "the decline of

these Utopian hopes was as breathtaking as their sudden arrival"; the free school movement faded as the rest of the movement faded. Free school participants felt the decline early in the 1970s, when total enrollment probably peaked well under fifteen thousand students. In the conservative restoration of the 1970s and 1980s, career education, back-to-basics, and academic excellence became the new hallmarks. Neumann, *Sixties Legacy*, 197–200. Some legacies remain, of course, such as the Brooklyn Free School and Summerhill itself.

274. Herbert R. Kohl, "Closing Time for Open Ed?," *New York Review of Books*, December 13, 1973, 48. He continued: "The school bureaucracy . . . proved rougher, more resilient, and cleverer than any of us had expected. The adults . . . often acted in selfish, competitive, and destructive ways. . . . We saw the open classroom approach being adopted by many administrators . . . as a new technique for keeping students quiet and occupied, for making school and classrooms slightly more pleasant, without changing the lines of power and authority. . . . [and] the young people interpreted the hands-off attitude of grown-ups as helplessness or rejection." Other Ways began under Kohl and Allan Kaprow (SUNY) in 1968 thanks to a Carnegie grant, and developed into a free school with additional support from a US Office of Education's Experimental Schools Program grant. It then became a public alternative school under a special agreement with the teachers' union—an unusual arrangement among free schools, which generally remained independent at that time, running off grants and nominal tuition. Neumann, *Sixties Legacy*, 87.

275. George Dennison, George Dennison, Paul Goodman, Nat Hentoff, John Holt, and Jonathan Kozol, et al. "New Nation Seed Fund," *New York Review of Books*, February 11, 1971, quoted in Miller, *Free Schools, Free People*, 125.

276. Kozol, *Free Schools*, 13, 8; see also chap. 2. Indeed, a 1971 study found that 80% of free school students were white; additionally, Black and Hispanic students tended to be concentrated in a few schools. Over 80% of the schools charged tuition higher than $2,500 a year (current dollars), putting the schools out of reach of most poor families. (Cooper cites $425 annually, which we convert using the inflation calculator at http://www.saving.org/inflation/.) Further, combining Ned O'Gorman's Storefront School in East Harlem, New York City, or the struggle for community control in Ocean Hill–Brownsville in Brooklyn, within the same movement as freethinking learning refuges in the western hills of Massachusetts seems a stretch; see Michael C. Johanek and John L. Puckett, *Leonard Covello and the Making of Benjamin Franklin High School: Education as If Citizenship Mattered* (Philadelphia: Temple University Press, 2007), 345–46n66.

277. Kozol was hyperbolic in his critique: "An isolated upper-class rural Free School for the children for the white and rich within a land like the Unites States and in a time of torment such as 1972, is a great deal too much like a sandbox for the children of the SS Guards at Auschwitz. . . . At best, . . . these schools are obviating pain and etherizing evil; at worst, they constitute a registered escape-valve for political rebellion." Kozol, *Free Schools*, 11–12. In the spring of 1972, several hundred free schoolers gathered in New Orleans, where the movement's splits were evident. Editor Bill Harwood of the *New Schools Exchange Newsletter* observed that "the romantic folks, characterized by the California contingent, were at odds with the folks who were working in urban areas with poor kids and concentrating on survival skills." Beyond this split, though, was a shared contempt for "the folks . . . working within the established system." But the latter would soon overwhelm the faded free and freedom school movements. Ron Miller, *Free Schools, Free People*, 123–24. The historical accounts to date generally do not take into account the resistance from those accepting the traditional culture that many free schools were pushing against. For school reform from this perspective (though not regarding free schools), see Adam Laats, *The Other School Reformers: Conservative Activism in American Education* (Cambridge, MA: Harvard University Press, 2015).

278. Forman, "Secret History of School Choice," 1303. Lawrence did not wish to "do away with public schools and establish a privately run system for the poor" (ibid.).

279. If we consider vocational, evening, and other variations from any era's standard day schools—that is, schooling meant to address those for whom the dominant mode was not working—then alternative schools have existed for hundreds of years. Free evening schools operated in the early 1800s in the United States; see, for example, Arthur J. Jones, *The Continuation School in the United States* (Washington, DC: Department of Interior, Bureau of Education, 1907). Yet the more recent wave corresponded to the rise of the other alternatives to the public system described above—free schools, freedom schools, magnets, and so on—and grew considerably from the 1970s forward.

280. Thomas E. Wolf, Michael Walker, and Robert A. Mackin, *Summary of the NASP Survey, 1974* (Amherst: University of Massachusetts, 1975), quoted in Deal and Nolan, *Alternative Schools,* 5.

281. Richard Neumann, *Sixties Legacy: A History of the Public Alternative Schools Movement, 1967–2001,* History of Schools and Schooling (New York: P. Lang, 2003), 107.

282. Sally H. Wertheim, *Alternative Programs in Public Secondary Schools in Greater Cleveland: A Descriptive Study* (Cleveland, OH: Martha Holden Jennings Foundation, 1974), 5; original italics.

283. Wertheim, 5.

284. As word spread, other sites inspired by Parkway emerged, including Metro in Chicago, the School without Walls in DC, the Newport Plan in California, the Gateway High School in New Orleans, and others.

285. Wertheim, "Alternative Programs," 7. Students at Brown School could also take courses at other area schools and universities.

286. Neumann, *Sixties Legacy,* 110. John Adams High in Portland adopted a "problem-solving approach to learning," spending half the day exploring "social problems such as racial tensions, pollution, crime, unemployment, welfare, and student unrest" (ibid.).

287. Wertheim, *Alternative Programs,* 4–11.

288. Seymour Fliegel and James MacGuire, *Miracle in East Harlem: The Fight for Choice in Public Education,* 1st ed. (New York: Times Books, 1993).

289. Wertheim, *Alternative Programs,* 4–11. On regional alternatives, see also Neumann, *Sixties Legacy,* chap. 4; Daniel Linden Duke, *The Retransformation of the School: The Emergence of Contemporary Alternative Schools in the United States* (Chicago: Nelson-Hall, 1978); and Deal and Nolan, *Alternative Schools.* Regional examples included Shanti School in central Connecticut, and the Alternatives Project in Pennsylvania. In the latter, two alternative high schools served six area systems; each participating district contributed either $10,000 or one staff member in return for each group of eighteen students that they sent.

290. See Charles E. Silberman, *Crisis in the Classroom: The Remaking of American Education,* 1st ed. (New York: Random House, 1970).

291. Silberman, 11.

292. Silberman, 11.

293. Parents surveyed indicated that the lack of good options also motivated their choice of alternative schools, at least in the Parkway Program. Joan Wofford and Joanne Ross, *Philadelphia's Parkway Program: An Evaluation,* (Newtown, MA: Organization for Social and Technical Innovation; sponsored by the Philadelphia School District, 1973), 8–12.

294. Quoted in Deal and Nolan, *Alternative Schools,* 337.

295. Sears and Marshall quoted in Neumann, *Sixties Legacy,* 122.

296. Neumann, *Sixties Legacy*, 127–28; see also Duke, *Retransformation of the School*, esp. chap. 6.

297. Mario Fantini, "Alternative Educational Programs: Promise or Problems?," *Educational Leadership*, November 1974, 84. For other work by Fantini, see "Options for Students, Parents, and Teachers: Public Schools of Choice," *Phi Delta Kappan* 52, no. 9 (1971): 541–43; Fantini, "Alternatives within Public Schools," *Phi Delta Kappan* 54, no. 7 (1973): 444–48; and Fantini, "Humanizing the Humanism Movement," *Phi Delta Kappan* 55, no. 6 (1974): 400–402.

298. Fantini, "Alternatives within Public Schools," 444.

299. Laats, *The Other School Reformers*, loc. 5333.

300. Laats, loc. 5334, 5335–38. This is Laats's summary of their argument.

301. Fantini, "Alternatives within Public Schools," 444.

302. Fantini, 444. By 2014, a study of state definitions of alternative education found that "alternative education serves primarily students with behavioral problems." The report notes that "The lack of a commonly accepted definition of "alternative education" indicates the fluidity of related policies and legislation, the diversity of contexts and settings, and the various groups of at-risk youth who may benefit from alternative education options." L. Y. Aron quoted in Allan Porowski, Rosemarie O'Conner, and Jia Lisa Luo, *How Do States Define Alternative Education?* (Washington, DC: US Department of Education, Institute of Education Sciences, National Center for Educational Evaluation and Regional Assistance; Regional Educational Laboratory Mid-Atlantic, 2014).

303. Fantini, "Alternatives within Public Schools," 448.

304. Malcolm Levin, "Understanding the Alternative Schools Movement," *Curriculum Inquiry* 9, no. 4 (1979): 338.

305. Fantini, "Alternative Educational Programs," 87.

306. Fantini, 87.

307. Fantini, 87. Beyond the conservative turn, Donald Erickson at Simon Fraser University noted another perhaps unanticipated implication of the public alternative schools movement, especially on the road to variety. In 1975, as Fantini, reformer Robert Barr (*Alternatives in Education, Phi Delta Kappan*, Bicentennial Publication, 1976, and others were making their case for parental choice of alternative public schools, Erickson noted it as "a startling abandonment of the professional educator's traditional ideology." Observing that medical doctors do not let patients choose their favorite medicines, he concluded that "the alternative schools movement makes only limited educational sense unless educators lack the scientific knowledge they need, or perhaps the unbiased attitudes they need, to diagnose the pedagogical ills of children from varying background and to prescribe appropriate remedies. Alternative schools imply that parents and students can often make better choices intuitively than educators can make on the basis of professional expertise." Indeed, why stop at the walls of the public system? Why not a blended "educational marketplace," a "public-private consortium," physically "a centrally located instructional complex" drawing students from around a city? The center would broker public-private educational services, tapping the unique strengths of both sectors. Erickson argued this only reflected historical precedents, from the pedagogical entrepreneurs of colonial times, or the private ethnic schools, or Catholic parochial schools, or Dewey's lab school, or free and Freedom Schools, and so on. While doubtful that the alternative schools movement would advance such a vision, he did view it as a step toward "the educational flexibility we need." Erickson, "Public School Alternatives: How Sweeping a Reform?," *Religious Education* 70, no. 2 (1975): 164, 170.

308. Albert Shanker, president, American Federation of Teachers, "Speech to the National Press Club," Washington, DC, 1988, 2.

309. Shanker, 2.

310. Shanker, 7; Unlike a doctor seeing a patient for whom the pill does not work, "we don't have the flexibility; we don't adjust. . . . We just assume that we are a God-created institution; that if some individual doesn't respond to us, then something is wrong with that individual. . . . We'll help, but usually by doing more or even less of the same thing that didn't work." Shanker, 7–8.

311. Shanker, 10. See also John Goodlad, *A Place Called School: Prospects for the Future* (New York: McGraw-Hill, 1984); and Goodlad and Pamela Keating, *Access to Knowledge: An Agenda for Our Nation's Schools*, 1st ed. (New York: College Entrance Examination Board, 1990). For more on this "radical and tiny movement," see the National Network for Educational Renewal, http://www.nnerpartnerships.org/, and the Coalition of Essential Schools, http://essentialschools.org/; see also Theodore R. Sizer, *Horace's Hope: What Works for the American High School* (Boston: Houghton Mifflin, 1996); Sizer, *Horace's School: Redesigning the American High School* (Boston: Houghton Mifflin, 1992); Sizer, *The New American High School*, 1st ed. (San Francisco: Jossey-Bass, 2013); Sizer, National Association of Secondary School Principals (US), and National Association of Independent Schools. Commission on Educational Issues, *Horace's Compromise: The Dilemma of the American High School: With a New Preface* (Boston: Houghton Mifflin, 2004); and Theodore R. Sizer and Nancy Faust Sizer, *The Students Are Watching: Schools and the Moral Contract* (Boston: Beacon Press, 1999).

312. Shanker, 11.

313. "Convention Plots New Course—A Charter for Change" (column sponsored by the New York State United Teachers and the American Federal of Teachers), *New York Times*, July 10, 1988, accessed July 26, 2018, http://source.nysut.org/weblink7/PDF/az3xahf1j2neic45lxkv4z45/2/88-07 -10.pdf. Apparently, Joe Loftus, from the Center for Child Welfare Strategy, floated a similar proposal in Chicago in 1988, and a group of teachers in California had proposed running their own schools. See Andy Smarick, *The Urban School System of the Future: Applying the Principles and Lessons of Chartering*, New Frontiers in Education (Lanham, MD.: Rowman & Littlefield Education, 2012); and "Joe Loftus' 1988 Proposal for 'Chartered Schools,'" accessed at Education Evolving, July 6, 2015, http://www.educationevolving.org/pdf/JoeLoftus1988CharterProposal .pdf. Budde wrote his charter concept piece, "Education by Charter," in 1974, and then had it republished via the Northeast Regional Lab and distributes it widely (per Kolderie, Education Evolving timeline). Ray Budde, "Education by Charter," *Phi Delta Kappan*, March 1989, 518–20. Shanker visited Gesamtschule Holweide in Cologne, Germany, a school that still exists, with a long history of teacher teams, Das Team-Kleingruppen-Modell (TKM); (see the school website at http://www.gehw.de/jts/index.php); Max Larkin, "Charter Schools Began in a Surprising Way: With a Union Leader," *Edify*, WBUR, Boston, MA, November 4, 2016; http://www.wbur.org/edify /2016/11/04/charter-school-union-roots.

314. Shanker, "Speech to the National Press Club," 14; Shanker indicated that "I like tests, and I even like standardized tests. I would like to have a standardized reading test where you have to read something that is worthwhile, or write something that is worthwhile. But what we have now is a national scandal in testing. . . . I would love to have standardized tests that we could have confidence in. . . . I am a strong believer in testing. . . . The public has a right to know what the schools are doing and what the schools are not doing. They are not getting that today with the tests that are out there" (ibid., 29).

315. Shanker, 26–27.

316. Shanker, 24. Interestingly, initial reaction from conservatives was tepid, see Richard D. Kahlenberg and Halley Potter, "The Original Charter School Vision," *New York Times*, August 30, 2014; and Kahlenberg and Potter, "Restoring Shanker's Vision for Charter Schools," excerpted

from Richard D. Kahlenberg and Halley Potter, *A Smarter Charter: Finding What Works for Charter Schools and Public Education* (New York: Teachers College Press, 2014).

317. Kristol quoted in Richard D. Kahlenberg, *Tough Liberal: Albert Shanker and the Battles over Schools, Unions, Race, and Democracy* (New York: Columbia University Press, 2007), 312, cited in Kahlenberg and Potter, "Restoring Shanker's Vision for Charter Schools," accessed July 25, 2018, https://www.aft.org/ae/winter2014-2015/kahlenberg_potter.

318. Minnesota passed the Postsecondary Enrollment Options Act in 1985, allowing high school students to enroll in public postsecondary institutions for academic credit that would count toward their high school degree. See Laws of Minnesota for 1985 First Special Session, chapter 12, H.F. no. 3, Office of the Revisor of Statutes, State of Minnesota, accessed July 25, 2018, https://www.revisor.mn.gov/laws/1985/1/12/.

319. Paul E. Peterson, "No, Al Shanker Did Not Invent the Charter School," *Education Next*, July 21, 2010, https://www.educationnext.org/no-al-shanker-did-not-invent-the-charter-school/. Sy Fleigel of New York City's District Four also joined the Itasca Seminar at Gull Lake, Minnesota, that fall.

320. John Rollwagen and Donn McLellan, "Chartered Schools = Choices for Educators + Quality for All Students," Citizens League, November 17, 1988.

321. This seems an underexplored shift, ripe for further historical investigation.

322. Ted Kolderie, "Origins of Chartering Timeline," Education Evolving, September 2010, www.educationevolving.org/system/chartering/history-and-origins-of-chartering; "Getting to Know: Senator Gary K. Hart, Author of the California Charter School Act," *In the News*, May 3, 2011, http://www.ccsa.org/blog/2011/05/getting-to-know-senator-gary-k-hart-author-of -the-california-charter-schools-act.html; Ember Reichgott Junge, *Zero Chance of Passage: The Pioneering Charter School Story* (Edina, MN: Beaver's Pond Press, 2012); and Bruce Fuller, "The Verdict on Charter Schools?," *Atlantic*, July 8, 2015, https://www.theatlantic.com/education /archive/2015/07/the-verdict-on-charter-schools/397820/. Key players included Secretary of Education Richard Riley and his special assistant Jon Schnur; Schnur later served as senior policy advisor on education to Vice President Gore, White House associate director for educational policy under President Clinton, before cofounding New Leaders for New Schools; he also served as senior advisor to President Obama's presidential transition team and to US Secretary of Education Arne Duncan. A Princeton classmate of Wendy Kopp, he is credited as the key architect of Obama's Race to the Top Program.

323. Albert Shanker, "Goals Not Gimmicks," *New York Times*, November 7, 1993, found at http://locals.nysut.org/shanker. See more at Kahlenberg and Potter, "Restoring Shanker's Vision for Charter Schools."

324. Hassel quoted in Kenneth K. Wong and Warren E. Langevin, "Policy Expansion of School Choice in the American States," *Peabody Journal of Education* 82, no. 2–3, 440–72.

325. Wong and Langevin, 465.

326. For the school year 2016/17, charter schools in Arizona, California, Ohio, Florida, Texas, and Michigan represented 56% of the national total, per National Alliance for Public Charter Schools, "Estimated Charter Public School Enrollment, 2016–17," accessed July 26, 2018, http:// www.publiccharters.org/sites/default/files/migrated/wp-content/uploads/2017/01/EER_Report _V5.pdf. Solely for New York City, Harlem represented this concentration pattern within the city: "With 44 charter schools, Harlem housed 75% of Manhattan's 59 total charter schools by 2013, indicating both a steady growth and concentration of charter schools in the community." Terrenda Corisa White, "Culture, Power, & Pedagogy(S) in Market-Driven Times: Embedded Case-Studies of Instructional Approaches across Four Charter Schools in Harlem, NY" (PhD

diss., Columbia University, 2014), 80. "Indeed the NYC Charter School Center (2012) estimated nearly 77% of all charter schools in the city were located in three neighborhoods, including Harlem, Central Brooklyn, and South Bronx" (ibid., 83). In 2013/14, 66% of Harlem charters were managed by CMOs (ibid., 85).

327. National Center for Education Statistics, US Department of Education, "Public Charter School Enrollment," March 2018, http://nces.ed.gov/programs/coe/indicator_cgb.asp.

328. In the spirit of transparency, one of the authors served as a reviewer for RTTT funding, including the first round.

329. Danny Yadron, "How 'Race to the Top' Is Rewriting U.S. Education," McClatchy DC Bureau, August 8, 2010, http://www.mcclatchydc.com/news/politics-government/article24589378 .html#storylink=cpy.

330. Of course, the political left and right tended to oppose NCLB for differing reasons; very broadly, the left voiced more concern about dehumanizing accountability and privatization, while the right resented national standards as impositions of federal control into local affairs.

331. David Labaree, "The Winning Ways of a Losing Strategy: Educationalizing Social Problems in the United States," *Educational Theory* 58, no. 4 (2008): 447–60.

332. While in 1974, roughly a quarter of labor, private and public, was unionized, the sector trends diverge. From 1983 to 2004, as private labor force unionization dropped to 8.2 percent, public unionization rose to 37.1, largely based on an increase in local public labor force unionization, with teacher unions the largest subgroup (then police, fire). See Henry S. Farber, "Union Membership in the United States: The Divergence between the Public and Private Sectors," in *Working Papers, Industrial Relations Section* (Princeton, NJ: Princeton University, 2005), 1–29.

333. Dorothy Shipps, *School Reform, Corporate Style: Chicago, 1880–2000*, Studies in Government and Public Policy. (Lawrence: University Press of Kansas, 2006), chap. 5.

334. Frederick M. Hess and Jeffrey R. Henig, eds., *The New Education Philanthropy: Politics, Policy and Reform* (Cambridge, MA: Harvard Education Press, 2015), 2. For more on the education-industrial complex, see Anthony G. Picciano and Joel Spring, eds., *The Great American Education-Industrial Complex: Ideology, Technology, and Profit* (New York : Routledge, 2013); and Dipti Desai, "Educational Industrial Complex," accessed July 25, 2018, https://greatschoolwars .files.wordpress.com/2015/10/eic-oct_11.pdf. For a different ideological lens on the term, see Victoria M. Young, "The Rising Education-Industrial Complex," Federalist Papers Project, June 4, 2013, http://www.thefederalistpapers.org/current-events/the-rising-education-industrial -complex-2.

335. Hess and Henig argue that, while philanthropy's role is not unprecedented, "the extent, intensity, coordination and directness are markedly different" (*The New Education Philanthropy*, 182); this may amount to the same thing; we think the sustained impact at multiple levels—the who, the what, the how of public schooling from classrooms to policy chambers—of a small and constant set of foundations is so "markedly different" as to be, well, unprecedented.

336. Joanne Barkan, "Got Dough? How Billionaires Rule Our Schools," *Dissent*, Winter 2011, https://www.dissentmagazine.org/article/got-dough-how-billionaires-rule-our-schools, 7; US Department of Education, "Education Secretary Announces Nine Senior Staff Appointments," May 19, 2009, http://www.ed.gov/news/press-releases/education-secretary-announces-nine -senior-staff-appointments; Susan Ohanian, "'Race to the Top' and the Bill Gates Connection," Fairness and Accuracy in Reporting, September 2010, http://fair.org/extra-online-articles/race -to-the-top-and-the-bill-gates-connection/.

337. *New York Times*, April 2, 2009, quoted in Barkan, "Got Dough?"

338. Joanne Weiss, "The Innovation Mismatch: 'Smart Capital' and Education Innovation,"

Harvard Business Review, March 31, 2011; Patricia Burch, *Hidden Markets: The New Education Privatization* (New York: Routledge, 2009). See also Wayne Au and Joseph J. Ferrare, *Mapping Corporate Education Reform: Power and Policy Networks in the Neoliberal State* (New York: Routledge, 2015).

339. Joanne Weiss, "The Innovation Mismatch: 'Smart Capital' and Education Innovation," *Harvard Business Review*, March 31, 2011.

340. Quoted in Burch, *Hidden Markets*, 21.

341. Along the lines of Barkan, "Got Dough?," see Linsey McGoey, *No Such Thing as a Free Gift: The Gates Foundation and the Price of Philanthropy* (London; New York: Verso, 2015); Hess and Henig, *The New Education Philanthropy*; Burch, *Hidden Markets*; Michael Fabricant and Michelle Fine, *Charter Schools and the Corporate Makeover of Public Education: What's at Stake?* (New York: Teachers College, 2012); Samuel E. Abrams, *Education and the Commercial Mindset* (Cambridge, MA: Harvard University Press, 2016); Patrick L. Baude, Marcus Casey, Eric A. Hanushek, and Steven G. Rivkin, *The Evolution of Charter School Quality* (Cambridge, MA: National Bureau of Economic Research, 2014); Helen F. Ladd, Charles T. Clotfelter, and John B. Holbein, "The Growing Segmentation of the Charter School Sector in North Carolina," NBER Working Paper No. 21078, April 2015; Dennis Epple, Richard Romano, and Ron Zimmer, *Charter Schools: A Survey of Research on Their Characteristics and Effectiveness* (Cambridge, MA: National Bureau of Economic Research, 2015); and Atila Abdulkadiroglu, Parag A. Pathak, and Christopher R. Walters, *School Vouchers and Student Achievement: First-Year Evidence from the Louisiana Scholarship Program* (Cambridge, MA: National Bureau of Economic Research, 2015).

342. Andrew Wiese, "'The House I Live In': Race, Class, and African American Suburban Dreams in the Postwar United States," chap. 5 in *The New Suburban History*, ed. Keven M. Kruse and Thomas J. Sugrue, Historical Studies of Urban America (Chicago: University of Chicago Press, 2006), 99–100.

343. Wiese, "'The House I Live In': Race, Class, and African American Suburban Dreams in the Postwar United States," chap. 5 in *The New Suburban History*, ed. Keven M. Kruse and Thomas J. Sugrue, Historical Studies of Urban America (Chicago: University of Chicago Press, 2006), 119.

344. On homeschooling history, see Milton Gaither, *Homeschool: An American History* (New York: Palgrave Macmillan, 2008); and Joseph Murphy, *Homeschooling in America: Capturing and Assessing the Movement* (Thousand Oaks, CA: Corwin Press, 2012).

345. Jim Carl, *Freedom of Choice: Vouchers in American Education*, Praeger Series on American Political Culture (Santa Barbara, CA: Praeger, 2011), 113–15. For the current school, see http://www.bgcsedu.org/BGCS.htm.

346. On how parents choose, see, for example, Gary Miron, *Exploring the School Choice Universe: Evidence and Recommendations*, National Education Policy Center Series (Charlotte, NC: Information Age Publishing, 2012); and Jack Buckley and Mark Schneider, *Charter Schools: Hope or Hype?* (Princeton, NJ: Princeton University Press, 2007), among many others.

347. Over 70% of the students in gifted and talented (G&T) programs in New York City are white or Asian; those groups constitute only 30% of all students there. Allison Roda, "Where Their Children Belong: Parents' Perceptions of the Boundaries Separating 'Gifted' and 'Non-Gifted' Educational Programs" (PhD diss., Columbia University, 2013), 1–2.

348. Roda, 120; see also Roda, *Inequality in Gifted and Talented Programs: Parental Choices About Status, School Opportunity, and Second-Generation Segregation*, Palgrave Studies in Urban Education (New York: Palgrave Macmillan, 2015).

349. Mark R. Warren and Karen L. Mapp, *A Match on Dry Grass: Community Organizing as a Catalyst for School Reform* (New York: Oxford University Press, 2011) There is a growing liter-

ature on community organizing for school reform. Per Warren, strategies include: "demanding greater resources for schools, building meaningful and powerful forms of parent engagement and leadership in schools, working to set up smaller schools that are more connected to communities and their cultures, collaborating with principals and teachers to create 'relational cultures' in schools that engage all stakeholders, and connecting school reform efforts with other efforts to strengthen communities, such as building affordable housing, creating safer neighborhoods, fostering economic development, and making improvements in public health." Warren, "Transforming Public Education: The Need for an Educational Justice Movement," *New England Journal of Public Policy* 26, no. 1: 9, http://scholarworks.umb.edu/nejpp/vol26/iss1/11. See also Warren, Soo Hong, Carolyn Heang Rubin, and Phitsamay Sychitkokhong Uy, "Beyond the Bake Sale: A Community-Based Relational Approach to Parent Engagement in Schools," *Teachers College Record* 111, no. 9 (2009): 2209–54; Hong, *A Cord of Three Strands: A New Approach to Parent Engagement in Schools* (Cambridge, MA: Harvard Education Press, 2011); Celina Su, *Streetwise for Book Smarts: Grassroots Organizing and Education Reform in the Bronx* (Ithaca, NY: Cornell University Press, 2009); and Jeannie Oakes, John Rogers, and Martin Lipton, *Learning Power: Organizing for Education and Justice*, The John Dewey Lecture (New York: Teachers College Press, 2006). For a longer view on parents' roles vis-à-vis schools, see William W. Cutler III, *Parents and Schools: The 150-Year Struggle for Control in American Education* (Chicago: University of Chicago Press, 2000).

350. Arthur Eugene Bestor, Clarence J. Karier, and Foster McMurray, *Educational Wastelands: The Retreat from Learning in Our Public Schools*, 2nd ed. (Urbana: University of Illinois Press, 1985), 7, quoted in Deborah Duncan Owens, *The Origins of the Common Core: How the Free Market Became Public Education Policy* (New York: Palgrave Macmillan, 2015), 48. Bestor also suggested how we might hold the system accountable, in ways absent in current debates: "Raising the intellectual level of the nation" might be "measured . . . by larger per capita of books and serious magazines, by definitely improved taste in movies and radio programs, by higher standards of political debate, by increased freedom of speech and of thought, by a marked decline in such evidences of mental retardation as the incessant reading of comic books by adults."

351. Friedman quotes are from fn2 in Friedman, "The Role of Government in Education," but not in the later book version of the argument in Friedman's *Capitalism and Freedom* (Chicago: University of Chicago Press, 1962). Friedman agreed that the state would need then to inspect schools "much as it now inspects restaurants," including for "a minimum common content" (Friedman, "The Role of Government in Education," 4).

352. Legislation allowing school district takeover by the state arose roughly contemporaneously with the expansion of charters. New Jersey passed the first state takeover law in 1989.

Part Two

1. See a defense of this right in Stephen G. Gilles, "On Educating Children: A Parentalist Manifesto," *University of Chicago Law Review* 63, no. 3 (1996): 937–1024; a discussion of these views in Harry Brighouse and Adam Swift, *Family Values: The Ethics of Parent-child Relationship* (Princeton, NJ: Princeton University Press, 2014); and a discussion on the morality of school choice in Adam Swift, *How Not to Be a Hypocrite: School Choice and the Morally Perplexed Parent* (London: Routledge, 2003).

2. We focus on parents' choices in this discussion therefore mostly avoid this dilemma, which is famously analyzed in Joel Feinberg, "The Child's Right to an Open Future," in *Whose Child?*, ed. W. Aiken and H. LaFollette (Totowa, NJ: Rowman & Littlefield, 1980), 124–53. See an argument regarding the tension between cultural accommodation and educational rights in Sigal

Ben-Porath, "Exit Rights and Entrance Paths: Accommodating Cultural Diversity in a Liberal Democracy," *Perspectives on Politics* 8, no. 4 (2010): 1021–33.

3. For school choice as a free market tool to increase quality, see John E. Chubb and Terry M. Moe, *Politics, Markets, and America's Schools* (Washington, DC: Brookings Institute, 1990); and Joseph P. Viteritti, *Choosing Equality: School Choice, the Constitution, and Civil Society* (Washington, DC: Brookings Institute, 1999). For school choice as reflecting liberal democratic values, see Amy Gutmann, *Democratic Education* (Princeton, NJ: Princeton University Press, 1999); and Meira Levinson, *The Demands of Liberal Education* (New York and Oxford: Oxford University Press, 1999). Egalitarian support of school choice programs as potentially contributing to social justice include Harry Brighouse, *School Choice and Social Justice* (New York and Oxford: Oxford University Press, 2000); and Adam Swift, *How Not to be a Hypocrite* (London: Routledge, 2003).

4. US Department of Education, National Center for Education Statistics, "Table 216.20: Number and Enrollment of Public Elementary and Secondary Schools, by School Level, Type, and Charter and Magnet Status: Selected Years, 1990–91 through 2013–14," Digest of Education Statistics 2015, September 2015, https://nces.ed.gov/programs/digest/d15/tables/dt15_216.20.asp; National Alliance for Public Charter Schools, total number of students, accessed May 2014, http://dashboard2.publiccharters.org/Home/?p=Home.

5. Frederick M. Hess, "Does School Choice 'Work'?" *National Affairs*, Fall 2010, http://www.nationalaffairs.com/publications/detail/does-school-choice-work.

6. Charles Hammond, "New England Academies and Classical Schools," excerpted in Theodore R. Sizer, *The Age of the Academies*. Classics in Education (New York: Bureau of Publications, Teachers College, Columbia University, 1964), 127–42.

7. Stephen Gilles, "On Educating Children: A Parentalist Manifesto," (Summer 1996): 944.; Shelley Burtt, "Religious Parents; Secular Schools," *Review of Politics* 56 (1994): 51–70; Burtt, "In Defense of Yoder: Parental Authority and the Public Schools" in *Political Order*, ed. Ian Shapiro and Russell Hardin, NOMOS, vol. 38 (New York: New York University Press, 1996), 412–37, and Melissa Moschella, *To Whom Do Children Belong? Parental Rights, Civic Education, and Children's Autonomy* (New York: Cambridge University Press, 2016).

8. See Milton Friedman, "The Role of Government in Education," in *Economics and the Public Interest*, ed. Robert A. Solo (Rutgers, NJ: Rutgers University Press, 1955).

9. Chubb and Moe, *Politics, Markets, and America's Schools*, 217.

10. Hess, "Does School Choice 'Work'?" For "some advocates of school choice," and "preliminary results," see Jay P. Greene and Greg Foster, *Vouchers for Special Education Students: An Evaluation of Florida's McKay Scholarship*, Manhattan Institute Report, 2003; and Will Dobbie and Roland G. Fryer, "The Medium-Term Impacts of High-Achieving Charter Schools," *Journal of Political Economy* 123, no. 5 (October 2015): 985–1037.

11. See the school's website at http://www.histcs.org/.

12. Matt Zwolinski, "A Libertarian Case for the Moral Limits of Markets," *Georgetown Journal of Legal and Public Policy* 13 (2015): 278.

13. See, for example, Gutmann, *Democratic Education*; Stephen Macedo, *Democracy and Distrust: Civic Education in a Multicultural Democracy* (Cambridge, MA: Harvard University Press. 2003); William A. Galston, *Liberal Purposes: Goods, Virtues, and Diversity in the Liberal State* (Cambridge: Cambridge University Press, 1991); and T. H. McLaughlin, *Liberalism, Education and Schooling: Essays by T.H. McLaughlin*, ed. David Carr, Mark Halstead, and Richard Pring (Exeter, UK: Imprint Academic, 2008).

14. Stephen D. Sugarman and Frank R. Kemerer, eds., *School Choice and Social Controversy: Politics, Policy, and Law* (Washington, DC: Brookings Institute Press 1999.

15. See Sarah Stitzlein, *American Public Education and the Responsibility of Its Citizens*

(Oxford University Press 2017). Stitzlein argues that public schools are spaces where people learn to negotiate the intersections of personal, communal, and shared civic interests, therefore allowing for democracy not only to be expressed through the statement of preferences and their aggregation, but also to be developed and practiced. Kathleen Knight-Abowitz, *Publics for Public Schools: Legitimacy, Democracy, and Leadership* (Routledge, 2014). In *Publics for Public Schools* and other publications, Knight-Abowitz maintains that public schools serve a unitary public mission in their overall national role, expressing a shared democratic and civic vision while also working at the local level to enable a smaller-scale public engagement with the specific functioning of local schools. The important democratic and civic role of public schools is best realized through attending to both of these roles, which is made uniquely feasible by assigned public schools. It is worth noting that this function can be made more significant by zoning schools to bring together families from different class and race communities.

16. The Democracy Prep charter network is a notable exception in this specific regard, as it devotes significant time to the civic development of its students; but this is clearly far from being common in other charters. Moreover, "choice schools" are not the best context for teaching democratic and civic practices, to the extent that they do not enable access to this opportunity in an equitable way.

17. Fabricant and Fine, *Charter Schools and the Corporate Makeover*, 3

18. Richard Rothstein, *The Color of Law: The Forgotten History of How Our Government Segregated America* (New York: Liveright Publishing, 2016).

19. Eamonn Callan, "The Great Sphere: Education against Servility," *Journal of Philosophy of Education* 31, no. 2 (1997): 2221–32.

20. Erica Frankenberg, Genevieve Siegel-Hawley, and Jia Wang, *Choice without Equity: Charter School Segregation and the Need for Civil Rights Standards.* (Los Angeles: Civil Rights Project / Proyecto Derechos Civiles, 2010), http://civilrightsproject.ucla.edu/research/k-12-education/integration-and-diversity/choice-without-equity-2009-report.

21. As was the case in *Mozert, in which the court dismissed the exemption request made by a group of devout Christian parents who saw the general English language arts reader their children's school was using as an affront to their reading of the Bible*; see Mozert v. Hawkins County Board of Education, 827 F.2d 1058 (6th Cir. 1987).

22. See Ben Justice and Colin Macleod, *Have a Little Faith: Religion, Democracy, and the American Public School* (Chicago: University of Chicago Press, 2016).

23. Adam Laats, *The Other School Reformers: Conservative Activism in American Education* (Cambridge, MA: Harvard University Press, 2015).

24. J. S. Mill, *On Liberty* (Scott Publishing, 1859), Project Gutenberg, http://www.gutenberg.org/ebooks/34901, 200.

25. See the discussion in Harry Brighouse, "Civic Education and Liberal Legitimacy," *Ethics* 108, no. 4 (July 1998): 719–45.

26. Susan Moller Okin, *Women in Western Political Thought* (Princeton, NJ: Princeton University Press, 1979), 285.

27. S. R. Ben-Porath, "School Choice as a Bounded Ideal," *Journal of Philosophy of Education* 43, no. 4 (2010): 527–44.

28. Carolyn Sattin-Bajaj, "Communication Breakdown: Informing Immigrant Parents about High School Choices in New York City'," in *School Choice and School Improvement*, ed. Mark Berends, Marisa Cannata, and Ellen B. Goldring (Cambridge, MA: Harvard Education Press, 2011), 147–75.

29. Mark Schneider, Paul Teske, and Melissa Marshall, *Choosing Schools: Consumer Choice*

and the Quality of American Schools (Princeton, NJ: Princeton University Press, 2002). See also Douglas N. Harris and Matthew F. Larsen, "What Schools do Families Want (and Why?)" Education Research Alliance for New Orleans Policy Brief, January 15, 2015; and Schneider, Teske, Marshall, and Christine Roch, "Shopping for Schools: In the Land of the Blind, the One-Eyed Parent May Be Enough," *American Journal of Political Science* 42, no. 3 (1998): 769–96.

30. Jesse Lee, "Taking On Education," *What's Happening* (blog), White House: President Barack Obama, March 10, 2009, http://www.whitehouse.gov/blog/2009/03/10/taking-education.

31. See Robin Lake, Melissa Bowen, Allison Demeritt, Moira McCullough, Joshua Haimson, and Brian Gill, *Learning from Charter School Management Organizations: Strategies for Student Behavior and Teacher Coaching* (Mathematica Policy Research and Center on Reinventing Public Education, 2012), http://www.crpe.org/sites/default/files/pub_CMO_Strategies_mar12_0.pdf.

32. Lake et al., 9.

33. Roland G. Fryer, "Creating 'No Excuses' (Traditional) Public Schools: Preliminary Evidence from an Experiment in Houston" (working paper 17494, National Bureau of Economic Research, Cambridge, MA, 2011).

34. D. Meyerson, A. Berger, and R. Quinn, "Playing the Field: Implications of Scaling in the California Charter School Movement," in *Scaling Social Impact: New Thinking*, ed. P. N. Bloom and E. Skloot (New York: Palgrave Macmillan, 2010).

35. Center on Reinventing Public Education, *Charter Management Organizations: Innovations, Opportunities, and Challenges*, National Charter School Research Project, June 2010, http://www.crpe.org/sites/default/files/cmo_brief_09_interimrep_jun10_0.pdf.

36. C. Farrell, C., M. B. Nayfack, J. Smith, P. Wohlstetter, and A. Wong, *Scaling Up Charter Management Organizations: Eight Key Lessons for Success* (California: National Resource Center on Charter School Finance & Governance, 2009).

37. Kevin Hall and Robin Lake, "The $500 Million Question," *Education Next*, Winter 2011, http://educationnext.org/the-500-million-question/.

38. Don Shalvey, "It's Report Card Time for Charter Schools," Bill & Melinda Gates Foundation, November 16, 2011, http://www.impatientoptimists.org/Posts/2011/11/Its-Report-Card-Time -for-Charter-Schools?p=1.

39. Sarah Reckhow and Jeffrey W. Snyder. "The Expanding Role of Philanthropy in Education Politics," *Educational Researcher* 43, no. 4 (2014): 186–95.

40. See a mostly favorable discussion, with some criticism, in John Merrow, "Thinking about Charters," *Learning Matters: Taking Note* (blog) June 22, 2012, http://takingnote.learningmatters .tv/?p=5807.

41. Helen Zelon, "Why Charter Schools Have High Teacher Turnover" City Limits, August 20, 2014. There is some disagreement among researchers as to whether teacher attrition is greater at charter schools as a result of a "charter effect" or merely in correlation with school demographic characteristics. It seems clear that some charter networks are characterized by very high attrition rates.

42. However, there are many important discussions on "the new managerialism" that explore the overall negative effect of the narrowed vision and the focus on testing, on all students and especially on more vulnerable and marginalized ones; see M. W. Apple, *Educating the Right Way: Markets, Standards, God, and Inequality* (New York: Routledge, 2006).

43. While some CMOs and charter operators are highly successful in improving their students' outcomes, as measured by test results, college admission, or other measures, some traditional public schools and districts have made equally impressive strides. Montgomery County (MD), Long Beach (CA), and Union City (NJ) are outstanding examples of the improvements

that can be made in public schools through reforms that do not include charters or the introduction of choice.

44. See G. Miron and C. Nelson, *What's Public about Charter Schools? Lessons Learned about Choice and Accountability* (Thousand Oaks, CA: Corwin Press, 2002).

45. The literature in political science that analyzes accountability is quite broad; see, for example, Andreas Schedler, "Conceptualizing Accountability," in *The Self-Restraining State: Power and Accountability in New Democracies*, ed. Andreas Schedler, Larry Diamond, and Marc F. Plattner, (Boulder, CO: Lynne Rienner, 1999), 13–28; and Robert Mulgan, *Holding Power to Account: Accountability in Modern Democracies* (New York: Palgrave, 2003). A variety of typologies are featured, and the one used here is common, though by no means exhaustive. It is nonetheless useful for covering much of the debate on the role and uses of accountability in democratic institutions in a way that allows us to pursue the question of the different forms of school accountability.

46. William L. Sherman and Paul Theobald, "Progressive Era Rural Reform: Creating Standard Schools in the Midwest," *Journal of Research in Rural Education* 17, no. 2 (Fall 2001): 84–91 Michael Johanek, "Preparing Pluribus for Unum: Historical Perspectives on Civic Education," in *Making Civics Count: Citizenship Education for a New Generation*, ed. David Campbell, Frederick Hess, and Meira Levinson (Cambridge, MA: Harvard Education Press, 2012), 57–87 For a history of testing in the United States back to colonial times, see William J. Reese, *Testing Wars in the Public Schools: A Forgotten History* (Cambridge, MA: Harvard University Press, 2013).

47. See an extended discussion of the way standardized tests are used in education reform today in Diane Ravitch, *The Death and Life of the Great American School System* (New York: Basic Books, 2010), esp. chap. 8.

48. As an example, the 2014/15 School District of Philadelphia offered an English-language list of high schools from which parents of eighth graders were to choose where to apply; it consisted of sixty-nine dense pages of information, including different types of schools, different types of admission, academic performance measures, types of services offered, and so on.

49. Ben-Porath, "School Choice as a Bounded Ideal," 541–42.

50. M. Orr and J. Rogers, "Unequal Schools, Unequal Voice: The Need for Public Engagement in Public Schools," in *Public Engagement for Public Good: Joining Forces to Revitalize Democracy and Equalize Schools* (Stanford, CA: Stanford University Press), 13.

51. Michael Johanek, "Preparing Pluribus for Unum: Historical Perspectives on Civic Education," in *Making Civics Count: Citizenship Education for a New Generation*, ed. David Campbell, Frederick Hess, and Meira Levinson (Cambridge, MA: Harvard Education Press, 2012), 63.

52. http://ciep.hunter.cuny.edu/school-elections-what-do-we-do-about-low-voter-turnout/.

53. Albert O. Hirschman, *Exit, Voice, and Loyalty: Responses to Decline in Firms, Organizations, and States* (Cambridge, MA: Harvard University Press, 1970).

54. Suzanne Dovi, *The Good Representative* (Oxford, UK: Blackwell, 2008). See a more detailed discussion in Dovi, "Accountability as Resistance: Helping Others Be Autonomous?" (American Political Science Association 2014 Annual Meeting Paper).

55. Kristen A. Graham, "Parents at Phila. School Reject Takeover by Charter," *Philadelphia Inquirer*, June 6, 2014.

56. Christopher Lubienski, Charisse Gulosino, and Peter Weitzel, "School Choice and Competitive Incentives: Mapping the Distribution of Educational Opportunities across Local Education Markets," *American Journal of Education*, August 2009, 604.

57. Alan Wolfe, introduction to *School Choice: The Moral Debate* (Princeton University Press, 2003).

58. Quoted in US Department of Education, "How *No Child Left Behind* Benefits African

Americans," NCLB/Stronger Accountability, last modified September 2, 2005, https://www2.ed .gov/nclb/accountability/achieve/nclb-aa.html.

59. Jennifer B. Ayscue and Brian Woodward with John Kucsera and Genevieve Siegel-Hawley, "Segregation Again: North Carolina's Transition from Leading Desegregation Then to Accepting Segregation Now," Civil Rights Project, May 14, 2014.

60. H. Lankford and J. Wyckoff, "Why are Schools Racially Segregated? Implications for School Choice Policy," in *School Choice and Diversity: What the Evidence Says*, ed. J. T. Scott (New York: Teachers College Press, 2005), 9–27.

61. Justine S. Hastings, Christopher A. Neilson, and Seth D. Zimmerman, "The Effect of School Choice on Intrinsic Motivation and Academic Outcomes" (NBER Working Paper No. 18324, August 2012), http://www.nber.org/papers/w18324.

62. John F. Witte, Patrick J. Wolf, Deven Carlson, and Alicia Dean, *Milwaukee Independent Charter Schools Study: Final Report on Four-Year Achievement Gains* (Fayetteville: University of Arkansas Department of Education Reform, 2012).

63. Kevin Booker, Tim R. Sass, Brian Gill, and Ron Zimmer, "The Effects of Charter High Schools on Educational Attainment," *Journal of Labor Economics* 29, no. 2 (April 2011): 377–415, http://www.jstor.org/discover/10.1086/658089?uid=3739864&uid=2129&uid=2&uid=70&uid=4 &uid=3739256&sid=21101326194901.

64. Julian R. Betts and Richard C. Atkinson, "Better Research Needed on the Impact of Charter Schools," Science 335 (January 13, 2012): 171–72, http://weber.ucsd.edu/~jbetts/Pub/A76 Science-2012-Betts-171-2.pdf.

65. CREDO, *Multiple Choice: Charter School Performance in 16 States*, (Stanford, CA: Center for Research on Education Outcomes [CREDO], 2009), https://credo.stanford.edu/reports /MULTIPLE_CHOICE_CREDO.pdf.

66. Center for Research on Educational Outcomes, *National Charter School Study* (Stanford, CA: Stanford University, 2013).

67. Philip Gleason, Melissa Clark, Christina Clark Tuttle, and Emily Dwoyer, *The Evaluation of Charter Schools Impacts: Final Report*, US Department of Education, Institute for Education Sciences, June 2010, https://ies.ed.gov/ncee/pubs/20104029/pdf/20104029.pdf.

68. J. L. Woodworth and M. E. Raymond, *Charter School Growth and Replication*, vol. 2 (Stanford, CA: Center for Research on Education Outcomes, 2013), http://credo.stanford.edu /pdfs/CGAR%20Growth%20Volume%20II.pdf.

69. B. Gill, R. Zimmer, J. Christman, and S. Blanc, *State Takeover, School Restructuring, Private Management, and Student Achievement in Philadelphia*, 2007. Retrieved from RAND at http://www.rand.org/pubs/monographs/MG533.

70. Greg J. Duncan and Richard J. Murnane. *Whither Opportunity? Rising Inequality, Schools, and Children's Life Chances* (New York, Chicago: Russell Sage Foundation, Spencer Foundation, 2011); see esp. chap. 9 and 10.

71. Martin Carnoy, "For the Love of Learning: Lessons from Chile's Voucher Reform Movement," National Education Policy Center, December 11, 2013, http://nepc.colorado.edu/blog /lessons-chiles-voucher-reform-movement.

72. Woodworth and Raymond, *Charter School Growth and Replication*, 2:47–48.

73. Gary Miron, Jessica L. Urschel, and Nicholas Saxton, *What Makes KIPP Work? A Study of Student Characteristics, Attrition, and School Finance* (National Center for the Study of Privatization in Education, Teachers College, Columbia University and the Study Group on Educational Management Organizations at Western Michigan University, 2011), http://www.edweek .org/media/kippstudy.pdf.

74. US Government Accountability Office, *Charter Schools: Additional Federal Attention Needed to Help Protect Access for Students with Disabilities* (Washington, DC: Government Accountability Office, 2012), http://www.gao.gov/assets/600/591435.pdf. Protection for students with disabilities were further deregulated during Betsy Devos's tenure as Secretary of Education (ibid.).

75. Rubén Donato, *The Other Struggle for Equal Schools: Mexican Americans during the Civil Rights Era"* (Albany: State University of New York Press, 1997), 71.

76. Helen F. Ladd, Charles T. Clotfelter, and John B. Holbein, "The Growing Segmentation of the Charter School Sector in North Carolina" (NBER Working Paper No. 21078, April 2015); Natalie Lacireno-Paquet, Thomas T. Holyoke, Michele Moser, and Jeffrey R. Henig, "Creaming versus Cropping: Charter School Enrollment Practices in Response to Market Incentives" Educational Evaluation and Policy Analysis 24, no. 2:145–58; G. R. and K. L. Tedin, "Does Choice Lead to Racially Distinctive Schools? Charter Schools and Household Preferences," *Journal of Policy Analysis Management* 21:79–92; and R. Bifulco and H. F. Ladd, "School Choice, Racial Segregation, and Test-Score Gaps: Evidence from North Carolina's Charter School Program," *Journal of Policy Analysis Management* 26 (2007): 31–56.

77. Elizabeth Anderson, *The Imperative of Integration* (Princeton, NJ: Princeton University Press, 2010), 2. See also Derrick Darby and John L. Rury, *The Color of Mind: Why the Origins of the Achievement Gap Matter for Justice* (Chicago: University of Chicago Press, 2018).

78. Quoted in Michael Alison Chandler, "Charters Grapple with Admission Policies, Question How Public They Should Be," *Washington Post*, October 31, 2015, https://www.washingtonpost.com/local/education/public-charter-schools-grapple-with-admissions-policies/2015/10/31/c40a4390-7128-11e5-8d93-0af317ed58c9_story.html.

79. Richard Arnott and John Rowse, "Peer Group Effects and Educational Attainment," *Journal of Public Economics* 32, no. 3 (1987): 287–305. For a report on an in-class study, see Caroline Hoxby, "The Power of Peers," *Education Next*, Summer 2002, http://educationnext.org/the-power-of-peers/. For a recent summary of research in economics, see Dennis Epple and Richard Romano, "Peer Effects in Education: A Survey of the Theory and Evidence," *Handbook of Social Economics* 1, no. 1 (2011): 1053–1163.

80. C. D. Cobb and G. V. Glass, "Ethnic Segregation in Arizona Charter Schools," *Education Policy Analysis Archives* 7, no. 1 (January 14, 1999), http://dx.doi.org/10.14507/epaa.v7n1.1999.

81. Michael Merry, "Equality, Self Respect and Voluntary Separation, *Critical Review of International Social and Political Philosophy* 15, no. 1(2012): 79–100; and Karolyn Tyson, *Integration Interrupted: Tracking, Black Students, and Acting White after Brown* (New York: Oxford University Press, 2011).

82. Bifulco and Ladd, 2007.

83. David R. Garcia "The Impact of School Choice on Racial Segregation in Charter Schools," *Educational Policy* 22, no. 6, 805.

84. "African Centered Schools: What You Need to Know," pamphlet, 2008, the Uhuru Collective, accessed at http://www.chereum.umontreal.ca/activites_pdf.

85. Martha Minow, "Confronting the Seduction of Choice: Law, Education, and American Pluralism," *Yale Law Journal* 120, no. 4 (2011): 814–56.

86. Michael S. Merry, "Social Exclusion of Muslim Youth in Flemish- and French-Speaking Belgian Schools," *Comparative Education Review* 49, no. 1: 1–23; and Merry and William New, "Constructing an Authentic Self: The Challenges and Promise of African-Centered Pedagogy," *American Journal of Education* 115, no. 1: 35–64.

87. A. J. Binder, *Contentious Curricula: Afrocentrism and Creationism in American Public Schools* (Princeton, NJ: Princeton University Press, 2004).

88. T. J. Yosso, "Whose Culture Has Capital? A Critical Race Theory Discussion of Community Cultural Wealth," *Race Ethnicity and Education* 8, no. 1: 69–91.

89. This figure is higher than the general number of black students in majority-minority schools, which in 2001 ranged from 30% to 50%, depending on the region. See a summary of recent data in Arianna Prothero, "Data and the Debate Over Diversity in Charters," *Education Week*, June 13, 2016, https://www.edweek.org/ew/articles/2016/06/03/data-and-the-debate-over-diversity-in.html; and Joseph S. Spoerl, "Justice and the Case for School Vouchers," *Public Affairs Quarterly* 9, no. 1 (January 1995): 75–86, https://www.jstor.org/stable/40435904.

90. Sigal R. Ben-Porath, "Deferring Virtue: The New Management of Students and the Civic Role of Schools," *Theory and Research in Education* 11, no. 2 (July 2013): 111–28; and Joanne W. Golann, "The Paradox of Success at a No-Excuses School," *Sociology of Education* 88, no. 2 (2015) 103–19.

Conclusion

1. A major text in the history of US education is David B. Tyack, *The One Best System: A History of American Urban Education* (Cambridge, MA: Harvard University Press, 1974).

2. While the most recent state law for compulsory schooling passed in 1917, enforcement lagged at more advanced levels. Earlier, school years were also shorter; combining low attendance rates and shorter years, students attended fewer than eighty days a year in 1870; that would rise during the world wars, eventually doubling by 1980. Yet the majority of 25- to 29-year-olds began completing high school only after World War II; the rate broke 90% just two years ago. Over the last century, as students attended school for more days per year and for more years, they also did so within fewer schools and fewer districts; from World War II to the early 1980s, the number of school districts dropped nearly 90%, and the number of schools dropped more than 60%.

3. Julian R. Betts and Tom Loveless, eds., *Getting Choice Right: Ensuring Equity and Efficiency in Education Policy* (Washington, DC: Brookings Institution Press, 2005); Mark Schneider, Melissa Marschall, Christine Roch, and Paul Teske, "Heuristics, Low Information Rationality, and Choosing Public Goods: Broken Windows as Shortcuts to Information about School Performance," *Urban Affairs Review* 34, no. 5: 729–41.

4. Teach for America founder Wendy Kopp, for example, cofounded Teach for All in 2007 to address a global issue: "Around the world, Teach For All network partners are developing leadership in classrooms and communities to ensure all children can fulfill their potential." Teach for All, "What We Do," accessed August 2, 2018, https://teachforall.org/what-we-do#27496.

5. Quoted in M. Johanek, "Getting to the Balcony from Chile," *School Administrator*, December 2014, 41. An intriguing analysis of the reform experiences of Sweden and Finland can be found in Samuel E. Abrams, *Education and the Commercial Mindset* (Cambridge, MA: Harvard University Press, 2016), chap. 11–12.

6. Pasi Sahlberg, email message, November 10, 2015, conversation at Global Education Forum, University of Pennsylvania, October 16–17, 2015.

7. Sahlberg, email message, November 10, 2015. In a related vein, in the United States recently, a fairly innocuous private, nonrequired set of curricular standards in US history caused a bit of a firestorm, as they were not considered by some to be respectful enough of the United States' "exceptional" role in the world. Yet few would stand for a required national curriculum in history, insisting on a curricular freedom of choice that would seem quite odd in most countries regarding their national curricula.

8. Jeffrey R. Henig, "Mayors, Governors, and Presidents: The New Education Executives

and the End of Educational Exceptionalism," *Peabody Journal of Education: Issues of Leadership, Policy, and Organizations* 84, no. 3 (2009): 283-299.

9. "Youth and student travel organisations continue to expand significantly, with 31 percent having opened a new office in their home country in 2011 and 17 percent having established a branch office abroad." WYSE Travel Confederation, "New WYSE Travel Confederation Research Launched: Youth and Student Travel Market Industry Review #4," March 26, 2014, https://www.wysetc.org/2014/03/26/new-wyse-travel-confederation-research-launched-youth-and-student-travel-market-industry-review-4-marketing/. Estimates on global industry size are from Sara Custer, "Educational Travel to Grow Dramatically by 2020," *Pie News*, February 8, 2013, http://thepienews.com/news/educational-travel-to-grow-dramatically-by-2020/. Estimates of study travel within this estimate—defined as travel involving language development or training—represents about 40% of the total, though, arguably, any youth travel might be considered educative.

10. Duncan and Murnane, *Whither Opportunity*, 11. See also Bruce Bradbury, Miles Corak, Jane Waldfogel, and Elizabeth Washbrook, *Too Many Children Left Behind: The U.S. Achievement Gap in Comparative Perspective* (New York: Russell Sage Foundation, 2015); and Duncan and Murnane, "Rising Inequality in Family Incomes and Children's Educational Outcomes," *Russell Sage Foundation Journal of the Social Sciences* 2, no. 2 (May 1, 2016): 142–58.

11. Greg J. Duncan and Richard J. Murname, "Rising Inequality in Family Incomes and Children's Educational Outcomes," *RSF: The Russell Sage Foundation Journal of the Social Sciences* 2, no. 2 (May 2016): 146.

12. Lawrence Cremin, "The Free School Movement," in *Alternative Schools: Ideologies, Realities, Guidelines*, ed. Terrence E. Deal and Robert R. Nolan (Chicago: Nelson-Hall, 1978), 206.

13. Cremin, 206.

14. Chris Lubienski and Janelle Scott, *The Politics of Venture Philanthropy in Charter School Policy and Advocacy*, Working Paper Series (Goldman School of Public Policy at Univeristy of California Berkeley, 2009), https://gspp.berkeley.edu/research/working-paper-series/the-politics-of-venture-philanthropy-in-charter-school-policy-and-advocacy.

15. Michael Johanek, "Preparing Pluribus for Unum: Historical Perspectives on Civic Education," in *Making Civics Count: Citizenship Education for a New Generation*, ed. David Campbell, Meira Levinson, and Frederick Hess (Cambridge, MA: Harvard Education Press, 2012), 57–87.

16. Some five thousand "community schools" exist today—fewer than charters, it would appear, though the likely larger size of community schools would suggest approximate enrollments, with caveats regarding overlap, definitions, and so on. On the history of community schools, see Michael C. Johanek and John L. Puckett, *Leonard Covello and the Making of Benjamin Franklin High School: Education as If Citizenship Mattered* (Philadelphia: Temple University Press, 2007). Much of the current drive for community schooling also reflects a "one-stop" consumer impulse, the "full-service" notion popularized more recently by Joy Dryfoos and others; see Dryfoos, *Full Service Schools* (San Francisco: Jossey-Bass, 1994). Such a drive need not be inconsistent with schools also serving public work purposes, though we have found the latter, if persistently present, less frequently enacted.

17. Shanker quoted in Diane Ravitch, "How to Fix the Charter School Movement," *Answer Sheet Blog, Washington Post*, July 16, 2012, https://www.washingtonpost.com/blogs/answer-sheet/post/how-to-fix-the-charter-school-movement-and-what-albert-shanker-really-said/2012/07/16/gJQAjxW4oW_blog.html. Regarding EMOs, see G. Miron and C. Gulosino, *Profiles of For-Profit and Nonprofit Education Management Organizations: Fourteenth Edition—2011-2012*, (Boulder, CO: National Education Policy Center), http://nepc.colorado.edu/publication/EMO-profiles-11-12.

18. "Network Partners," Teach for All, accessed February 1, 2018, https://teachforall.org/network-partners; 990 report for Teach for All for 2015, ProPublica, Nonprofit Explorer, accessed February 1, 2018, https://projects.propublica.org/nonprofits/organizations/262122566. See also Diane Ravitch, "Big Money Rules," *New York Review of Books*, December 7, 2017, http://www.nybooks.com/articles/2017/12/07/big-money-rules/?pagination=false&printpage=true; and Megan E. Tompkins-Stange, *Policy Patrons: Philanthropy, Education Reform, and the Politics of Influence*, Educational Innovations Series (Cambridge, MA: Harvard Education Press, 2016).

19. Mark Stern, Sheila Clonan, Laura Jaffee, and Anna Lee, "The Normative Limits of Choice: Charter Schools, Disability Studies, and Questions of Inclusion," *Educational Policy* 29, no. 3: 448–77.

20. Illustrative perhaps of a US tradition of blurred public/private boundaries, as well as shifting definitions of those spheres, we see the expansion of various "partnership" school or "empowerment zone" models, where efforts are made to blend charter and district design elements; one organization, Empower Schools, describes their work as "part of a national Third Way movement that leverages and fuses the best of districts and charters." Empower Schools, "About Us," accessed February 5, 2018, http://empowerschools.org/about-us/. In Springfield, Massachusetts, the Springfield Empowerment Zone Partnership (SEZP), a private 501(c)(3) nonprofit, describes itself as "a results-oriented steward of eleven public schools, forged through an innovative partnership of the Springfield Public Schools (SPS), the Springfield Education Association (SEA), and the Massachusetts Department of Elementary & Secondary Education (DESE)." Springfield Empowerment Zone Partnership, "Empowering Partnerships," accessed February 5, 2018, http://www.springfieldempowerment.org/about.html.

Index

Page numbers in *italics* refer to figures and illustrations.